Personal and Community Health

I wish to acknowledge the following organizations and people:

Blackwell Scientific Publications
Bristol Cancer Help Centre
Harper & Row Ltd
Health Education Authority
International Council of Nurses
John Wiley & Sons
Methuen and Co. Ltd
Premenstrual Tension Advisory Service
Professor Peter Townsend
Royal Society for the Prevention of Accidents
Terence Higgins Trust
Valentine, Mitchell and Co. Ltd.

Personal and Community Health

Anne Barnes BSc (Social Science Nursing Edin) RGN, DN, HVCert

Third edition

Baillière Tindall
London   Philadelphia   Toronto
Sydney   Tokyo

Baillière Tindall 24–28 Oval Road
  W.B. Saunders London NW1 7DX, UK

West Washington Square
Philadelphia, PA 19105, USA

1 Goldthorne Avenue
Toronto, Ontario M8Z 5T9, Canada

ABP Australia Ltd, 44–50 Waterloo Road
North Ryde, NSW 2113, Australia

Harcourt Brace Jovanovich Japan Inc.
Ichibancho Central Building, 22–1 Ichibancho
Chiyoda-ku, Tokyo 102, Japan

First published 1975
Second edition 1981
Third edition 1987

Typeset by Photo·graphics, Honiton, Devon
Printed and bound in Great Britain by The Alden Press, Oxford

British Library Cataloguing in Publication Data

Barnes, Anne
  Personal and community health. — 3rd ed.
  1. Health   2. Nursing
  I. Title   II. Jackson, Sheila M. Personal
  and community health
  613′.024613   RT67

ISBN 0–7020–1234–3

Contents

To my mother and father

Preface

Health is valued above all else. We aim to maintain it, and, at times of ill-health, we strive to regain it. The commitment of nurses to health is embodied in the UKCC training rules which expect student nurses 'to acquire the competencies required to advise on the promotion of health and the prevention of illness'. In 1978 at Alma-Ata the World Health Organization declared its commitment to 'Health for all by the year 2000'.

In recent years there has been a significant increase in the potential for the prevention of illness through the identification of risk factors associated with certain diseases. At the same time there has been an upsurge of interest in the concept of wellbeing as more and more people aim to adopt a healthy lifestyle in order to preserve and protect their health. People are increasingly recognizing that they need not be passive recipients of illness but have a considerable capacity to influence their health. But health is not only a personal affair. 'No man is an island', and the health of each person is inextricably linked with the health of their family and the health of the community in which they live. The nurse's role in health promotion therefore has to take account of issues relating to personal, family and community health.

This book has been completely rewritten to take account of this increase in knowledge and change in attitudes, although the overall plan remains unchanged. The first part of the book describes health and wellbeing in its widest sense, the second part focuses on the 'seven ages of man', and the final part considers health problems and indicates the main responsibilities which the community must undertake in order to promote health and some of the means by which improvements in health can be measured.

The book is designed both for easy reference and to provide a comprehensive outline so that a nurse reading it would, at the end, understand some of the principles involved in promoting a sense of wellbeing. Above all, it is intended to be a practical guide on health issues, and a source for further reading.

I am greatly indebted to Sheila Jackson for devising the original format and for setting the standard of this book. It has been my intention to continue in the tradition set by her so that its usefulness to the nurse and its function in the nurses' library will remain unchanged.

Anne Barnes

1

What is Health?

All people value health yet many do not give it a great deal of consideration until they are unwell and most would probably have to think very carefully if asked what health means to them. It can mean very different things to different people. For some it may mean a high-level wellness described by Dunn (1961) as 'alive to the tips of his fingers, with energy to burn, tingling with vitality. At times like these the world is a glorious place!'. For others it may mean the absence of obvious disease or starvation. The *Good Health Guide* lists the following statements which people may consider in trying to find out what 'health' really means to them:

For me being healthy is:

1 enjoying being with my family and friends;
2 living to be very old;
3 being able to run for a bus without getting out of breath;
4 hardly ever taking any pills or medicines;
5 being the ideal weight for my height;
6 taking part in lots of games or sports;
7 having a clear skin, bright eyes and shiny hair;
8 never suffering from anything more than a mild cold or tummy upset;
9 being able to adapt easily to changes in life, e.g. getting married, becoming a parent, changing jobs;
10 feeling glad to be alive when I wake up in the morning;

11 being able to touch my toes or run a mile in 10 minutes;
12 enjoying my job and being able to do it without much stress and strain;
13 having all the bits of my body in perfect working condition;
14 eating the 'right' food;
15 enjoying some form of relaxation or recreation;
16 never smoking;
17 hardly ever going to the doctor;
18 drinking only moderate amounts of alcohol.

Health may mean being fit (statements 3, 6, 11, 15), not being ill (statements 4, 8, 13, 17), living to an old age (statements 2, 5, 14, 16, 18) and many other things. Who sets the standard for health? Is there a universal state of wellbeing which everyone can aspire to or is it up to each individual person to decide for themselves what standard of health they desire and can reasonably expect?

Health is clearly not a simple nor a single issue. It involves a number of different dimensions. The World Health Organization has stated that it is 'the optimum condition of physical, social and mental wellbeing'. It has been likened to an equilateral triangle where the weakening of one side upsets the other two and therefore the balance of health (see Figure 1). Ewles and Simnett (1985) recognize more dimensions and describe these as:

1

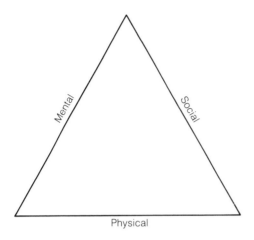

Figure 1.   *Balance of health.*

- *physical health*: the mechanistic functioning of the body;
- *mental health*: the ability to think clearly and coherently;
- *emotional health*: the ability to recognize emotions such as fear, joy, grief and anger and to express them appropriately;
- *social health*: the ability to make and maintain relationships with other people;
- *spiritual health*: the formation of personal creeds, principles of behaviour and ways of achieving peace of mind which for some people will involve religious beliefs and practices;
- *societal health*: involving the society in which the person lives: clearly health is dependent on the environment and societies where there is famine, oppression or racism are not conducive to health.

DEFINITIONS OF HEALTH

Definitions of health differ greatly and most, inevitably, seem incomplete. In 1947, the World Health Organization gave the following definition:

'Health is a state of complete physical, mental and social wellbeing and not merely the absence of disease or infirmity.'

This definition has been criticized for being overly idealistic and for implying that health is a static entity. Using this definition few people could claim that they enjoyed health and most would spend a lifetime striving towards it.

Subsequent definitions have concentrated on the positive aspects of health rather than on the negative absence of disease, and have tended to view it as a continuous process of adaptation and change. In 1958, Dunn defined health as '. . . an integrated method of functioning which is orientated toward maximizing the potential of which the individual is capable, within the environment where he is functioning'. Katherine Mansfield's much quoted definition of health is similar: 'By health I mean the power to live a full, adult, living, breathing life in close contact with what I love — the earth and the wonders thereof . . . I want to be all that I am capable of becoming'.

Some definitions focus strongly on the power of the person to adapt to life's changes and the personal responsibility implicit in gaining and maintaining health. Illich (1975) states, 'Health designates a process of adaptation. It designates the ability to adapt to changing environments, to growing up and to ageing, to healing when damaged, to suffering, and to the peaceful expectation of death'.

Recently, attention has been given to concepts of wellness as well as to health. Traditionally, absence of discernible illness constituted health or wellness. Some practitioners now recognize that there are as many degrees of wellness as there are degrees of illness. Blattner (1981) uses a model to illustrate this concept (see Figure 2). Ardell (1977) states, '. . . high level wellness is a lifestyle-focused approach which you design for the purpose of pursuing the highest level of

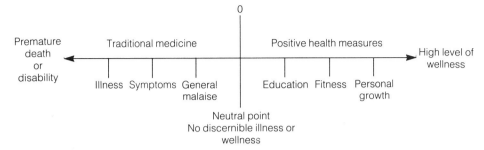

Figure 2. *Scale of wellness and illness. Illness/Wellness continuum used with permission.* © *1972, 1981, John W. Travis, M. D., Wellness Association, Box 5433, Mill Valley, CA 94942. From Wellness Workbook, Ryan & Travis, Ten Speed Press, 1981.*

health within your capability. A wellness lifestyle is dynamic or ever-changing as you evolve through life. It is an integrated lifestyle in that you incorporate some approach or aspect of each wellness dimension (self-responsibility, nutritional awareness, stress management, physical fitness, and environmental sensitivity)'.

THE HISTORICAL PERSPECTIVE

In recent years the term 'holistic health' has come into common usage. The words 'holistic' and 'health' are both derived from the same Anglo-Saxon root, *hal*, meaning 'whole' and 'to heal'. Holistic health involves an understanding of every influence on health together with a belief that health is a state of balance and harmony. This is a rather different approach from that of modern medicine which has tended to focus on a particular problem within a specific bodily system. Holistic health is however a very old idea.

In ancient Greece, around 500 BC, the god Hygieia was worshipped by those who believed that good health resulted from man's understanding of how to live. Pythagoras introduced the concept of physiological harmony, seeing disease as an imbalance of the constitutional elements of man. Hippocrates, the father of modern medicine, also believed that health was a state of balance (mental, emotional and physical) which depended on an equilibrium of the fluid essences,

or 'humours', of blood, bile, phlegm and choler. He placed great emphasis on natural living and correct habits, and used drugs for 'humour-balancing'. By the fourth century the Greeks were beginning to understand the essential nature of things including anatomy and physiology and Aristotle reorganized this knowledge into spirit and matter. Gradually, the idea that the mind or the spirit could influence physical health was disregarded.

Also at about this time, attention became increasingly focused on the discovery of specific causes for physical ailments. The 'miasma' theory postulated causes for disease outside the body, an idea eventually supported by Pasteur's work which demonstrated the existence of micro-organisms. This heralded intense activity in medicine aimed at tracking down the cause of disease and finding its cure. In the west it was not until the 1970s that serious consideration was again given to the possibility that mind and body could be intimately linked and that promoting health should be considered as well as combating disease. It is interesting that both Pasteur and Florence Nightingale urged practitioners to examine the factors which caused people to remain healthy as well as those which led them to ill-health. In the east this had always been so.

The Eastern philosophies of India, China and Japan developed their own concepts of health and systems of health

Figure 3. *The t'ai-chi t'u symbol. The circle represents the tao or t'ai chi (supreme ultimate). The white is the yang force (heat, expansion, the creative, male, positive); the black is the yin force (cold, contraction, the receptive, female, negative).*

care. They, however, did not shed their philosophical and religious origins, and they did not separate mind and body. Hindus consider the body to be an integral part of the human being, unseparated from the spirit. Similarly, Buddhism considers mind and body in unison. The Four Noble Truths which it preaches emphasize the natural ebb and flow of nature and the importance of the human spirit in coping with a never ending chain of cause and effect. In China the Taoists advocated following the natural order of things and trusting intuition. In the world of the Taoists everything is held in a state of balance between the yin and the yang. This is symbolized as the 'supreme ultimate' which is not stationary but in constant cyclic movement (see Figure 3). The value placed on health in China is highlighted by their system, in traditional medicine, whereby the practitioner is paid for maintaining one's health rather than for treating sickness.

NURSING AND HEALTH

At the heart of nursing lies the helping and healing relationship between nurse and patient/client. Four factors are present in models of nursing; health, person, nurse and environment. There are many models of nursing each with its own invaluable contribution to the practice of nursing and to the understanding of health. The following illustrate some of the ways in which the interrelationship of these four factors have been interpreted.

The forerunner of nursing theory was Florence Nightingale whose 'laws of nursing' were aimed at promoting health as well as relieving the suffering of humanity. She identified two types of nursing; sick nursing and health nursing. The latter, which would require some practical teaching, was to be practised by all women and its goal was the prevention of disease. Considerable attention was paid to the person's environment and its effect on health, particularly 'dirt, drink, diet, damp, draughts and drains'. She was greatly concerned for the 'health of houses' and claimed that one could better predict health problems if one checked houses, conditions and ways of life rather than the physical body. Her understanding of the person included physical, intellectual, emotional, social and spiritual needs. She saw health as a complex process, not merely the opposite of disease but, 'being able to use every power we have to use'.

Henderson (1969) states, 'The unique function of the nurse is to assist the individual, sick or well, in the performance of those activities contributing to health or its recovery (or peaceful death) that he/she would perform unaided if he/she had the necessary strength, will or knowledge. And to do this in such a way as to help him/her gain independence as rapidly as possible.' Health is equated with independence on a continuum that equates illness with dependence. This level of independence involves 14 components:

1   Breathe normally.
2   Eat and drink adequately.
3   Eliminate body waste.

4 Move and maintain desirable postures.
5 Sleep and rest.
6 Select suitable clothes — dress and undress.
7 Maintain body temperature within a normal range by adjusting clothing and modifying the environment.
8 Keep the body clean and well groomed and protect the integument.
9 Avoid changes in the environment and avoid injuring others.
10 Communicate with others expressing emotions, needs, fears or opinions.
11 Worship according to one's faith.
12 Work in such a way that there is a sense of accomplishment.
13 Play or participate in various forms of recreation.
14 Learn, discover or satisfy the curiosity that leads to normal development and health and use the available health facilities.

Implicit in this understanding of health is the recognition that the person makes the choices regarding their state of health and while the nurse may facilitate these choices the ultimate responsibility for health is borne by the person. Although the 14 components will always be present the interpretation of them for each individual person is unique. Henderson's definition of nursing includes the assumptions that independence is valued by the nurse and the patient more than dependence and that people desire health and will act in a way to achieve this if they have the knowledge, capacity or will.

Dorothea Orem's model centres on self-care. She defines health as a state of wholeness, or integrity of the individual human being, and the capacity to live within one's physical, biological and social environments and achieve some measure of one's potential. Universal self-care requisites include:

- sufficient intake of air, water, and food;

- provision of care associated with elimination;
- the maintenance of a balance between activity and rest, and between solitude and social interaction;
- the prevention of hazards to life, functioning and wellbeing;
- the promotion of human functioning and development within social groups in accord with human potential and limitations.

Man, she states, is self-reliant and responsible for both self-care and the wellbeing of his/her dependents. The behaviour necessary to sustain health is developed through experiences with the environment which offers conditions conducive to health and development. Activities of self-care are learned relative to the beliefs, habits and practices which characterize the cultural group to which one belongs. Nursing is necessary when a person is unable to meet their self-care needs and its aims are to enable the person to become self-directing.

Roy's model of nursing uses adaptation as the central component. The person is seen as a biological, psychological and social being, constantly interacting with a changing environment. To cope with this changing world the person must adapt. Adaptation behaviour may be innate or learned. For instance on a warm day a person may adapt by sweating, removing a coat or seeking shade. Health is defined as a continuum ranging from peak wellness to death with varying degrees of health or wellness between these extremes. Interaction between the person and the environment will frequently lead to adaptation which may promote or restore health. The consequence of the adaptation process is an increase in coping ability so that gradually greater ranges of stimuli can be dealt with successfully. The person is constantly in a state of dynamic equilibrium leading to higher and higher levels of wellness. Nursing is needed when unusual stressors or weakened coping mechanisms make the person's attempts to cope ineffective. Nursing aims to promote the adaptation necessary by a person to fulfil their needs.

HEALTH EDUCATION AND HEALTH PROMOTION

One of the determinants of health and wellness appears to be the person's capacity to make his/her own choices. This choice is based on many factors which include the traditions of the cultural group and the family, self-awareness and knowledge. Self-awareness and knowledge are particularly important if there is to be progress and change. They allow a person to make an informed choice about his/her health. For instance, a child may grow up in an area where many people, including his family, smoke. He may begin to smoke with his young friends at school and continue smoking with his workmates. He may become aware that he has more coughs and colds than non-smoking friends and becomes more breathless when playing sport. However, an informed decision about whether to continue smoking or not cannot be made until he understands the risks associated with smoking, both in the present and in the future. Health education seeks ways of providing this information in meaningful ways so that people can make informed decisions about their health. In order to achieve this it sometimes uses advertising methods to neutralize the effects of the promotion of unhealthy practices, such as cigarette smoking.

The word 'education' is derived from the latin stem, *educo*, meaning, literally, to draw out. Health education is sometimes wrongly seen as forcing ideas onto people and coercing them into changing their ways of behaviour. It may also be seen as moralizing. This is not its aim. It seeks to empower people to take control of their own health by giving them choices rather than removing the power of choice

from them. As well as providing knowledge, health education helps to put people in touch with their feelings about certain behaviours, such as smoking or overeating, and their reasons for doing it. Increase in self-awareness can facilitate change. It is often the case that a person who has managed to change an unhealthy habit will influence other people. A woman who loses weight through eating a more healthy diet may influence the rest of her family, so preventing obesity and possibly heart disease. Someone who had an alcohol problem may start a support group for colleagues at work with a similar problem. In this way the principles of good health spread outwards rather like ripples on a pond.

Health promotion is an umbrella term which includes health education but has much wider aims. It seeks to change the environment so that healthy choices are easier, for instance through lobbying parliament for a ban on cigarette advertising and non-smoking areas in public places, or the promotion of non-alcoholic drinks in pubs. It makes use of marketing research and advertising methods to promote health in ways which are likely to be most effective. It constantly monitors the prevalence of health problems, such as drug abuse or alcoholism and plans accordingly. It may do this through interviewing sample groups within the population to discover their attitudes to a specific health issue and will then plan a health promotion campaign, for instance the 'Don't drink and drive' campaign at Christmas time. Most campaigns make use of the media, especially local radio, posters in public places and television. Some District Health Authorities have a Health Promotion Unit which includes Health Promotion Officers skilled in research and marketing methods. They actively promote good health, identify specific health problems, plan health education campaigns and evaluate their effectiveness. The information provided by this department and its resources is also invaluable to other health care workers, such as hospital nurses and health visitors, involved in the promotion of health.

PREVENTIVE HEALTH CARE

Illness is regarded as an interaction of agent, host and environment:

Agent⟷Host⟷Environment

In any community the constant threat of disease or illness must be controlled. This may be achieved through environmental measures such as the provision of an adequate and clean water supply, or through strengthening the 'defences' of the agent as in immunization and health education. In the past, the major threats to health came from infectious diseases. Today, many diseases are self-induced; the so-called 'lifestyle' diseases. Preventive health care is divided into primary prevention, secondary prevention and tertiary prevention.

Primary prevention is the eradication of the cause of disease before it attacks the host. It includes immunization against specific diseases such as poliomyelitis, pertussis, measles, diphtheria and tuberculosis; and specific measures such as the avoidance of accidents, a balanced diet, and not smoking.

Secondary prevention is the early identification of a disease before it manifests itself. It includes breast self-examination to detect any sign of changes or lumps, and the detection of congenital dislocation of the hip in babies. In both of the examples given early detection is crucial for effective treatment. Often self-awareness of any change in one's normal bodily functioning together with knowledge of certain signs and symptoms which require treatment will ensure that early treatment is sought. However, some people may ignore early warning signs because they do not realize their significance. Moreover, some diseases are not detectable to the person in the very early stages; for example, cervical cancer, phenylketonuria and tuberculosis. Some

such conditions can be detected through 'screening'. The principles behind screening and the criteria which must be met are:

1 The disease being searched for should always be a reasonably serious one.
2 The screening test should be simple to carry out and unequivocal in its interpretation.
3 As far as possible the test should be objective, not subjective, i.e. the presence of a chemical not normally found or the presence of abnormal cells.
4 The test should always be completely safe and should not produce undue fear or apprehension in the people tested. Also, they should fully understand the nature of the test and the consequences should it prove positive.
5 Effective treatment should be available for the abnormal condition or disease being screened for.

Tertiary prevention is the curing of disease, the prevention of complications, and the prevention of spread of disease. This includes medical and surgical intervention for established disease. The prevention of complications is as important as effective cures. For instance, a child who is found to have a hearing impairment will be given a hearing aid and possibly special education which will limit the problems associated with poor hearing even though the condition cannot be cured. Chronic illness and disabling conditions can cause the person to develop other associated problems such as depression and loneliness due to immobility. Such problems can be limited through sensitive health care at an early stage of the problem.

PERSONAL, FAMILY AND COMMUNITY HEALTH

Although health is often seen as a personal issue, it is intimately related to the

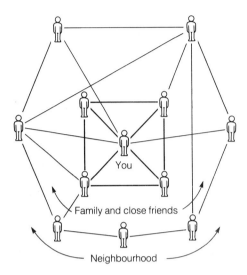

Figure 4. *Network of health care.*

family and the community (see Figure 4). 'No man is an island. . .', and a person's health will be influenced by those around them in the community within which they live. This is a two-way process in that a person will, in turn, influence the health status of their family and that community. Health within the family depends on the needs of each family member being met. Most families seem naturally to consider the 'holistic' health needs of each other. For instance, the care of a young child will involve not only adequate food and warmth but also the provision of emotional warmth and security, play, and the development of social relationships with family members, friends, playgroup leaders, childminders and so on. Similarly, a family caring for an elderly person will consider such things as outings, friendships, personal interests and their need to be respected for their wisdom and experience. Families develop their own attitudes towards health, and this is constantly changing as new ideas from outside the family are assimilated.

Communities are composed of individuals and families and so both reflect and enhance the health status of that community. In some communities there are natural caring networks where people share knowledge as well as their fears and problems. In this way people help each other to cope with life's difficulties. For instance, many new mothers learn about childcare from their own mother and grandmother, and from other mothers whom they meet within the local community. The care of frail, elderly people within the community is dependent upon family and neighbours visiting, chatting, doing shopping and generally offering support. Health services complement this system and are necessary when, for various reasons, health needs cannot be fulfilled. Health needs are more easily met within some communities than others, and are affected by such things as access to facilities for shopping, health care, leisure, public transport; prevalence of crime; employment; and type of housing (see Chapter 15).

MEASUREMENT OF HEALTH WITHIN A COMMUNITY

The health of a community can be assessed by the use of certain vital statistics which are connected with the life and health of the people within that community. At present, there are no satisfactory ways of measuring positive health or wellness. Most of the information gathered relates to the incidence and prevalence of disease (morbidity) and the number of persons dying from disease (mortality). Some improvements in health are particularly noteworthy. The major infectious scourges of the 19th century have largely been combated (see Figure 5). This has come about through specific public health measures such as ensuring a clean water supply to prevent cholera; immunization to prevent poliomyelitis, diphtheria, etc.; vaccination and mass screening to detect and treat tuberculosis; and general improvements in living with better housing, less overcrowding, better diet, more leisure time,

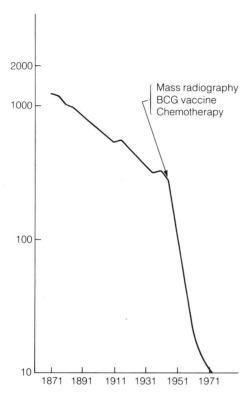

Figure 5. *Effectiveness of health measures in reducing mortality from tuberculosis. The graph shows mortality from tuberculosis, 1871–1971, in England and Wales.*

contraception and so on. The new scourges which are relevant today include Acquired Immune Deficiency Syndrome (AIDS), drug abuse and coronary heart disease (see also Chapter 17).

The health status of some sections of the community however still gives cause for concern. The Report of the Working Group on Inequalities in Health (The Black Report) (1980) showed that there were considerable differences in the health of people in Britain and that this was related to social class. In general terms, whereas the health status of people in social class 1 (professionals) has improved since the inception of the National Health Service there has been no such improvement in the health of people in social class 5 (unskilled workers) and in some instances it has even worsened. The relationship between type of employment (and unemployment) and health is clearly documented, illustrating again the relationship between the environment and health. There is a clear need for health care to be directed towards vulnerable groups in an attempt to redress these inequalities in health and to campaign for adequate facilities within communities to enhance health.

Health is not a single, static entity. It is a complex process which is continually evolving and which is influenced by many outer forces involving the family, community and environment as well as the inner personal forces determined by mind and body. The enhancement of health demands a constant, quiet vigilance based on self-awareness and the pleasure of experiencing a sense of wellness. There are times when extra attention is required to stave off threats to health or to restore it after a period of illness. It is also inevitable that some health potential will lie dormant for a time before it is realized. Change to any part of it will affect the whole system and this change may be enhancing or damaging. It is for each person to decide upon the direction which their health and personal sense of wellbeing will take, and it is the skill of the nurse to recognize and understand this and to sensitively enable that person to realize his/her own health potential.

References and further reading

Ardell, D.B. (1977) *High Level Wellness.* Emmaus, PA: Rodale Press.
Blattner, B. (1981) *Holistic Nursing*, Englewood Cliffs, NJ: Prentice-Hall.
Dalzell-Ward, A. J. (1974) *A Textbook of Health Education.* London: Tavistock Publications.
Dunn, H. L. (1961) *High-level Wellness.* Arlington, VA: R. W. Beatty.
Ewles, L. & Simnett, I. (1985) *Promoting Health. A Practical Guide to Health Education.* Chichester: John Wiley.
Fitzpatrick, J. & Whall, A. (1983) *Conceptual*

Models of Nursing. Analysis and Application. Bowie, MD: Robert J. Brady.

Fulder, S. (1984) *The Handbook of Complementary Medicine.* (Sevenoaks: Hodder & Stoughton (especially Chapter 1).

Henderson, V. (1969) *Basic Principles of Nursing Care*, revised edn. Geneva: International Council of Nurses.

Illich, I. (1975) *Medical Nemesis. The Exploration of Health.* London: Marion Boyars.

Kenyon, J. N. (1986) *21st Century Medicine. A Layman's Guide to the Medicine of the Future.* Wellingborough: Thorsons.

Mansfield, P. (1982) *Common Sense about Health.* Louth, Lincolnshire: Templegarth Trust.

Meredith Davies, J. B. (1983) *Community Health, Preventive Medicine and Social Services*, 5th edn. London: Baillière Tindall.

Open University (1980) *The Good Health Guide.* London: Pan Books.

Prevention and Health: Everybody's Business. A Reassessment of Public and Personal Health (1976) London: HMSO.

Riehl, J. P. & Roy, C. (1980) *Conceptual Models for Nursing Practice*, 2nd edn. New York: Appleton-Century-Crofts.

Townsend, P. & Davidson, N. (1982) *Inequalities in Health. The Black Report.* Harmondsworth: Penguin.

2

General Health Measures

Health is a complex issue. We may easily assume that we know what it entails and yet it can mean quite different things to different people. It will also change throughout the course of a lifetime and be influenced by many different factors. There is no 'blueprint' for good health but there are general guidelines which can safely be taken to be pointing in the direction of health. We must surely all have heard stories of people who smoke and drink alcohol copiously and still live to a 'ripe old age'. The evidence that exists suggests that the risks of ill-health associated with such a lifestyle are high. But ultimately it is for each of us to weigh relative risks against relative benefits and consider the general health measures, make our choices and act according to our personal beliefs and lifestyle.

Below are guidelines of some general health measures. It is not intended as a definitive list.

PERSONAL HYGIENE

Cleanliness is important for several reasons: it protects against micro-organisms which may cause infection or disease, it is socially acceptable and it helps a person to look and feel more comfortable and attractive.

The Skin

The skin has a number of functions including protection of the underlying organs, retention of water in the body, regulation of body temperature, excretion of water and nitrogenous waste in sweat, storage of fat, and sensation. These functions can be carried out most effectively if the skin is clean. After a normal day the skin has accumulated debris in the form of dried sebum, salts from evaporated sweat, dust, and scales from dead cells. This is an attractive environment for bacteria and fungi. On hot days, or following exercise when sweating has been excessive, and in dusty areas where there is a greater accumulation of debris, there is an increased need for washing.

Cleanliness of the skin can be achieved by washing all over with warm water and soap. Dry skin may require an emollient preparation in place of soap. This rehydrates the skin and is especially beneficial to those with a condition such as eczema. Not everyone has access to a bath or shower but an adequate wash can be managed using a basin or bowl of water. Washing removes the micro-organisms and debris which cause the characteristic odour. Sweating is particularly heavy in the axillae where, because two skin surfaces touch, the warm moist area makes a good breeding ground for bacteria. After washing some people choose to use either an antiperspirant (to help prevent heavy sweating) or a deodorant (to reduce the smell of sweat), and both need to be renewed daily. The genital area requires special care and a daily wash with particular attention to the penis

11

or vulval area. Soft toilet paper should be used and it is important for females to wipe backwards towards the anus as this will reduce the likelihood of infection entering the urinary tract from the anal area. A change of underwear daily will help to maintain freshness, and in hot climates cotton is preferable to synthetic materials because it absorbs sweat.

Neglect of personal hygiene may occur as a result of conditions such as senility or depression, or where people are living in close proximity with inadequate sanitation. Infestation may occur with various parasites which easily transfer between people in close contact in these circumstances.

Pediculus corporis (the body louse, see Figure 6) is a light grey insect about 4 mm in length which lives on the skin but lays its eggs mainly in the seams of clothing. The rows of tiny, white, oval eggs can be seen with the naked eye. It causes irritation to the skin and scratching may cause secondary infection or impetigo. In some countries they can spread serious diseases such as typhus. Infestation is less likely to occur if baths are taken regularly and if bed linen and clothes are washed frequently.

Phthirus pubis (the pubic or crab louse, see Figure 6) affects the body hair, particularly the pubic hair. Eyebrows and even eyelashes can become infested but not scalp hair. It can be transferred through intimate contact.

Pulex irritans (fleas, see Figure 7) is a wingless insect which lives on the blood it sucks after biting the host. These bites leave small, red, highly irritating papules

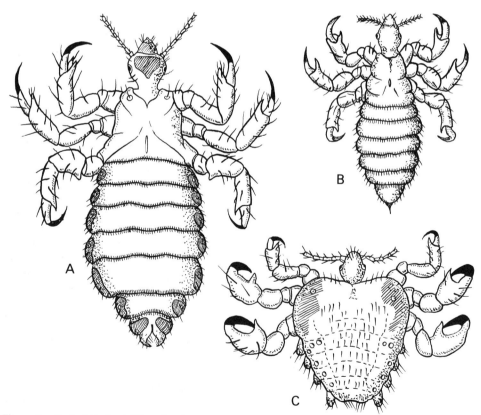

Figure 6.   *Body (A), head (B) and pubic (C) lice. The drawing shows the relative sizes. By permission of HMSO.*

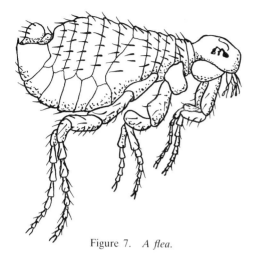

Figure 7. *A flea.*

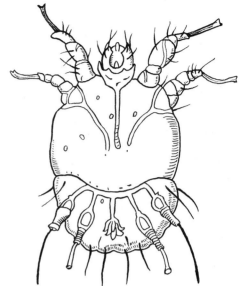

Figure 8. *A scabies mite.*

due to the allergic reaction to the bites. Fleas have strong back legs which enable them to jump considerable distances. The common flea does not carry disease but bites may become infected through scratching. The rat flea (*Xenopsylla cheopsis*) may transfer disease from rat to man. Cat fleas do not live on humans but may bite them in the absence of cats. Eggs are laid in bedding, dust or rubbish and cracks in the floor and the partially developed flea may lie dormant for long periods before completing its life cycle.

The treatment for all infestations is basically the same; a bath to cleanse the skin and hair, treatment of clothing (or provision of new clothing) and treatment of bed linen (and, for fleas, treatment of carpets and furnishings).

Scabies is a contagious disease caused by infestation with *Sarcoptes scabei* (the scabies mite, see Figure 8). The female mite burrows into the horny layer of the skin to lay its eggs. This burrow is diagnostic of the condition and can be seen as a raised line often ending in a papule and typically found on the wrist or between the fingers. The mite is most commonly found in warm skin folds around the lower part of the body. The infected person becomes sensitive to the secretion produced by the mite and a papular, allergic reaction occurs which is intensely itchy. It occurs most commonly in children and often spreads throughout the family. Treatment must therefore include the whole family.

Warts are small growths caused by a virus which occur mainly on the hands. Verrucae are warts which occur on the soles of the feet. Warts and verrucae will eventually disappear spontaneously but can be removed if they cause discomfort. They can be passed from one person to another and so the affected person should avoid walking barefoot in a public place. Special socks can be worn by swimmers with verrucae to prevent them from being passed onto others using swimming baths.

Acne is the most common skin problem between 15 and 25 years of age. Of teenagers, 80–90% have some degree of spots, pimples and blackheads on their face or shoulders. As this is a time of intense self-awareness it can lead to embarrassment and misery. The cause of acne is thought to be an imbalance of hormones which in turn causes an increase in the size and activity of the sebaceous glands. The duct of the gland becomes blocked with the increased amount of sebum and a comedone or blackhead appears. Inflammation may follow producing a pus-filled pimple or pustule. In young women, the normal increase in progesterone towards the end of the menstrual cycle further aggravates the endocrine imbalance and acne may therefore be worse during menstruation. The condition may however improve whilst taking the combined oral contraceptive pill. There is no evidence that diet has a direct effect on acne, although a healthy lifestyle with careful cleansing of the affected areas, clean hair, good diet, exercise and adequate rest may help. Sunlight can help decrease excess oil secretion and so improve acne.

Over the past few years suntans have become less fashionable Response to sunshine is influenced by a variety of factors including skin type, age, extent of exposure, time of year, environment, endocrine balance and use of suntan lotions. During the tanning process ultraviolet rays cause the dermis to produce the brown pigment, melanin, to protect it from burning. As ultraviolet rays do not give heat or light it is possible to suffer sunburn on even cool or cloudy days especially if on snow, white sand or water. The rays cause a concentration of white blood cells in the area and dilatation of blood vessels in the dermis. This process takes from 12 to 24 hours when congestion of the blood vessels cause reddening of the skin and pain. Particular care should be taken of children and by people with fair skins. Sunlamps and solariums have a similar effect on the skin. Exposure to sunlight will, over time, cause slackening in the connective tissue of the skin decreasing its tone and elasticity and will also thicken and coarsen the skin. However, the greatest associated health risk is malignant melanoma which is the main cause of death from diseases of the skin. Friedman (1985) states that in the USA one in 150 people will develop a malignant melanoma during their lifetime and that this is expected to rise to one in 100 by the year 2000. The mortality rate is rising faster than in any other cancer except lung cancer. The factors mainly involved are genetic influence, excessive exposure to ultraviolet light, immunological defect, oncogenic virus and chemical carcinogens. If the melanoma is detected at an early stage the prognosis is excellent with virtually 100%' cure rate. However, if it is left until it thickens the prognosis becomes less optimistic. Friedman suggests periodic self-examination of the skin of the whole body. When teaching people how to differentiate between a suspicious skin lesion and an inocuous one he uses the following guide. A malignant melanoma has A—asymmetrical shape, B—a border which is irregular, C—colour variation and D—diameter usually in excess of 6 mm.

In addition to tanning the skin, ultraviolet rays act on fatty substances called sterols and stimulate production of vitamin D which is necessary for the assimilation of calcium and phosphorus. During the summer months extra amounts of this vitamin are stored to be distributed to the other parts of the body during the winter. Asian people in Britain may become deficient in vitamin D owing to lack of sunlight, the screening effect of melanin pigment in the skin, a deficiency in the diet and the wearing of clothes which cover their arms and legs. A dietary supplement may be required especially for lactating women and children. Vitamin supplements can prevent the deficiency disorder rickets, which has been diagnosed in Asian and Rastafarian children. The problem may also exist for elderly people who are housebound. Glass filters out the ultraviolet rays and so even sitting by a window in direct sunlight will not stimulate production of vitamin D. Supplements may therefore be necessary.

The sun also seems to have the capacity to enhance our sense of emotional wellbeing. Its rays through their warmth encourage relaxation and help to reduce stress and fatigue. Many people comment that they feel generally better when the sun is shining, and conversely feel tired and even depressed after a wet, sunless summer or a long cold winter. Research is being carried out into the effects of seasonal changes on emotional and mental states. The term SAD (seasonally affected disorders) has been coined.

Hair

Along with clothes, hairstyle is a major way of expressing one's personality and also one's ethnic group. It is also something which affects the way we feel about ourselves. Patients who have spent many hours in bed may feel much better simply for having their hair washed. Unkempt hair may be an early sign of fatigue or depression if it is uncharacteristic for that person. The frequency with which hair actually needs washing is difficult to determine. The secretion of sebum makes the hair greasy and it therefore picks up dirt more easily. This varies from person to person but many people will choose to wash their hair at least once a week, mainly for social reasons. Warm water and shampoo are required to remove oil and dirt which must be thoroughly rinsed from the hair. Washing hairbrushes at the same time will prevent oil and debris from being redeposited on clean hair.

Seborrhoeic dermatitis, dandruff, is a chronic oiliness and scaling of the scalp which produces a degree of inflammation. It typically occurs during adolescence. The dead cells, sebum, dust and bacteria produce the characteristic white flakes. The cause is not known although there is some evidence that it may be caused by a fungus infection. It is not contagious nor infectious but it can be socially embarrassing. Regular hair washing with a medicated shampoo usually helps.

Pediculus capitis (the head louse) lives on the scalp (see Figure 6) and can easily be seen when the hair is parted. The eggs (nits) are regular in shape and firmly fixed to the hair shaft (unlike dandruff). They are laid at the base of the hair close to the scalp and are camouflaged and so very difficult to see. Once hatched, the empty egg case appears white and is quite distinctive. Hair grows at approximately one centimetre a month and so the duration of the infection can be estimated. The louse can transfer from one person to another only through direct contact which needs to be no more than a casual brush of heads for instance in a queue or in the school playground. Consequently the whole family may soon be affected. The louse does not discriminate between washed and unwashed hair. The condition often passes unnoticed although it may lead to irritation and occasionally secondary infection through scratching. Treatment with carbaryl or malathion must include the whole family. The highest incidence of infection is amongst preschool children and good grooming campaigns are helpful in playgroups, nurseries and infant schools. As a preventative measure brushing and combing is helpful because it can damage the legs of the louse so preventing it from laying eggs. Routine checks by school nurses have failed to eradicate this social problem and the focus now is on health promotion, teaching good grooming, and encouraging parents to check their children's hair regularly and treat appropriately.

Dental Care

One of the main aims of dental care is to prevent dental caries and periodontal disease, the commonest ailments to affect people in the UK. By the age of 15 years about 97% of children have some caries, and a 1978 survey of adult dental health showed that 30% of people aged over 16 years in the UK had no natural teeth (39% in Scotland). Both diseases are preventable. The main threat to teeth is plaque, a colourless film of material composed of masses of bacteria in a sticky polysaccharide matrix which adheres to the surface of the teeth. It tends to accumulate and thicken unless regularly removed. When sugar comes into contact with bacteria in the plaque acids are formed which cause tooth decay, or caries. Plaque which forms on the gum margin can cause inflammation of the gums and eventually destruction of the bony support of the tooth; periodontal disease.

Prevention involves the following:

- Thorough cleaning of the teeth. This includes brushing at least twice a day to remove the build-up of plaque. Plaque-disclosing tablets will highlight faulty technique. Dental floss removes plaque and debris from between teeth.
- A diet low in sugar. The most damaging foods are those which stick to the teeth such as toffee and dried fruits. Sweet foods are better taken over a short period of time than spread throughout the day.
- Fluoride, either in toothpaste or in the water supply in areas which are naturally deficient. The benefits are most significant during childhood. In Britain the recommended level is one part fluoride to every million parts of water.
- Regular dental checks at least yearly beginning between two and three years of age. This will include advice on dental care and the detection of problems at an early stage.

Hands

Hands can transport infective organisms to the mouth either directly, through nail biting, or onto food which is then eaten. Hands which are kept clean reduce the risk of faeces-borne infections. The most important times to wash hands are before preparing or eating food, after going to the toilet, and whenever they look or feel dirty. Of all the parts of the body hands need washing most often (a point which needs to be considered by nurses caring for patients in bed). It is important to lather all surfaces of the hands thoroughly (including under the nails), rinse under running water and dry carefully on a clean (or paper) towel. Hand washing has been found to be the most important aspect in preventing acquired hospital infection. Careful drying of the skin will reduce the risk of roughness and cracking of the skin, and a barrier cream will protect hands against the harsh effects of wind and water. Hands are not only useful for manipulative skills, they are also used to communicate ideas and feelings through gestures and touch and so their care is especially important.

The Feet

Many foot problems can be avoided with a little care and attention. The Society of Chiropodists claims that with proper foot care you will forget you have feet. Foot care involves cutting the nails straight across (not too short) with scissors, or if they are thick filing them down frequently to thin them down on top as well as shortening their length. A daily wash soothes and relaxes the feet and prevents foot odour, although long soaking in warm water softens the skin making it more vulnerable to blisters. They must be carefully dried especially between the toes. Well fitting shoes are important. The ideal shoe is one which is the correct fit, grips the heel and instep, and has a low or medium heel. At least one pair of such shoes is essential for people who are on their feet a lot. Feet can then tolerate other styles for short periods. Tights and socks are best changed daily especially during hot weather. On cold days it may help to warm the feet gently before going out and wear wollen socks or tights to keep them warm (warm legs also help feet). Feet must not be cramped because this can retard the circulation and cause chilblains. If feet do get cold they can be warmed gently in a bath or 'contrast' baths (alternate warm and cold baths). Children's feet are especially vulnerable and require special care (see Chapter 3).

Feet need extra care during sports. The forces which are applied to the feet during exercise are extreme. A planned programme of exercise gradually building up to more prolonged and vigorous exercise will prevent muscle strain. The selection of correct footwear is vital. It should fit correctly and must not rub. It should also absorb shock, especially for exercise such as road running. Socks are more absorbent and porous if they are made from natural materials. Minor skin infections are a potential hazard and so minor abrasions need attention. Strenuous exercise causes excess sweating and therefore careful hygiene is essential.

Infection of the skin by fungal organisms (athlete's foot) is more likely to occur amongst those who share changing rooms and shower facilities. Moist skin due to sweating and abrasion is particularly prone to this type of infection especially between the toes. Care must be taken to prevent the spread of the infection to others.

POSTURE

It is only relatively recently, in evolutionary terms, that man has walked upright. The back is a vulnerable part of the body and everyday events such as picking up children, carrying heavy shopping, lifting patients, bending over a production line and slouching in a chair place considerable strain on the back. Posture also reflects emotion; someone who feels depressed or dejected may droop their shoulders and upper spine whereas someone anxious and tense may adopt an overly stiff posture. Back pain is a common complaint especially amongst nurses. Strain and damage can be reduced through correct posture (see Figure 9). Whether sitting or standing the body must be correctly balanced. People who spend long periods at desks, e.g. typists, may find a kneeling seat (e.g. the Back Chair) restful because it holds the spine in a straight line and reduces strain (see Figure 10).

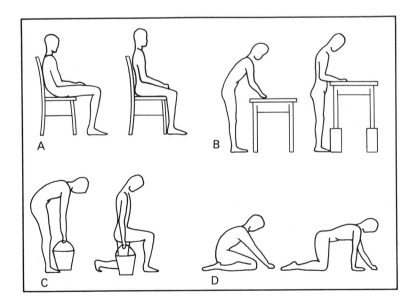

Figure 9. *The pairs of figures illustrate the incorrect (left) and correct (right) posture for (A) sitting in a chair, (B) working at a bench or table, (C) lifting a weight, and (D) working while kneeling.*

Figure 10.   *The Back Chair.*

EXERCISE AND SPORT

Over the course of evolution the human body has become accustomed to exercise and has not adapted to the more sedentary modern life style. Exercise is beneficial for the following reasons:

- It improves the staying power of the heart and circulation and may protect against coronary heart disease.
- It keeps the neck, back and joints supple and corrects posture. It may strengthen the back muscles which support the spine.
- It tightens flabby muscles and develops strength.
- It helps to maintain weight within normal limits.
- It helps to combat stress.
- It helps you to feel good in mind as well as body.
- It can be great fun.

Physical fitness has three basic ingredients:

- Stamina involves rhythmic movement of large groups of muscles for sustained periods. This improves the circulation and strengthens the heart muscles leading to a slower, more powerful heart beat. It makes it easier to cope with prolonged or heavy exertion and may reduce the risk of heart disease.
- Strength increases muscle power, including the abdominal muscles, and so makes lifting easier.
- Suppleness gives the maximum range of movement in the neck, spine and joints. It reduces the likelihood of sprained ligaments and pulled muscles and tendons as well as aches and pains brought on by stiffness.

There is a wide variation in individual differences and any exercise programme should build up gradually. At least 5 minutes of 'warm-up' time is necessary before embarking on any arduous exercise, such as jogging, with a cooling-off period at the end of the session. It generally takes at least three 20-minute sessions of vigorous exercise for 6 weeks before there are any noticeable benefits. Exercise must be enjoyable and an integral part of the general lifestyle. If it is boring or gruelling it does not promote a feeling of wellbeing and will probably soon be discarded.

Sport is a popular way of taking physical exercise because it affords other benefits as well as fitness. It is usually associated with a social occasion and an opportunity to spend time with people who have similar interests. A pint in the pub following a game of football or a cricket match is all part of the pleasure. Sport also enhances mental fitness through competition and tactics. Gallwey (1975) describes a radically new way of learning to play tennis which he later applied to other sports such as golf and skiing. 'Inner Game' methods draw on the skills of the inner self and not the outward, critical, doubting self. Considerable attention is now being given to mental training for those involved in competition. Some sports people (at all levels) describe 'peak experiences' when everything seems to go right without any effort. These are rare moments but for some athletes the intense feeling of wellbeing generated by sports such as marathon running is the primary motivating factor.

REST AND SLEEP

Everyone needs rest in order to combat physical and mental fatigue. There is a saying that 'a change is as good as a rest'. What most people need is a rest from something which they spend a significant part of their time doing. Therefore a sales assistant might find exercise restful, a housewife may do an Open University course, an office cleaner may sit and knit in the evenings, and a nurse may enjoy a good novel. Most people will have a variety of pastimes which they find restful perhaps the most popular of which is watching television. After a hard day it can be extremely restful to watch an engrossing television serial. Holidays may provide a contrast to the normal environment and are often chosen with this in mind.

The amount of sleep required by an adult varies considerably from one person to another, but the average is probably between 6 and 8 hours. Human beings are to some extent controlled in when they sleep by a 'biological clock' known as the circadian rhythm which is a natural cycle of sleep and wakefulness covering 24–25 hours. As anyone who has worked night duty or unsocial hours will know, this can be consciously altered. However, it may take some time for a new pattern to be adjusted to, hence the problem of 'jet lag'. There are generally regarded to be five stages of sleep, representing a scale of depth from 1 to 4 and a stage known as 'rapid eye movement' (REM). When an awake person closes their eyes

and relaxes, brain waves characteristically show the slow regular pattern of 'alpha waves'. The deeper stages of sleep are recognized by theta and then delta waves. After about an hour of sleep, and then at intervals throughout the night, REM sleep occurs. In terms of brain activity this is similar to the near-waking state and is the time at which dreams occur. It is quite difficult to rouse a person during this stage although they may wake spontaneously if the dream is disturbing.

Factors conducive to sound sleep include warmth, comfort, quietness and physical tiredness. Many people find a walk in the evening and a warm bath before going to bed restful. A warm milky drink (not tea or coffee) may also help. The main adverse factor is worry which may prevent sleep or cause early waking. Insomnia is a common problem amongst people of all age groups. Relaxation and visualization exercises may help particularly if a picture of an ideal place of relaxation, such as a warm beach, is created in the mind.

STRESS AND RELAXATION

Stress is generally considered to have an adverse effect on health, contributing to many chronic health problems such as coronary heart disease, hypertension and irritable bowel syndrome. A certain amount of tension is necessary in order to perform effectively; too little and we become bored which may in itself lead to stress; too much and our performance begins to deteriorate and we may become exhausted or ill (see Figure 11). In evolutionary terms stress was originally intended to provide us with a 'fight or flight' reaction necessary for our survival. The body prepares for intense physical activity which in the modern world is seldom appropriate. Someone doing precision desk work may have a physiological response similar to someone doing physical work. For short periods this is not a problem but it can cause health problems

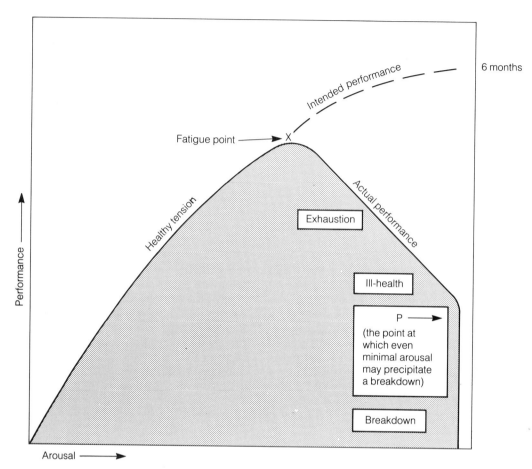

Figure 11.   *The stress curve. When the fatigue point X is reached, the harder the person tries the less they achieve. If arousal continues at a high level it can lead to exhaustion, ill-health and eventually breakdown. Relaxation techniques can reduce fatigue and raise the level of performance.*

Macdonald Orbis

if the reactions are prolonged, excessive and inappropriate. There are various ways of dealing with stress; physical activity particularly for people doing sedentary jobs can 'burn off' some of the physical tension; hobbies and leisure pursuits which distract from the events causing stress; and relaxation.

Relaxation is different from rest in that it is a specific technique which reduces physical tension in the body and brings about specific physiological changes. These include slowing of the heart rate, lowering of blood pressure and a change

of brain wave activity to predominantly alpha waves which are characteristic of meditative states. Some people seem to have the natural ability to relax but others need to learn the skill. The first stage is to recognize tension in oneself. There are many different methods of relaxation such as those described by Bond (1986), Silva and Miele (1980) and Benson (1976). Benson suggests that there are four essential elements; a quiet environment, a mental device such as a word or phrase repeated in a specific fashion over and over again, the adoption of a passive attitude, and a comfortable position. It is suggested that relaxation should be practised for 10–20 minutes once or twice daily in order to markedly enhance wellbeing. Silva and Miele (1980) include positive affirmations to promote health and to prevent illhealth. Silva and others also advocate creative visualization and guided imagery by which a mental image of a specific health goal is created. Tape recordings of relaxation exercises which often feature soothing music or natural sounds are available at health shops. Biofeedback may be useful when learning how to relax. This device is a skin resistance galvanometer which indicates changes in the level of arousal. An auditory signal changes as the person becomes more relaxed and through this learns how to relax at will.

YOGA

The word 'yoga' comes from the Sanscrit word for oneness. It is a personal self-help system of health care and spiritual development. There are several different types of yoga but the one usually practised in the west is hatha yoga which is mainly concerned with health through the mastery of the body. It concentrates on physical exercises and relaxation which are done calmly with carefully controlled breathing. Meditation allows the mind to relax through concentration on words or phrases (a mantra), or visual symbols (a mandala). There is considerable experimental evidence that it can produce predictable beneficial effects on the body's function. Most people practising yoga even over a short period generally experience a feeling of improved mental and physical wellbeing. Other 'medical' benefits require serious devotion.

DIET

In western society eating habits have changed markedly over the years, especially the post-war years. This has been due to a number of factors; changes in food production and processing, greater availability of imported foods, food marketing, 'convenience' foods, as well as changes in attitudes regarding what we believe to be 'good for us'. After the war, the consumption of refined foods, fat and protein greatly increased. Carbohydrate, the staple foodstuff of the past was neglected. The previously 'luxury' foods became more typical of family meals during the 'you've never had it so good' days of the 1960s.

Meanwhile, in developing countries, many people continued to live at or just above starvation level because of crop failure due to lack of water, crop destruction due to disease and pests, natural disasters such as floods and earthquakes, and inefficient traditional farming methods. The result of famine can be divided into three groups: diseases of malnutrition and death from starvation which particularly affect the old and the very young; disorganization of social structures as people search for food and may become refugees in other countries; and the spread of epidemics as a result of overcrowding and lack of hygienic precautions. Third world countries free of famine often have a diet which is largely based on carbohydrates such as maize or rice. It has been noted that in these countries very few people are overweight and there is a markedly low incidence of the 'diseases of affluence' such as coronary heart disease, diabetes and bowel cancer. Increasingly, therefore, the west is turning to the third world to learn about 'healthy' eating.

It has generally been accepted that the basis of a good diet is a mixture of the various foods as this ensures that all the necessary nutrients will be consumed over the day's meals. However, it is increasingly recognized that the amounts of unrefined carbohydrates should be increased with a corresponding decrease in fat intake. In Britain the average diet provides about twice as much protein as is needed. Protein from animal sources is usually associated with high fat intake whereas protein from vegetables will reduce fat intake and also fill the energy gap left by the reduction of fat and sugar. The NACNE Report (1983) advocates a substantial reduction in the consumption of fat from 38% towards 30% of total energy intake together with a reduction in sugar intake to a value of half that being consumed. To facilitate this it recommended the production of leaner meat and improved labelling of food to indicate 'hidden' fat and sugar. Likewise the COMA Report (1984) in considering the prevention of heart disease recommended a reduction in fat intake to no more than 35% of total food energy, including 15% from saturated fatty acids. There is some evidence that a reduction in salt intake is advisable because of an association with hypertension in certain people. The DHSS guidelines in *Present Day Practice in Infant Feeding* (1980) recommend a low salt intake in infancy because of a theoretical association with hypertension in later life. For many people this entails a significant change in eating habits.

In western countries obesity is the most common form of malnutrition. The NACNE Report (1983) states that in Britain the prevalence of overweight increases from 15% in 16 to 19-year-olds, to 54% in men and 50% in women 60–65 years of age. If all adults are considered, 39% of men and 32% of women are overweight with 6% of men and 8% of women being classified as obese (see Figure 12). There is a wide range in what is generally considered to be a reasonable body weight for one's height which is based on averages from a sample group of people. Body weight is maintained when the intake of food matches energy output. It increases when requirements are misjudged so that over a period of time more food is taken than is needed. One of the most important factors is feeling comfortable, physically, emotionally and socially, with one's weight and this varies considerably from person to person. Problems begin when overweight begins to affect the way in which one sees oneself or the way in which one leads one's life.

Dally and Gomez (1980) suggest a number of factors which may contribute to excessive weight gain. There appears to be an inherited predisposition in certain families to put weight on easily. This supports the notion that some people seem to be able to eat what they like and not gain weight whereas others gain weight quickly if they step outside their modest diet. The people who do not gain weight seem to be able to deal with excess

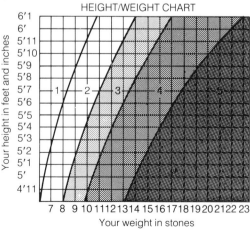

Figure 12.   *Height/weight chart. Reproduced by permission of the HEA.*

food by burning it off and converting it into heat rather than storing it. Storage seems to predominate in those who gain weight readily. Lack of exercise can contribute to weight gain because the energy expenditure is relatively low. Another complex factor is the attitude to food which develops through childhood. Food may be used to comfort the child in every circumstance so that in later life it is used to deal with such diverse problems as loneliness, anxiety or boredom. Or a habit of overeating may have developed in childhood as a result of parental anxiety over the child not gaining enough weight.

Orbach (1978) estimates that more than half of the female population (in western countries) between the ages of 15 and 50 years suffer from some form of eating problem and are constantly concerned with their weight. She examines some of the reasons, other than hunger, which cause people to eat and suggests that the need for food as a comfort conflicts with the expectations of society for slimness. These incompatible needs set up a self-hating struggle whereby one can never be entirely happy with either oneself or one's eating habits.

Weight loss occurs when the intake of food is lower than the requirements of the body for energy. The energy value of foodstuffs and body tissues is measured in calories or kilocalories. When food intake is reduced in starvation conditions or slimming the glycogen store in the liver and muscles is quickly used up along with the water store. This accounts for a rapid weight loss of about 7 pounds. Then, equal proportions of protein and fat are used for a few days and then a higher proportion of fat to protein is used. Fat is not as heavy as protein and so weight loss becomes slower. When the fat reserves are used up serious health problems begin because the body must then draw on protein from muscles including the heart muscle. 'Slimming diets' are extremely difficult to sustain and bodyweight lost is usually regained when old eating habits are reverted to. It is

therefore preferable to make gradual but permanent dietary changes reducing fats and sugar over a period of time and replacing refined foods with wholegrains and chips with jacket potatoes. As the changes are for life it is important that the foods are enjoyable and the diet varied and balanced.

MAINTAINING CONTINENCE

Incontinence of urine is a relatively common problem amongst people of all ages although it gradually becomes more likely with increasing age. A study by Thomas et al in 1980 found that in the UK one in four women and one in ten men had some incontinence, and for about 5% of the population this was regular incontinence which was defined as 'involuntary excretion or leakage of urine in inappropriate places or at inappropriate times twice or more a month, regardless of the quantity of urine lost'. From these results Norton (1986) estimates that between two and three million people in the UK are regularly incontinent of urine.

Incontinence can, to a great extent, be prevented through exercises designed to strengthen the pelvic floor muscles. Women in western countries are not taught how to use these muscles and so they become weak from disuse. In addition they may become strained during childbirth especially during a long labour or with a large baby. One exercise is to stop the flow of urine midstream. This is important for identifying the pelvic floor muscles and for getting the feel of contracting them. Exercises involving alternately contracting and then relaxing the pelvic floor mucles should be carried out daily and can be done at specific times associated with chores such as doing the washing up or ironing. Eileen Montgomery (1983) describes these exercises in detail. They are especially important following childbirth and abdominal surgery but the message is really that they are for everyone and for life. An adequate daily intake of fluid, which for most people is the equivalent of eight cups, prevents the bladder from becoming irritated by overly concentrated urine.

SEXUAL BEHAVIOUR

Sexuality encompasses a lifetime of feelings beginning with the caresses and explorations of early childhood. It is a reflection of how we see ourselves and how we see others; how we show affection and how we seek affection; what gives us comfort and how we give comfort to others. It is also bound up with love, the choice of sexual partners and childbirth. Society sets rules which to some extent control sexual behaviour. These social norms are constantly changing. Relatively recently homosexuality was seen as deviant, and adultery shameful. In Britain today being gay is normal and extramarital relationships are commonplace. Many adults will have several sexual partners before marriage (or a permanent relationship) and an increasing number will have other sexual partners afterwards. Couples may refer to their relationship as 'open' or 'closed' to describe their agreement in relation to taking other sexual partners. When there is a violation of the trust within a relationship there may be feelings of unhappiness, insecurity and emotional trauma.

Frequent changes of sexual partners creates the risk of sexually transmitted disease, also known as genito-urinary infections (sexually transmitted diseases and Acquired Immune Deficiency Syndrome are covered in Chapter 16). Recent evidence also suggests that cancer of the cervix may be linked to a virus which can be transmitted during sexual intercourse. The risk is increased if the woman becomes sexually active at an early age, has many partners or if her partner has many different sexual partners (see also Chapter 8). The risks of becoming infected can be lessened and the following precautions are suggested by the Health Education Council:

- Limit the number of sexual partners.
- Avoid sexual intercourse with a partner who has any inflammation, sore or unusual discharge around the genital area, and oral sex with a partner who has cold sores around the mouth.
- Use the sheath or diaphragm which gives some protection against infection if used properly.
- Pass urine and wash the genital area as soon as possible after intercourse. This may help to prevent cystitis and urethritis.
- Inform sexual partners of a suspected or diagnosed infection.

ALCOHOL

At one end of the scale alcohol may actually enhance health. It can be pleasurable, sociable and relaxing. However, at the other end of the scale is alcoholism which can be devastating for both sufferer and family. Sensible drinking entails limiting alcohol to reasonable amounts, and avoiding it totally when driving, handling machinery or working. Alcohol affects the body by acting as a depressant on the central nervous system. It removes inhibition, reduces visual acuity, impairs taste, smell and hearing, reduces muscular coordination and prolongs reaction time. Obviously small amounts have a small effect but it can still affect decisions and impair judgement. Alcohol also causes dilatation of the blood vessels thereby increasing heat loss and is not recommended whilst out in cold weather or for elderly people at risk of hypothermia.

The Health Education Council's booklet *That's the Limit* is designed as a guide to sensible drinking and clearly indicates, in general terms, safe limits. It is now generally agreed that there is no safe limit during pregnancy because of the possible teratogenic effect of alcohol. Alcohol should also be avoided by those with liver disease. It is a useful exercise to note down the amount of alcohol consumed as it is quite easy to consume more than one realizes. Everyone's tolerance level is different. The important thing is to become aware of how alcohol is affecting oneself. However, the following guidelines will keep most people within safe limits (women are more affected than men due to the fact that water constitutes 55–65% of body content in men, whereas in women water content is between 45–55%. Alcohol is therefore more diluted in men. Also, a woman's liver is more likely to suffer damage):

- *For men*: up to 21 units throughout the week.
- *For women*: up to 14 units throughout the week.

(Note: 1 unit = $\frac{1}{2}$ pint of ordinary beer or lager = a single measure of spirits = a glass of wine = a small glass of sherry = a measure of vermouth or aperitif.)

SMOKING

Smoking is essentially a social habit. Many smokers state that it helps them either to relax or, conversely, improves their concentration and increases alertness. However, the relationship between cigarette smoking and ill-heath is now so clearly established that in general health terms the disadvantages massively outweigh any advantages. A report by The Royal College of Physicians in 1962 drew together previous surveys and research. (A follow-up report was presented in 1983.) The evidence suggested that it was responsible for about 90% of lung cancer and chronic bronchitis, a major cause of cardiovascular disease, and an important factor in other cancers such as those of the mouth, throat, oesophagus and bladder. The Royal College of Physicians estimated in 1979 that cigarette smoking in the UK was responsible for more than 50 000 premature deaths annually. (It is now believed that this could be nearer 100 000.) That does not take account of those people whose quality of life is severely diminished by respiratory disease. Cigarette smoke contains innumerable potentially harmful substances. The main ones affect the body in various ways:

- Tar has a direct effect on the lungs. It damages the cilia and so prevents the removal of mucus and irritants. It also contains carcinogens which can have a direct effect on the respiratory tract.
- Nicotine is believed to be the substance which causes addiction to smoking. It increases the heart rate, raises blood pressure and may cause blood to clot more readily. It may also have a direct effect on the lining of blood vessels increasing atherosclerosis.
- Carbon monoxide is readily picked up by haemoglobin and so reduces the amount of oxygen which is transported throughout the body. It can exacerbate existing heart disease by depleting cardiac muscle of oxygen.

The number of people smoking is gradually declining and there are now more non-smokers than smokers in all social classes. A major cause of concern is the increase in number of school children smoking and the age at which they start (see Chapter 5). It is interesting to note that although the number of doctors smoking has declined rapidly since 1962, the same effect has not been seen amongst nurses. Hawkins (1982) showed that nurses smoked as much as their counterparts outside the profession which prompts the question, why do they not smoke less?

It is notoriously difficult to give up cigarette smoking even though the majority of smokers would like to and most will have tried to at some stage. Ironically it may be particularly difficult during a period of ill-health because it may be a way of coping with stress. Some people set a day when they aim to stop, others cut down gradually. It is often easier with the support of the family, or a small group. There are 'Smoke Stop' groups which provide intensive group support. The Health Education leaflet *So You Want to Stop Smoking* is useful. However, the main factor is motivation; anyone can do it if they really want to.

SELF-AWARENESS

Perhaps the key to good health is self-awareness. Above all it is important to keep in touch with how you feel and how you look. If you spend most of your life feeling fine then the health formula which you have devised for yourself is successful. Health is, after all, about enjoying life and getting the best out of yourself. However, it is unrealistic to expect to feel good all the time and perhaps our expectations of health are more centred on fantasy than reality. The media tend to portray health as a stereotype of youth, slimness and glamour. We all have ups and downs and we are certainly all different. It is, however, important to be aware enough of our bodies to be able to pick up early signs that all is not well so that we can act appropriately. It is easy for the smoker to ignore the cough or for the overweight person to ignore a shortness of breath. Awareness alone can prompt the person to adopt a lifestyle which is more healthy for them. Health is not about worrying about which disease is most likely to affect us. Neither is it about spending time and energy doing things which we loathe or eating foods which we dislike. It is about incorporating into our lifestyle these general health measures and developing a personal sense of wellness, enjoyment and perhaps even happiness.

References and further reading

Benson, H. (1976) *The Relaxation Response*. Glasgow: Collins.

Bond, M. (1986) *Stress and Self-Awareness: A Guide for Nurses*. London: Heinemann Nursing.

COMA (Committee on Medical Aspects of Food Policy), Panel on Diet in Relation to Cardiovascular Disease (1984) *Diet and Cardiovascular Disease*. London: DHSS.

Dally, P. & Gomez, J. (1980) *Obesity and Anorexia Nervosa. A Question of Shape*. London: Faber & Faber.

Davis, A. (1892) *Let's Stay Healthy*. London: George Allen and Unwin.

Department of Health and Social Security (1980) *Present Day Practice in Infant Feeding*. London: HMSO.

Friedman, R. J. (1985) Early detection of malignant melanoma: the role of physical examination and self-examination of the skin. *CAA Cancer Journal for Clinicians* **35** (3), 130–151.

Gallwey, T. (1975) *The Inner Game of Tennis*. London: Jonathan Cape.

Hawkins, L. et al (1982) Smoking, stress and nurses. *Nursing Mirror*, 13 October.

Health Education Authority. Various leaflets, including:
Eating for a Healthier Heart
Fibre in Your Food
Guide to a Healthy Sex Life
Herpes. What it Is, and How to Cope
Incontinence. A Very Common Complaint
Keep it Clean. A Guide to Personal Hygiene
Mind Your Back
Notes on Dental Health Education
So You Want to Stop Smoking
That's The Limit. A Guide to Sensible Drinking
The Fluoridation of Public Water Supplies

Huskisson, J. M. (1985) *Nutrition and Dietetics in Health and Disease*, 2nd edn. London: Baillière Tindall.

Kendall, S. (1986) Helping people to stop smoking. *Professional Nurse* **1** (6), 120–123.

Llewellyn-Jones, D. (1890) *Everybody. A Nutritional Guide to Life*. Oxford: Oxford University Press.

Madders, J. (1891) *Stress and Relaxation*. London: Martin Dunitz.

Montgomery, E. (1983) *Regaining Bladder Control*. Bristol: John Wright.

NACNE (National Advisory Committee on Nutrition Education) (1983) *Proposals for Nutritional Guidelines for Health Education in Britain*. London: Health Education Council.

Norton, C. (1986) *Nursing for Continence*. Beaconsfield: Beaconsfield Publishers.

O'Neill, P. (1982) *Health Crisis 2000*. London: William Heinemann.

Open University (1980) *The Good Health*

Guide. London: Pan Books.

Orbach, S (1978) *Fat Is a Feminist Issue*. London: Hamlyn.

Royal College of Physicians (1962) *Summary of a Report of the Royal College of Physicians of London on Smoking in Relation to Cancer of the Lung and Other Diseases*. London: Pitman Medical.

Royal College of Physicians (1979) *Smoking or Health*? London: Pitman.

Royal College of Physicians (1983) *Health or Smoking? Follow-up Report of the Royal College of Physicians of London*. London: Pitman.

Silva, J. & Miele, P. (1980) *The Silva Mind Control Method*. Reading: Granada.

Society of Chiropodists (1979) *Care of your Feet*. London: Society of Chiropodists.

Thomas, T. M. et al (1980) Prevalence of urinary incontinence. *British Medical Journal* **281**, 1243–1245.

Tyrer, P. (1980) *Stress. Why it Happens and How to Overcome it*. London: Sheldon Press.

3

The Infant

Infancy is generally regarded as that stage of life which begins at birth and ends at about 12 months. It is a time of total dependency on others, of rapid growth and of equally rapid learning. Interestingly it is also a time which is rarely remembered. It is therefore impossible for an adult to imagine those early experiences or to comprehend the ways in which a baby seeks to overcome feelings of hunger, discomfort or insecurity when in the womb only a short time previously everything was catered for and life was a state of balance and harmony. Of all the achievements possibly the most significant is the development of relationships between the baby and carers. A baby is reliant on others to fulfil its needs and can only survive as part of a social group, which is usually a family. From these relationships stem love, joy, trust, language and rich experiences. When a child at about the time of its first birthday stands up and toddles off to face new challenges it is the beginning of independence which is deeply rooted in the feelings of security developed in infancy.

BONDING AND ATTACHMENT

At the heart of human emotion is something which most people call love. Bowlby uses the term, 'affectional bond', a special kind of attraction which one human being has for another. It is now generally accepted that the foundation for this capacity to love, or to form affectional bonds, develops in early infancy. Bowlby (1953) states that an essential requirement for mental health is that 'an infant and young child should experience a warm, intimate and continuous relationship with his mother (or permanent mother-substitute — one person who steadily mothers him) in which both find satisfaction and enjoyment'. Physical contact between the mother and baby immediately after delivery seems to be critical in establishing this bond. Bowlby (1981) suggests that there may be 'sensitive periods' when contact is especially important to the relationship. In addition to the mother there are usually subsidiary attachment figures with whom the baby develops a special relationship, notably the father, but also grandparents, siblings and childminders. (Babies in special care units require careful nursing to ensure that they are not deprived of this essential early experience, and nurses make use of this knowledge to encourage mothers and fathers to handle and soothe their babies as much as possible during this time.)

There appear to be two basic processes involved in attachment. Firstly, responses to signals which may be initiated by either baby or carer; for instance a shriek of delight from the baby will usually bring coos of joy from the carer, and a smile from the carer will often be returned (after a variable length of time) by the baby. Secondly, the establishment of an association between feelings of pleasure and relief of distress with the presence of the carer. The importance of comfort to the infant was convincingly demonstrated by Harlow (1966). Using young monkeys he showed that a soft, cuddly surrogate mother was preferable to a hard, wiry mother even if the latter provided the food. This process of attachment appears to be essential for the development of health. Children who miss out on this experience may later experience developmental delay, psychological distress and difficulties in relating to others.

At the opposite end from love on the spectrum of human emotion is grief. They are inexorably linked so that when the source of love goes away grief inevitably follows. In adult life this occurs at the time of permanent separation or death. For a young child with no concept of time however even short periods of separation from the mother, such as occurs when a baby is admitted to hospital, may cause grief and the accompanying emotions of anxiety and despair. From the age of about six months, and possibly before, the baby knows that mother is special and different and will not readily accept substitutes. Mothers are now encouraged, wherever possible, to stay in hospital with their sick babies and remain the primary carer working alongside nurses. When this is not possible nurses can to some extent minimize the distress by limiting the number of carers.

DEVELOPMENT

During infancy the basic developmental pathways for all human skills and thought processes are laid down. Bower (1977) demonstrated through experimentation with babies that they have an enormous capacity for learning. Within hours of birth they seem capable of complex learning tasks. Parents are sometimes amazed at how quickly their very young baby will develop different sounding cries for different needs, and how very 'knowing' they seem to be. Older babies can even

relearn to wake up in the middle of the night if by chance they discover that a nice warm drink and fun and games are waiting for them, as many parents have discovered to their cost.

Babies tend to acquire certain skills at about the same age, and these are sometimes termed 'developmental milestones'. Some of these are illustrated in Figure 13. It should always be remembered that babies are all individuals and will therefore differ in the age at which they, for instance, start to walk or talk. Developmental milestones are only intended as a guide. However, a baby who is significantly delayed in developmental progress, either in one specific area or generally, merits more detailed assessment in order to exclude any illness or handicapping condition. For instance, a child who is not walking at the age of eighteen months would probably be referred to a paediatrician. However, delay may not only be caused by a physical defect; it may be due to adverse factors within the family which lead to long periods in a cot or strapped in a pushchair. The solution to the problem may therefore be in teaching the parents how to encourage walking by giving the baby greater freedom to crawl and move around.

Most parents would probably agree that differences in temperament are present at birth. Babies, even in the early weeks, will respond differently to situations; some seem very contented whilst others seem restless, wakeful and discontented, demanding a great deal of their mother's attention. Also, parents find that some babies are 'cuddlers' whereas others tend to go stiff and struggle if cuddled. It seems therefore that to some extent personality is determined before birth and that this will be affected by the ways in which the parents cope and how the child responds.

Psychoanalytic theory was postulated by Freud who saw personality in terms of three major systems: the id, the instinctive drives closely linked to biological

1 month

Held sitting

3 months

Prone

Held standing takes weight on legs

9 months

Attempts to crawl

12 months

Walks one hand held

18 months

Walks up and down stairs with help

2 years

Walks into large ball

3 years

Walks upstairs and down carrying large toy

4 years

Climbs trees

5 years

Stands on one foot with arms folded

Figure 13.   *Developmental milestones. From Sheridan, M.D. (1983)* From Birth to Five Years. *Reproduced with permission of NFER-Nelson Publishing Co. Ltd.*

processes and providing the energy
source; the ego, the 'executive' function
which considers reality and decides which
actions are appropriate; and the super-
ego, or conscience, which is the interna-
lized representation of values which
judges whether actions are right or wrong.
Gradually a balance between the different
aspects of personality develops. Freud
believed that the personality developed
largely as a result of what occurred at
fixed stages during the first 5 years of
life. These include: the oral phase from
birth to 1 year when pleasure comes from
sucking; the anal phase during the second
year when gratification is obtained
through holding or expelling faeces; and
the phallic stage from about 3 to 6 years
when pleasure is obtained from fondling
the genitals. Failure to gain satisfaction at
any stage results in arrested development,
'fixation', or 'regression' to an earlier
method of gaining satisfaction.

FEEDING

Babies in the first months of their lives
need milk. The addition of vitamins A,
C and D from the age of 1 month to at
least 2 years of age and preferably 5 years
is recommended by the DHSS (1980) to
ensure against deficiency. The number of
feeds required during the day will vary
according to their individual needs. Most
babies are fed 'on demand' but gradually
adopt a more regular feeding pattern of
three to four hourly within the first few
weeks of life. This is achieved through
adjustment and compromise on the part
of both mother and baby. In Britain
women have the choice of breast or
artificial feeding. Feeding is a time of
great pleasure and comfort, and providing
the baby is held closely and comfortably
and receives the full attention of the
mother both methods are perfectly
adequate (see Figure 14).

(Left) Sitting up in bed, back well supported, with
baby's head resting in the crook of your arm.
(Right) Sitting on a chair, back supported, with baby
on a pillow in your lap.

(Left) A useful position when stitches may be sore,
or for relaxed night feeding. To feed on the other
side just turn over.
(Right) Try this position if your tummy is sore after a
Caesarean. Baby's feet are behind you, and he lies
on a pillow placed under your arm, with your hand
supporting his head.

Figure 14. *Feeding positions.*

Breast Feeding

Breast feeding is the ideal way to feed a
new baby and in 1980 the DHSS report
on Present Day Practice in Infant Feeding
recommended that 'mothers should be
encouraged to continue breast feeding
for at least three months'. It is naturally
designed to be the perfect food, is freely
available at the right temperature, quantity and quality, and the amount and
composition of breast milk has the
capacity to alter in accordance with the
baby's changing needs. It also contains
qualities which are irreplaceable by artificial feeding. During the first 5 days
colostrum is produced which helps the
baby to make the adjustment from placental to oral feeding. It is a rich source
of antibodies which help protect the baby

against infection and allergies, and both colostrum and mature human milk contain substantial quantities of immunoglobulin A which acts as a barrier against infection, particularly gastro-enteritis. Because breast milk passes directly from the mother to the baby there is little risk of contamination from external organisms, and there is of course no danger of over-concentrated feeds. Finally, breast feeding can have beneficial effects on the mother's health. Many mothers experience pleasure and a feeling of contentment while they are breast feeding and satisfaction afterwards. Loss of excess weight put on during pregnancy (average 10–12 kg) is quicker for breast feeding mothers due to the energy demands of lactation. Also, lactational amenorrhoea can last for the duration of breast feeding and in developing countries this can have an important family spacing effect. In the western world there appears to be less of an effect and breast feeding cannot be relied upon as a method of contraception (see Chapter 7).

Breast feeding is the most natural and safest method of feeding and there is evidence that in Britain the number of babies being fed in this way is gradually increasing. However some mothers are not able to breast feed and some choose not to for various reasons. There is a small minority of babies who are unable to digest and absorb human milk, for instance those with lactose intolerance. These babies require specially formulated artificial milks.

Bottle Feeding

Bottle feeding is an adequate alternative to breast feeding in the western world, providing that a 'modified' milk is used, but can create serious health problems in developing countries. Most artificial milks are based on cow's milk which has been 'modified' so that it is similar to breast milk in respect of certain constituents — sodium, phosphate, calcium and protein — and adequately meets the nutritional demands of the baby. (Some artificial milks are based on soya protein.) Cow's milk contains relatively high levels of protein, sodium and phosphorus which can lead to hypernatraemia. Normally a baby is able to excrete excess sodium in the urine but if insufficient water is given, if the feeds are made up in too concentrated a form, or if the baby has fluid loss through, for instance, diarrhoea, then hypertonic dehydration may occur. The relative high levels of phosphorus compared with those of calcium in unmodified milk may result in neonatal tetany especially in the first 2 weeks. In hot climates it is important to offer freshly prepared boiled water between feeds to prevent the baby becoming unduly thirsty.

Successful bottle feeding therefore depends on a modified milk being correctly reconstituted, and, in addition, a clean water supply and a means of sterilizing bottle feeding equipment. This method of feeding requires careful teaching particularly if the mother is illiterate or if conditions are generally unhygienic. However it can also have certain advantages as it allows feeding to be shared by other carers, which may be especially important if the mother chooses to work outside the home.

Weaning and Mixed Feeding

Solid foods are generally introduced between 3 and 6 months. Before this time they may lead to obesity, and there is also a possible link between the introduction of foreign proteins at an early stage in the development of the immunological system and the subsequent development of allergies. Also, the relative high renal solute load (sodium, potassium chloride, protein) present in food puts a stress on the young kidney which may be a contributing factor in the later development of renal disease.

The main aim in weaning is to make the infant less nutritionally dependent on milk so that by the age of 1 year it provides only about 40% of the calorie intake. It also establishes the acceptance of a wide range of foods with differing tastes and textures which will ultimately become the family meals. The introduction of foods containing iron is important after 6 months when the reserves from the mother begin to become depleted. The addition of vitamin C to the diet is important as soon as the baby changes to cow's milk (not usually before 6 months). Foods in a variety of flavours and textures can be gradually introduced, although salt should not be added and as a general health measure it is advisable to keep sugar to a minimum so that it does not become an acquired taste.

Although convenience baby foods are marketed, the baby can eat more or less the same foods as the rest of the family if it is suitably prepared. A suggested infant weaning schedule is given in Figure 15. The foods offered in the first months are sieved or strained to a smooth consistency. Around the age of 6 months teeth appear and a baby is able to bite and chew lumpy foods as well as attempt to drink from a cup. From 7 months onwards most babies are able to cope with pieces of hard food such as a crust or piece of carrot but should never be left alone with these foods because of the risk of choking. (Exercise in chewing is also important for the development of speech and children with developmental delay, such as those with Down's Syndrome, may need special encouragement.) At about this age babies usually decide that they want to feed themselves and parents need patience to cope with their 'hit and miss' attempts and the inevitable mess. At about $1\frac{1}{2} - 2$ years most children are having the same mixed diet as the rest of the family.

As the number of vegetarians gradually increases, more babies are being weaned onto vegetarian, vegan and macrobiotic diets. Such diets can supply all the essential nutrients needed by a growing baby, but the best sources may be different from the 'normal' western diet, and there are potential problem areas. A vegetarian diet excludes meat, fish and poultry and any products derived from them but includes dairy produce; a vegan diet excludes all animal produce; a macrobiotic diet relies mainly on vegetable sources for protein but will occasionally include small quantities of eggs and fish. In these diets protein is obtained from four groups of foods (three for vegans): grains, pulses, seeds and nuts, and dairy produce. Most nutrients are quite easily obtained in the correct quantities but some may be more difficult. For instance, vegans and macrobiotics must obtain calcium and B vitamins from non-dairy sources. Supplements which vegans and macrobiotics are likely to find necessary are vitamin B12, vitamin D and iodine. Another problem for babies can be excess fibre which may lead to the food passing too rapidly through the gut. Frequent dirty nappies and a sore bottom will indicate that the diet needs adjusting to less fibre.

Meal times are an opportunity for the developing child to gain new experiences and acquire social skills. The taste and texture of foods together with the use of cutlery pose new challenges. Many babies enjoy the feel of food through their fingers, and the sight of it plopping onto the floor only adds to its interest. They like to play as well as eat. Mealtimes are also important social occasions when the family meets together. The developing child will gradually learn that this is a time of compromise between fun and the expectations of others.

SLEEP

Many people assume that babies sleep whenever they are not being fed or handled. This is not generally the case. The average sleeping time at the age of 3 weeks is about 15 hours although there is wide variation between individual babies. Some babies seem to sleep almost continuously whereas others may sleep for only 10 hours or less. Many babies

This chart tells you what sort of foods you can give your baby at each stage of weaning. Remember that babies enjoy trying different tastes, so vary the foods you give. Your baby may not like them all, but don't worry. It's best to let your baby choose and not to fight over food

*Remember: the age babies need to start solid food varies. Your baby may start earlier or later than four months and you should adjust the chart accordingly.

	Stage 1 e.g. 4 months*	Stage 2 4½ months	Stage 3 4¾ months	Stage 4 5–6 months	Stage 5 6–7 months	Stage 6 7–8 months	Stage 7 9–12 months
Early morning:	Breast or bottle feed.	Breast or bottle feed.	Breast or bottle feed.	Breast or bottle feed.	Breast or bottle feed, if still needed.	Try giving a drink of water or fruit juice.	Drink of water or fruit juice.
Breakfast:	Try one or two teaspoons of baby rice as well as the breast or bottle feed.	One or two teaspoons of baby rice then breast or bottle feed.	One or two teaspoons of baby rice then breast or bottle feed.	Still give baby rice, but try a few teaspoons of lightly boiled egg yolk too. Then breast or bottle feed	Try cereal or porridge and lightly scrambled egg. Try giving a drink of milk instead of the breast or bottle feed. Ask your health visitor whether the milk should be boiled first. Remember, as soon as your baby starts on household milk, it's important to give vitamin drops. Ask your health visitor for advice.	Still give cereal and the boiled egg with wholemeal toast and butter. Give a drink of milk.	Cereal then bacon, egg or fish with toast and butter and a drink of milk.
Lunch:	Breast or bottle feed.	Try one or two teaspoons of sieved vegetables or strained broth. Then breast or bottle feed	Try puréed meat or fish with sieved vegetables. Then breast or bottle feed	Puréed meat or fish with sieved vegetables. Then a little stewed fruit. Try giving a drink of water or well diluted fruit juice instead of the feed.	Try giving minced or mashed food instead of puréed food. Give meat or fish with vegetables. Then try ground rice or semolina, egg custard or jelly. Give a drink of water or well diluted fruit juice	Try cheese or fish, or minced meat, chicken or liver, with mashed vegetables. Then milk pudding or stewed fruit and a drink of water or fruit juice.	Try giving chopped food instead of minced or mashed food. Give meat, fish or cheese. Then milk pudding, fruit or egg custard with a drink of water or fruit juice.
Tea:	Breast or bottle feed.	Breast or bottle feed.	Try a little fruit purée as well as the breast or bottle feed	Try a mashed banana or other soft fruit as well as the breast or bottle feed.	Try a cheese or other savoury sandwich. Then fruit or yogurt. Try giving a drink of milk instead of the feed.	Bread and butter with savoury spread or cottage cheese. Then fruit or yogurt and a drink of milk.	Fish, meat or cheese sandwiches with a drink of milk.
Evening:	Breast or bottle feed.	Breast or bottle feed.	Breast or bottle feed.	Breast or bottle feed if your baby is still hungry.			

Figure 15.   *Weaning schedules.*

fairly quickly begin to associate a place or a situation with sleep. Often mothers have a routine after feeding or prior to bed which tells the baby when it is sleep time. The now largely unfashionable lullaby and pram-rocking were such signals. Probably a reasonably fixed routine is just as useful, and will encourage the baby to adopt a regular pattern of behaviour which will continue into childhood. The opportunity for undisturbed sleep is important for the rapidly growing child, and a baby who is clean, comfortable, satisfied and warm will often settle quickly.

Some parents find it convenient, as well as reassuring, to have the baby with them in their own room in the early weeks. If another room is available it is helpful to move the baby into it within the first few months so that the situation becomes familiar from an early age. Babies should not be placed on their backs to sleep because of the risk of suffocation as they are unable to roll over before about 6 months. The room should be well ventilated but free of draughts and a temperature of 15.5–18.5° C (60–65°F) is ideal. A soft light may also help to create a restful atmosphere and will allow parents to check the baby without disturbance. The mattress should be soft, firm and waterproof; bedclothes should be light and warm. Baby nests and quilted sleeping bags are not suitable because of the risk of suffocation and babies do not need a pillow for the same reason. In hot climates pure cotton bedclothes are more comfortable and reduce sweating. A net fastened securely around the pram can protect against flies, mosquitoes and other insects, as well as cats.

Fresh air has long been advocated as beneficial for babies provided that the weather is not too hot, too cold or foggy. It must certainly be refreshing for babies in homes with uniformly warm central heating. It also offers a new range of sounds, sights and smells for the baby to experience and helps to develop an understanding of the wider environment.

CLOTHING

Articles of clothing for a baby need to be soft, non-irritating, absorbent and easily laundered. Clothes containing man-made fibres are easily washed but are less absorbent than natural fibres and may be too hot in summer or cause a heat rash on a sensitive skin. Loosely woven garments can cause autoamputation if a finger is caught and for this reason tightly woven materials are recommended for children under 1 year. All-in-one garments are both neat and convenient but it is important to ensure that they are loose, especially in length, so that feet and toes are not cramped as this may damage the growth of the foot. Shoes are not necessary until the child starts to walk and are best avoided until then in case they also cramp the foot. Socks or bootees, mittens and a hat are necessary in cold weather to prevent excess loss of body heat.

WARMTH

Newborn babies are susceptible to the effects of heat and cold because their heat-regulating mechanism is only partly developed at birth. In a cold environment a baby will use up a great deal of physiological energy to maintain a stable temperature and will have little energy left for anything else. If the body temperature continues to drop a condition known as neonatal cold injury may develop. The baby will be quiet, sleepy and difficult to feed but because the hands, feet and cheeks are pink the true nature of the problem may not be realised. If undetected this can eventually lead to death. At night the cot can be warmed before the baby is put in. A reasonably constant temperature is necessary, and it should be noted that even in the summer the temperature can drop sharply before dawn.

It has generally been thought that babies tolerate heat better than cold.

However there is now some suggestion that babies becoming excessively hot may be a predisposing factor to 'cot death'. This is unsubstantiated but it is probably best to prevent the baby from becoming so hot that sweating, redness, irritability and heat rashes appear.

HYGIENE

The main aim is to ensure that the baby is always comfortable and free from the risk of infection. Bathtime does however, in addition, provide an opportunity for play.To keep the nappy area free from irritation and rashes it is generally advisable to cleanse the area at each nappy change. Many babies love to lie for a while unfettered and this gives them an opportunity to kick and move freely. Soiled nappies may contain organisms responsible for gastroenteritis and so care must be taken to ensure that any contamination is not transferred to the baby's mouth.

Many babies are bathed every day, at a regular time, as part of a set routine. This ensures cleanliness and provides the parent with an opportunity to check for rashes, dry skin, etc. When bathing a boy it should be remembered that the foreskin is normally adherent after birth and so should not be retracted. Separation will occur naturally after some months. An oil-based cream or a specially formulated nappy cream can be used to protect the skin from urine and prevent nappy rash. For safety it is wise to develop the habit of filling the bath with cold water first and then adding hot to avoid the risk of scalding. The bath can be on either a secure surface or the floor, whichever is easier. Provided the parent is confident the baby is likely to feel secure and therefore happy.

PLAY

Play is an essential part of an infant's life and appears to be a natural product of intellectual, emotional and physical growth. However, continuous encouragement and stimulation are needed if the capacity to play, and its benefits, are to be developed to their full extent. Play enables an infant to develop relationships. Carers can enhance this by singing lullabies, telling nursery rhymes and playing games such as 'peek-a-boo'. From the earliest weeks this also helps the development of language. From around 6 weeks much of the play activity centres on encouraging smiles and, later, laughter. This may involve bouncing on the knee, repeated hoistings into the air and tickling. Skills begin to develop through finger play, which start with reaching out for pram mobiles, banging rattles, matching shapes and other games which involve hand and eye coordination. Much of the play is repetitive in nature and the infant derives immense joy from being able to cause events to recur time and time again. An understanding of the importance of play in infancy is essential to nurses in paediatric wards in order to encourage parents to play with their babies and to integrate play into care when parents are not present.

HEALTH SERVICES

If the aim of the antenatal service is to produce a healthy mother and child then the aim of the child health service is to maintain that health. In Britain, and in many western and third world countries, health services aim to reach all children and offer a health surveillance and screening programme which will promote health, detect ill-health or handicap at the earliest possible stage, and provide care for children with identified problems.

Community Midwifery

In Britain a midwife is responsible for the care of mother and baby both in hospital and at home. Following transfer from hospital, or after a home delivery, she is required to visit daily to monitor the health of mother and baby. She can give help and support on matters such as infant feeding and family planning. She is also responsible for certain screening procedures (see later). Around the tenth day she hands over their care to the health visitor.

Health Visiting

The health visitor is the main health educator to the family and is responsible for supporting and guiding the parent in all aspects connected with health care. He/she maintains contact with the family by visiting them at home throughout the first 5 years. This will vary according to the needs of the family. For instance, a young single mother living in a new town away from her mother and female relatives would be likely to need far more support from a health visitor than a supported mother in an established city suburb with her mother living two streets away and Gran nearby. Because the health of the child is so dependent on the care which it receives it is vital that health services work with the parents and consider the needs not just of the child but of the whole family and take account of the community and culture.

Many health visitors offer postnatal support groups so that discussions which began in parentcraft classes can continue and parents can build up friendships with others who have children of a similar age. In addition to working directly with parents, health visitors can also encourage Mother and Baby Groups on a self-help basis. They are familiar with national self-help groups and local centres and can put parents in contact with the Association of Breast Feeding Mothers, The Assocation for Post-Natal Illness, Gingerbread, etc.

Child Health Clinics

Health visitors hold regular Child Health Clinics in a clinic building or community room which is easily accessible to all parents. They are usually held in the daytime although in areas where a high proportion of mothers go out to work there may be evening clinics. Here parents can bring their babies and discuss any aspect of child care, be given advice on minor health problems and have their baby's health monitored. Sometimes a doctor is present to see children for developmental screening. Increasingly, these clinics are using health promotion exhibits and videos to inform parents on issues relating to childcare and healthy living. Child Health Clinics also provide a regular opportunity for parents to meet and socialize.

Child Development Programme

The project, undertaken by the Early Childhood Development Unit at Bristol University, aims to help in the development of infant children living in some of the most disadvantaged urban areas of the UK and Ireland. Health visitors are specially trained to offer support and guidance to the parents and to enable them to develop their parenting skills. A feature of the project is that it concentrates on changing the human environment surrounding the child rather than trying to change the child directly. It does this by recognizing mothers as experts on their children and helping them to set easily achievable tasks which would begin to overcome their sense of failure or imagined inability to cope with life. In an earlier experimental phase of the programme, the home environments and the children were assessed before and after health visitor intervention and preliminary results indicate that the approach was successful. Mothers were more aware of development, of the need to spend time fostering language and skills, and had a better understanding of good nutrition. The children were more alert, inquisitive, talkative and willing to play games than previously. The parents spoke very highly of the project and acknowledged that they had gained confidence and an insight into their children's development which they otherwise would not have had.

Developmental Screening

Developmental screening is usually shared between the maternity hospital and the Primary Health Care Team. The aim is to detect any abnormality at the earliest possible stage and refer for treatment where appropriate. Health Authorities decide their own screening programme, which usually involves about four routine developmental screening checks in the pre-school years.

Development screening has in the past usually been carried out by either the general practitioner or the community medical officer. However, recently there has been a move for health visitors to undertake screening and only refer to doctors those children whose development is outside normal limits or where the parent is concerned about the child. The health visitor is an appropriate person for this because he/she will be familiar with the family situation and therefore will be aware of any factors which might affect development. He/she can also see the child in its own home and therefore ensure that the most disadvantaged children who might not attend a clinic receive this service. All aspects of the child's development including vision and hearing are considered; a growth and development record is kept (Figure 16), height and weight being charted on a percentile graph (see Figure 16).

The Guthrie test detects a rare condition called phenylketonuria, an inherited metabolic disorder in which there is a failure to metabolize phenylalanine, an essential amino acid present in all natural protein foods. The test is reliable after the first week of life. Milk feeds cause the level of phenylalanine in the blood to rise and phenylketone bodies are excreted in the urine. The effect of this on the brain leads to severe mental retardation if untreated. Treatment involves a special type of milk feed which strictly limits the amount of amino acids. At the same time as the Guthrie test blood is also taken to test for hypothyroidism, a congenital condition which if untreated causes cretinism in children.

Congenital dislocation of the hip is another condition which, if diagnosed very early, can be treated successfully. It is usually screened for several times in the first few months of a child's life. Inadequate development of the acetabulum of the pelvis causes the femoral head to displace and the hip joint will therefore fail to develop fully. The test consists of abducting the hips, and a positive result is indicated by a 'click' as the dislocated head moves back. Treatment consists of keeping the hips abducted in a splint. If this condition remains undetected until the child begins to weight bear, surgery may be required and the joint may thereafter be subject to arthritis.

Immunization

Prevention of disease is one of the most important aims in child health care. During infancy preventive measures can be carried out against several infectious diseases. To be effective the immunization rate within a community must be maintained at a certain level to prevent the outbreak of an epidemic, the so-called 'herd immunity'. However, in Britain no immunizations are compulsory, and are given only with parental consent. The programme begins at about 3–6 months of age in order to afford protection as early as possible. If started too early the immunization may not be successful as the immune system may be too immature to produce the necessary antibodies. Contraindications to immunization include acute febrile illness and any treatment which depresses antibody formation such as steroid therapy or irradiation, and two live vaccines should not be given within 3 weeks of each other. Severe febrile or severe neurological reactions following routine immunization are contraindications to further doses of the

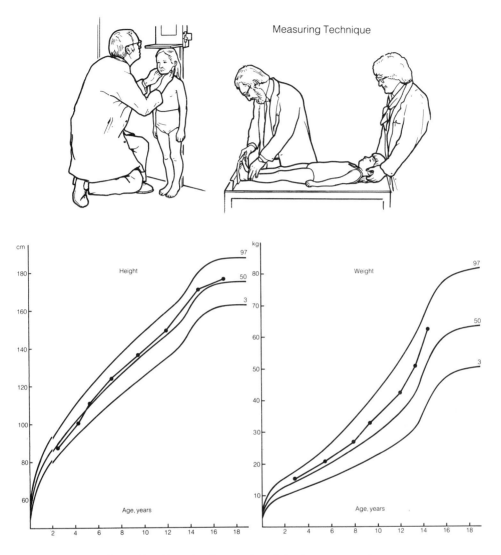

Figure 16. *Example of a growth and development record card.*

same antigen(s). The programme varies from country to country but the regimen shown in Table 1 is typical. Possible side-effects of vaccination are shown in Table 2.

In recent years there has been controversy over pertussis immunization with the claim that it has caused epileptic fits with ensuing brain damage in some children. Retrospective studies suggest that in general terms it is still safer for the child to have the immunization than risk developing the disease (which can also lead to permanent disability or death in a small number of children). Absolute contraindications to this immunization are a history of cerebral irritation or cerebral damage in the neonatal period, a history of fits or convulsions, and a history of severe local or general reaction

Table 1. *Immunization schedule.*

Age	Vaccination		
3–6 months	Diphtheria Whooping cough (pertussis) Tetanus Polio	injection	DOSE 1
5–8 months	Diphtheria Whooping cough (pertussis) Tetanus Polio	injection	DOSE 2
9–14 months	Diphtheria Whooping cough (pertussis) Tetanus Polio	injection	DOSE 3
1–2 years	Measles		
5 years, after school entry	Diphtheria Tetanus Polio	booster injection	
10–13 years	BCG to give protection against tuberculosis (no longer offered in some health authorities)		
11–13 years	German measles (rubella) for girls only to prevent them catching German measles in later years at a time when they could be pregnant, as this infection can seriously damage an unborn baby in the womb.		
15–19 years	Tetanus, booster injection Polio		

Table 2. *Possible side-effects of vaccination.*

Vaccination	Risk of side-effects
Polio	Very small. About one in a million children get some symptoms.
Diphtheria	Too small to measure.
Tetanus	Too small to measure.
BCG for tuberculosis	Very small. A preliminary test carried out the week before BCG is planned detects any children who might be sensitive. Most children have a painful spot where the BCG was performed. Sometimes a small open ulcer forms.
Measles	Very small risk of serious reaction, much lower than risk from disease itself. Vaccination is *much safer* than getting measles.
German measles	Too small to measure.
Whooping cough	There are side-effects but they are very rare and vaccination is recommended against whooping cough *except when:* • the child has a history of fits, epilepsy, 'funny turns', seizures, cerebral irritation or convulsions of any sort; • anyone in the child's family has a history of fits, epilepsy, 'funny turns' or convulsions of any sort; • the child is unwell, particularly with a respiratory complaint or has been unwell in the last two weeks; *this applies to all vaccinations*; • there was any local or general reaction to a preceding dose; • the child has any developmental or other defects.

to a preceding dose. A medical opinion should be sought for children with neurological impairment or delay, those with neurological disease, or where there is a close family history of idiopathic epilepsy.

During the second year of life measles vaccine is offered and it may be combined with mumps and rubella vaccine in some countries. Only one injection is necessary and it is delayed until after the first year because antibodies acquired naturally from the mother are still active during the first year and may prevent immunity in the infant.

In countries where tuberculosis is endemic BCG (bacille Calmette–Guerin) may be given in infancy before the child has been in contact with the disease. In Britain it may also be given at this time if there is a family history of the disease or if the family are immigrants from a country where it is endemic.

Vaccination against influenza may be given to infants who are at special risk, such as those with heart defects, to afford them extra protection against a disease which for them could be especially threatening.

SOCIAL SERVICES

The Social Services department of the local authority is responsible for the provision of social workers, fostering and adoption, and pre-school residential and day care. Under The Children's and Young Persons' Act, 1969, it has many statutory responsibilities including the supervision of certain children at risk or those brought before the courts, as well as the reception of children into care. Their overall aim is to support the family and this involves the provision of certain services.

Infants may require day care because their parent(s) go out to work, or are ill or handicapped and therefore unable to cope with the full-time demands of a young child. For babies day care usually means either a day nursery or a childminder.

Childminders have been used by working mothers for many years. The care they provide is very similar to that of a 'normal' family. They must be registered with social services and normally care for no more than three preschool children at any one time. A research study in Oxfordshire by Bruner (1980) criticized the quality of the care provided and found it often unstimulating. However, childminders have done a great deal recently to improve their image and develop their natural skills. The presence of one 'mother' figure and the general homeliness of the care given is convincing enough for many to see it as preferable to institution-based care. Some social services departments, such as the County of Avon, have successfully introduced a Sponsored Childminding Scheme whereby certain children are placed with childminders and their fees are paid by that department (Harbert and Rogers, 1983).

Day nurseries are discussed in Chapter 4.

If a crisis arises within the family a social worker may visit to help them resolve specific problems. Although every effort is made to keep the family together there are times when a baby needs to be 'received into care'. If this happens the baby is likely to be placed with foster parents and this may be a short- or long-term placement. Because young children need above all a stable loving relationship, care is always taken to ensure that they are not moved frequently between different foster parents and there is a trend towards adoption rather than long-term fostering for babies coming into care.

CHILD ABUSE

Child abuse is not a modern problem. Throughout the ages some children have always been subjected to abuse. It was certainly recognized in the 19th century

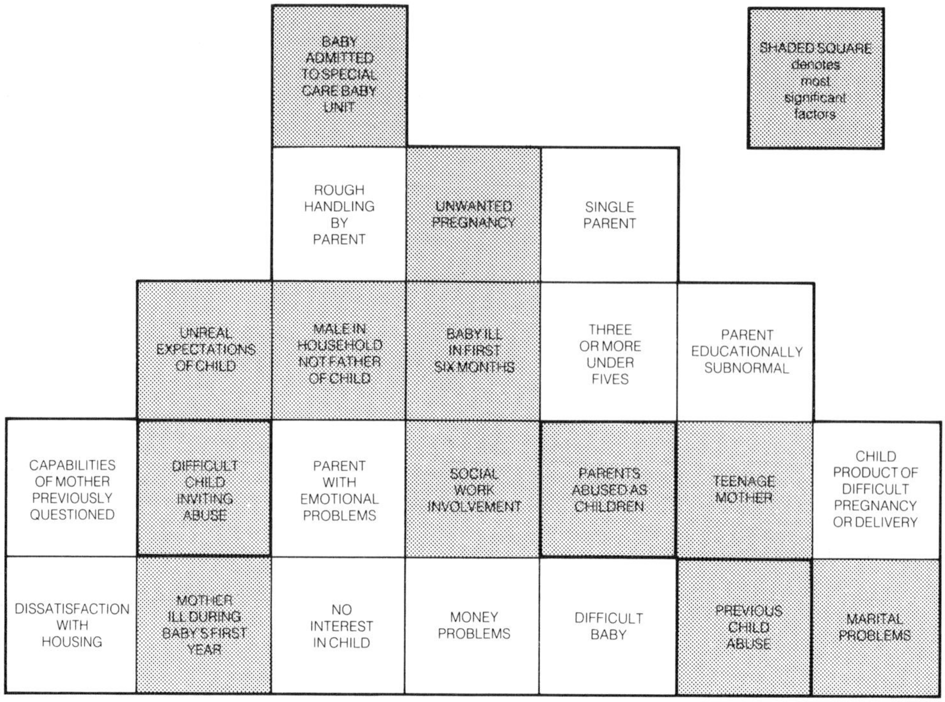

Figure 17.   *Risk factors in child abuse.*

and the work of the NSPCC, Barnardos and the Shaftesbury Society developed in response to the needs of destitute and ill-treated children. By the late 1800s it was reasonably well documented in Britain, the United States and France. However, our current understanding of the nature and extent of the problem stems largely from the work of Kempe in the 1960s.

The Select Committee on Violence in the Family (1977) concluded that in England and Wales an estimated 3000 children are severely injured each year and that six of them die each week. In addition 40 000 children receive mild to moderate injuries at the hands of their parents each year.

Abuse generally falls into three main categories:

- physical abuse, including nutritional and general neglect;
- emotional abuse;
- sexual abuse.

Studies of families where child abuse has occurred has led to a more sensitive understanding of those families and others who may need help. There seems to be a combination of circumstances or factors which suggest that child abuse might occur (see Figure 17). These are:

1   Factors relating to the child including: pre-term baby requiring special nursing care especially if separated from its mother; management problems such as feeding difficulties or persistent crying; generalized failure to thrive; abnormality or 'unwholesomeness, in some way producing feelings of revulsion rather than protection; negative behaviour or stubbornness in a toddler.

2   Factors relating to the parent or care-

giver including: aggression in a person with a previous history of violence; dull/immature personality; young age at the birth of the child; low toleration of stress or presence of severe strain; inability to cope well with life generally including money and relationships; history of physical and/or mental ill-health; history of being abused as a child or receiving inadequate care from parents.

3 Factors relating to family relationships including: three or more children born close together; little evidence of mother–child attachment; marital strife (one partner may not be the parent of the child, e.g. step-father or co-habitee); carers having unrealistic expectations of a child's behaviour or performance; obsessional behaviour by parents who regard the child as a young adult; the child being seen as the scapegoat for family problems; carers feeling that the child is rejecting their attempts to care; abnormal sexual behaviour in the family which may lead to sexual abuse.

4 Social factors including: social isolation such as the father being away for long periods, no extended family, no neighbourhood or friendship support; poor housing; poverty; general deprivation; cultural difficulties, especially stress arising out of differing cultural expectations; social mobility, especially a succession of male partners; alcohol or drug abuse; resentment in the mother at being confined to the home.

Some of the main clinical features are shown in Figure 18. A classical feature is the frozen, watchful expression which these children often have. Infants are the most vulnerable group and even apparently trivial injuries should be regarded as a possible sign of abuse.

Physical abuse usually produces signs such as bruising, burns and scalds.

Emotional deprivation and neglect may be more difficult to recognize. The picture may emerge over a period of time in a multitude of covert ways from developmental delay to failure to thrive.

Sexual abuse is also difficult to detect in the younger age groups although examination of the genitalia may reveal bruising and lacerations. There may also be evidence of sexually transmitted disease. Sexual abuse of infant boys is believed to be rare although it has been identified sometimes through the diagnosis of genital infections. Older children who are being sexually abused may appear sexually promiscuous as a consequence of the expectations of those who are abusing them and they may have knowledge of sexual practices which would not be expected for a child of their age.

Other forms of abuse which have been identified include smothering and poisoning. Munchausen syndrome by proxy was first described in 1977 by Meadow. It is the creation of physical illness in the child, usually by the mother, through the administration of drugs or other substances which will produce physical symptoms often warranting hospital investigation.

Prevention is possible through the elimination wherever possible of adverse factors such as separation of parents and child at delivery. A skilled midwife can give extra support to the mother who does not initially 'take to' her baby. The primary health care team, especially the health visitor, have a vital role to play in prevention by identifying social factors which may give rise to stress, and by offering support and help to families at critical times such as the postnatal period. They can also detect a problem at an early stage and give help to the family before a tragedy occurs, referring to the appropriate specialist services as necessary. All local authorities maintain a register of families who have abused their children or are suspected of having done so (see also Chapter 18).

SUDDEN INFANT DEATH SYNDROME

The sudden and unexpected death of an apparently healthy baby is one of the most

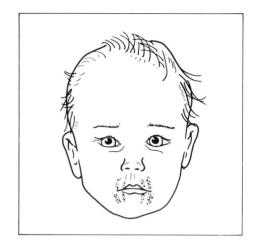

(a)   FACIAL SQUEEZING
– caused by forcibly feeding with a bottle;
associated with other mouth injuries.

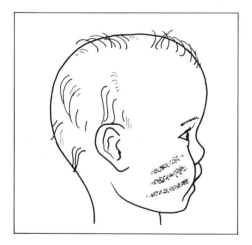

(b)   DIFFUSE FACIAL
        BRUISING
– caused by blows or forceful slapping. Ears
should be closely inspected for pin-point
haemorrhages.

(c)   PINCH MARKS
– on cheeks, ears, body or limbs.

Figure 18.   *Clinical features of child abuse.*

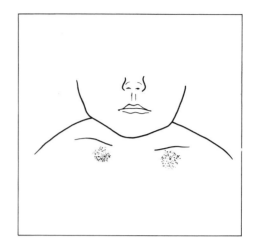

(d) GRIP MARKS
– on limbs, shoulders, neck or body, due to excessive pressure applied during grasping or shaking. Look for thumb and reciprocal finger marks.

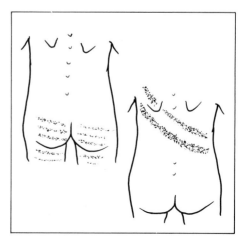

(e) BODY BRUISING
– bruise in protected or 'well-padded' area should alert suspicion. May be caused by hand, throwing, or with a particular object leaving an identifiable imprint

(f) IDENTIFIABLE LESIONS
    Unusual bruising or abrasions should raise one's suspicions that an object may have been used to inflict injury. As with all suspect injuries, it is of great importance to match the injury with the description given. Straight line bruising is frequently caused by sticks, whilst curved bruising may be caused by lashing with a flexible object such as a belt or wire.

(g)   BITE MARKS
Another identifiable imprint – note that the human bite usually produces two hemispherical lines.

(h)   BURNS OR SCALDS
   There may be great difficulty in distinguishing accidental and non-accidental burns or scalds, but developmental status and the symmetry of immersion scalds and additional grip marks may provide clues to the truth.

'Dunking' into very hot water is typical of non-accidental injury

– note that both these injuries are likely to be inflicted; the infant/child does not willingly persist with an activity which produces such symmetry.

(i)   CIGARETTE BURNS
– particularly in clusters, often on the arms, but occasionally on the face where they produce marked swelling.

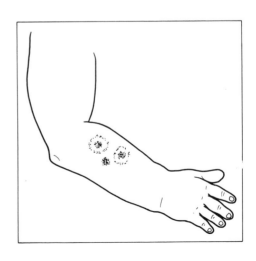

(j)   FRICTION BURNS
– usually caused by man made fabrics such as nylon. They are often seen on prominent areas of the nose, cheek and forehead and may be inflicted by ripping clothes off the child over the head.

(k)   BURNS
– from electric appliances. Often applied to the buttocks leaving an identifiable imprint of the heated element.

(l)   INJURIES FROM CONTACT WITH SOLID OBJECTS
Thumping a child with a closed fist or pushing/swinging him against the floor or wall is liable to produce swelling, which may be localized or diffuse, together with lacerations, abrasions and nosebleeds. 'Black eyes', where there is bruising and swelling of the eyelids, must be differentiated from bruising without swelling under the eyes which can result from a fracture of the anterior part of the base of the skull, though both can be a manifestation of child abuse. True accidental 'black eye' is nearly always unilateral.

(m)   MOUTH INJURIES
Internal injuries are most commonly seen in infants who are still being bottle fed, but will be easily missed in an incomplete examination. Forcible feeding with a bottle may produce tears of the labial frenulum (the band of tissue connecting the upper lip to the gum) together with bruising and swelling of the lips. Deeper penetrating injuries of the mouth and palate may result from aggressive feeding with a spoon.

Isolated swelling of the lips may well follow accidental falls in toddlers and children and may be confused with child abuse.

(n)   SEXUAL ABUSE
This form of child abuse is now recognized as a real and significant problem. A complete examination should include inspection of the genitalia for evidence of bruising and lacerations. In the older female child, tactful questioning about sleeping arrangements and habits may be necessary to identify incestuous relationships.

(o)   BONE INJURIES
Any fracture in an infant who is not yet mobile (less than eight months) is highly suspicious and skull fractures in toddlers are more likely to be produced by child abuse than by simple accidents. Fractures are a reflection of the force applied, as infant bones tend to be supple and are able to bend. They may be suspected by localized soft tissue swelling and a reluctance to use an affected limb in the acute phase, but, as healing is often rapid in this age group, may present as a hard swelling in the bone (due to callus formation) without loss of function after two or three weeks. Because so many bones are not easily accessible to detailed examination, a skeletal x-ray survey is of great importance in the assessment of suspected child abuse, with particular attention being paid to the ribs and the ends of 'long-bones'.

Figure 18.   *cont'd*

distressing experiences that can occur in a family. In Britain one baby in every 500 between the ages of 1 week and 2 years will die in this way (most of them in the first 8 months). A seemingly healthy baby is put to sleep in a cot or pram and when next looked at is found dead. Sometimes the baby may have had a snuffly nose or other minor symptoms but nothing to make the parents suspect a serious condition. A major study on Post Neonatal Mortality was undertaken in Sheffield (1985) and identified some instances where more appropriate response by health professionals might have prevented death.

A study by Camps (1970) found certain factors which seem to be significant:

1   low socioeconomic group,
2   low birthweight,
3   death occurring most commonly at night during sleep,
4   higher incidence during the winter months,
5   mothering skills below average,
6   illness symptoms prior to death.

A study in Sheffield by Emery and Carpenter (1977) identified babies at high risk who were then visited ten times by specially trained health visitors in the first 20 weeks of life. The results suggest that increased surveillance of high-risk groups can reduce sudden infant deaths. However, although this condition is gradually becoming better understood, it is still the case that SIDS cannot be foreseen by either parent or doctor.

The Foundation for the Study of Infant Deaths is a charity which exists to promote research and understanding, and to support bereaved parents.

References and further reading

Altschul, A. & Sinclair, H. C. (1981) *Psychology for Nurses*, 5th edn. London: Baillière Tindall.

Bower, T. G. R. (1977) *A Primer of Infant Development*. San Francisco: W. H. Freeman.

Bowlby, J. (1953) *Child Care and the Growth of Love*. Harmondsworth: Penguin.

Bowlby, J. (1981) *Attachment and Loss*, Vol. 1: *Attachment*. Harmondsworth: Penguin.

Bruner, J. (1980) *Under Five in Britain* (Oxford Preschool Research Project, 1). London: Grant McIntyre.

Camps, F. E. (1970) Sudden unexplained deaths in infancy. In: Clark, J. & Henderson, J., eds (1983) *Community Health*. Edinburgh: Churchill Livingstone.

Child Development Programme (1984) University of Bristol: Child Development Project.

DHSS (1980) *Present Day Practice in Infant Feeding*. London: HMSO.

Elliot, R. (1984) *The Vegetarian Mother and Baby*. London: Fontana.

Emery, J. L. & Carpenter, R. G. (1977) Final results of infants at risk of sudden infant deaths. In: Clark, J. & Henderson, J. (1983) *Community Health*. Edinburgh: Churchill Livingstone.

Feeding Children in the First Year, rev. edn. (1984) Edsall Summaries for Health Professionals. No. 1. London: B. Edsall.

Harbert, W. & Rogers, P., eds (1983) *Community Based Social Care. The Avon Experience*. London: Bedford Square Press/NCVO.

Harlow, H. F. (1959) Love in infant monkeys. *Scientific American* **200**, 68–74.

Huskisson, J. M. (1985) *Nutrition and Dietetics in Health and Disease*, 2nd edn. London: Baillière Tindall.

Kempe, R. S. & Kempe, C. H. (1978) *Child Abuse*. Glasgow: Fontana Press.

Leach, P. (1984) *Baby and Child*. Harmondsworth: Penguin.

Mussen, P. H., Conger, J. J. & Kagan, J. (1979) *Child Development and Personality*, 5th edn. London: Harper & Row.

O'Doherty, N. (1982) *The Battered Child*. London: Baillière Tindall.

Post Neonatal Mortality. A Multicentre Study undertaken by the Medical Care Research Unit, University of Sheffield (1985). London: HMSO.

Sheridan, M.D. (1983) *From Birth to Five Years. Children's Developmental Progress*. Windsor: NFER–Nelson.

Stern, D. (1977) *The First Relationship: Infant and Mother*. London: Open Books.

Weller, B. F. (1980) *Helping Sick Children Play*. London: Baillière Tindall.

Weller, B. F. and Barlow, S. (1983) *Paediatric Nursing*. London: Baillière Tindall.

4

The Preschool Child

'The magician sits in his high chair and looks upon the world with favor. He is at the height of his powers. If he closes his eyes, he causes the world to disappear. If he opens his eyes, he causes the world to come back. If there is harmony within him, the world is harmonious. If rage shatters his inner harmony, the unity of the world is shattered. If desire arises within him, he utters the magic syllables that cause the desired object to appear. His wishes, his thoughts, his gestures, his noises command the universe.'
(From Selma H. Fraiberg, *The Magic Years*, 1976. Reproduced with permission of Methuen & Co.)

This description of the child at 18 months sums up the world of the toddler. And yet, as the word implies, 'toddling' is also an uncertain and an unsteady time when walking, talking and all other actions and gestures are still embryonic. There will be much development and many changes before the start of school at around the age of 5 years.

DEVELOPMENT

The transition from total dependency in infancy to independence 5 years later when the child is able to cope with hours away from home indicates that this is a critical time in the child's development. It may be difficult for the carer to keep up with the pace of change, and to understand the conflict which is created for the child as he/she attempts mammoth new tasks whilst still needing to feel love and security close at hand. Toddlers who stamp their feet and insist on walking rather than going in a pushchair need a guiding hand and when they tumble,

Mum must be there with a kiss to make the knees better. The 'attachment figures' are keys to the toddler's new world; a world built on the confidence necessary to venture forth and to enquire.

Throughout early childhood the behaviour of the child is constantly being influenced by the responses of the carers. Behaviour which is appropriate such as smiles and coos is encouraged and therefore develops, whilst other forms of behaviour such as temper tantrums are ignored and gradually disappear. This interaction is largely responsible for shaping a child's development. Smiles and early words, if not encouraged, will soon disappear, and temper tantrums and night waking if encouraged will persist. Social learning theory is one theory of development which is particularly relevant to the preschool child. It suggests that behaviour develops through direct experience or through observing others. The outcome of actions will partially determine whether they are repeated. Reinforcement is crucial for the performance of learned behaviour.

LANGUAGE DEVELOPMENT

The development of language starts in the first weeks of life as a baby watches, and attempts to imitate, lip movements. At about 6 – 12 weeks babies begin to vocalize in response to coos and words from the carer. These vocalizations can sound so descriptive that parents sometimes describe it as 'story telling'. Babbling develops after around 6 months when the distinctive sounds of da-da, ma-ma, ga-ga are heard to the delight of parents. These sounds gradually develop into understandable single words which can be used to identify Mum, Dad, dog, bus, and other essential features of the child's world. During the second year most children have a small vocabulary and by the age of 2–3 years are able to string words together into understandable phrases.

By the age of 3 years most children are using speech as their main method of communication. They may have several hundred words which they can use, not only to name and describe, but also to illustrate their thoughts and ideas. This ability to bind conceptual thought with language is a major achievement which is still not fully understood. It is an essential part of the child's intellectual development. When a 3-year old child continually asks 'why' it is to increase understanding of how things work through the use of words. Children seem to love the repetitive sounds of nonsense and nursery rhymes and songs. Playgroups and preschool television programmes use this medium a great deal. They seem not only to entertain, but also to form an essential part of the development of speech.

Probably the single most important factor in the development of language is continuous contact with speech. Response to a child's vocalizations from the earliest age is essential, as is listening and encouragement as the child gets older. All new skills must be practised and so it is reasonable that children under five are not always 'word perfect'. However, it is important that the child can understand and be understood. Children who are deprived of this early experience may be delayed in their speech development.

Another reason for delayed speech may be loss of hearing. Most health authorities screen all children with a hearing test in the preschool years. Particular note should be taken of children with abnormal speech development, previous ear infections, those who come from families where there is a history of deafness and those whose parents are concerned.

FEEDING PRESCHOOL CHILDREN

By the beginning of the second year, the child will be able to share most family foods and the same mealtimes. For many families this means a wide variety of foods. A mixed diet should ensure that over several meals all the necessary nutrients are available. Many parents find that their child's appetite fluctuates over this period and they may notice that previously acceptable foods are rejected, or that they seem particularly hungry. A study by Richman et al (1975) cited in Douglas and Richman (1984) suggest that about 11% of 3-year-olds have food fads. The reason for this is not clear and it can be extremely frustrating and even worrying for parents. The most successful approach seems to be quiet encouragement.

During the period from 1 to 3 years the daily energy requirement increases slowly. Increased muscle tissue is deposited and increased mineralization of bone and teeth occurs. The inclusion of 600–700 ml (1 pint) of milk as a drink or in made-up dishes every day provides adequate protein and calcium intake. Cheese, bread and cereals also contain protein and calcium and are useful for the child who does not like milk drinks. Protein contains the vital amino acids in the correct balance in meat, fish, milk and dairy produce, but can also be obtained from a mixture of vegetable proteins found in bread, pulses, beans and nuts. Foods such as fish fingers and beans can therefore supply adequate protein for the child who will not eat 'meat and veg'. Supplements of vitamins A and D which are essential for the development of bones and teeth are especially important for Asian and Rastafarian children whose diet may lack them.

Preschool children may need a drink and snack mid-morning and/or mid-afternoon when they begin adjusting to family mealtimes. Many snack-type foods such as fruit, raw carrots, cheese sandwiches, and savoury biscuits are nutritious and form an essential supplement to the daily diet. Sweets as a snack have a low nutritive value and are particularly damaging to teeth. For these reasons they are best avoided.

Apart from its nutritional value, food is also important for its social connotations. Some children are given 'treats' when they are 'good', and are told that they are 'bad' if they don't eat all their meal. In this way they come to associate food with moral behaviour. Mealtimes can easily become battlegrounds if parents insist that the child eats everything on the plate. Rules and regulations at mealtimes are fair game to young children who can create turmoil by simply refusing to eat cabbage, or whatever.

However, mealtimes are social occasions and part of growing up is learning those social skills. Children need practice and there is usually a long period of messy eating before the age of five when most are reasonably adept at the social graces of their particular cultural group. Children learn these skills mainly from watching others. They therefore need ample opportunity to share mealtimes with the family, and most day nurseries nowadays encourage nursery nurses to eat meals with the children for this reason. A child's understanding of food can be further developed by joining in with the shopping and food preparation.

HYGIENE AND PHYSICAL CARE

For many toddlers and young children their day ends with a bath. As with any other activity at this age this will itself be part play and part learning. The bath is as good a place as any for water play. A child will gradually come to understand the merits of clean hair and skin and short neat finger nails if this is part of a regular nightly routine which is in part a game. As children become older they can be increasingly involved in self care such as brushing their teeth.

Toilet Training

At some stage, usually at about the age of 2 years, toilet training begins. Until about 15 months a child passes urine and faeces without any real sensation of what is happening because the nervous system is still immature. Sometime after 15 months the child begins to make a connection between a 'feeling' and 'having gone'. If a potty or toilet is introduced at this stage an association will begin to be made, and as the child begins to develop that feeling before going the potty will be used for the purpose for which it was intended to the inevitable joy of the parent and thus the child. At least, that is the theory. In practice there are probably about as many methods tried as there are toddlers. The cardinal rules are not to start too early (few children are ready before 18 months), not to apply pressure to the child to 'perform', and for all parents to realize that children are rarely reliable, even during the day, before the third year.

Foot Health

Foot health begins the first time a new baby is put into a babygrow. Young feet are easily damaged if moulded into unnatural shapes. In cultures where people go barefoot there are few deformed feet, and feet seem able to withstand very rugged terrain. In developed countries babies need shoes for protection when they start walking outdoors. Indoors, bare feet, or slipper socks during cold weather, are advocated for healthy foot growth. Shoes should be properly fitted for length and width and new ones bought as soon as old ones are outgrown. Socks should always be worn to prevent shoes from rubbing, and it is also important to ensure that socks fit correctly. Anything tight on the feet is likely to be damaging.

Dental Health

The formation of strong teeth which will resist decay depends on diet. A baby's first teeth are formed during pregnancy and their formation is influenced by the diet of the mother at that time. By the age of 2 years most toddlers will have all of their first set of teeth, and to ensure the health of these and the second set a diet with adequate amounts of calcium and vitamin D is essential. Probably one of the most crucial factors is control of sugar intake. The most damaging effect on teeth appears to come from sugar deposits which remain on the teeth for some time. Sweets or foods which contain sugar and which are either sucked or which stick to the teeth are probably the worst offenders. If sweets are to be given those which dissolve quickly are preferable. Even apples at the end of meals may be harmful as fructose-containing particles can become trapped between the teeth. A drink of water after a meal is probably useful in flushing away excess sugar deposits, and brushing the teeth after eating sweets is especially important.

A child can be gradually introduced to the tooth brush and toothpaste as soon as the first teeth appear. However regular brushing becomes especially important after the molars are cut. Teeth should be cleaned before bedtime and again sometime in the morning. There is convincing evidence that the trace mineral, fluoride, confers protection against tooth decay and can be obtained from toothpaste, in drop or tablet form, and in some areas it is routinely added to the water supply. To be effective fluoride needs to given from 2 weeks of age to 16 years. Excess fluoride can cause mottling of the teeth and it is important therefore that it is only given as a supplement when the level in the water supply is low.

A visit to the dentist sometime before the second birthday will accustom the child to the life-long recommended habit of six-monthly routine checks. Dental supervision during these early years is an essential part of preventative dental care and can sometimes save orthodontic treatment later.

SLEEP

Children, like adults, vary in the amount of sleep which they require, but many sleep for 12–14 hours each night. In Britain there is a cultural tendency for children to be put to bed in the early evening. Children also vary in their willingness to go to bed at the stated hour, and a routine from early infancy is important. Some, but not all, need a morning or an afternoon nap and this will of necessity need to be abandoned before school starts.

As a child moves out of the toddler stage bedtime becomes even more important. It may become associated with a particularly pleasant activity such as story time when the child and parent are alone together sharing the experience of the imagined world within the book. The treasured belongings and the personal space, even if it is not an 'own' room, become increasingly significant.

TRANSITIONAL OBJECTS

Many children have special toys or objects, such as teddies or blankets, to which they are especially attached. Winnicott suggested that they form a link between the child's inner and outer world; a bridge between the security of the familiar and the strangeness of new experiences. They have a soothing function at times of distress and may help a child in the process of separation from attachment figures. Whatever their purpose they seem to be essential to a child's sense of security and happiness, and are particularly comforting at times of stress such as admission to hospital.

PLAY

Play is one of the basic needs of all children and has several functions all of which involve learning. To a child learning is fun. It is only later at school that they separate out. Many children, particularly those in third world countries and rural areas, will learn about their world through play because the child shares the world of the adult. In developed countries the child is to a large extent isolated from the workplace of the adult and play therefore tends to be more sophisticated and structured.

By the age of 18 months most toddlers are on their feet and walking towards their first adventures. They will already have explored their immediate environment; now their world becomes bigger and they are able to explore further. The toddler is interested in how things work and this involves experimentation; water splashing makes things wet, wet sand is different from dry sand, mud and dough is squidgy and can be shaped and moulded. The world is an endlessly fascinating place full of shapes and textures. The toddler is, in short, rediscovering the laws of the universe.

By the age of two a great deal of play is imitative in nature and through this social roles are learnt. A father or mother busy doing the housework or cleaning the car will find their youngster keen to 'help'. This type of play also promotes speech development as children often pick up words and phrases from their parents and repeat them when recreating similar situations in play. There is much debate on the extent to which children ought, or ought not, to be encouraged to adopt sex-role conventions. Elena Belotti (1975) argues that little girls are often pressed into a submissive position preparing them for the role of housewife and mother. Attitudes on this subject are constantly changing and families all differ in what they see as the best way to develop their child's qualities.

Weller (1980) has described the stage from 2 to 3 years as parallel play when the child plays happily alongside other children and will interact briefly but basically continues to play independently. Role-playing games become increasingly important. Between the ages of three and four children develop social play when they play with others, usually in small groups. They take it in turns to dress up and play the part of people they come into contact with; mother, father, shopkeeper, doctor, nurse. In this way children learn to cooperate with each other, to share and to take turns. They also develop their imagination and begin to appreciate the feelings and experiences of adults. This may be especially important if they have had an unpleasant experience with adults, such as tests in hospital, when it may help to act out the roles.

A child's fantasies and imagination can be enhanced by story telling; a traditional bedtime activity. Fairy stories which centre around the good and bad characters of fairies and witches seem essential listening for a child who will often request a favourite story over and over again. The advent of television as a major influence in children's lives means that mental images are now created for children. Its impact is difficult to assess and both advantages and disadvantages are claimed. It is a powerful medium for the transmission of ideas and factual information, and technological advances ensure that it is conveyed in an appealing way. Television programmes produced specifically for preschool children seem to have considerable appeal as well as educational value. Conversely, television can have an adverse effect if preschool children are left on their own to watch television for long periods and if it is allowed to stifle conversation within the family (see also Chapter 5).

Play is essential for physical development. Running, jumping and climbing all develop neuromuscular coordination and strength. The child's environment will in part dictate the amount of exercise possible. A toddler needs floor space in which to crawl and walk, free from possible dangers. As children get older they need space outdoors and freedom to explore bigger challenges. Many cities have parks with play areas for children, and adventure playgrounds aim to combine an interesting design with safety features. There is a move to encourage physical development at a young age. 'Tumble Tots' is an organization which aims to enhance physical play in children as young as 6 months. Through various exercises on specially designed equipment they claim to enhance the toddler's natural instincts, abilities and self-confidence. Swimming is a useful form of physical exercise which is likely to be of enormous benefit in later life. Many swimming pools run classes for young children, some from as young as a few months.

PLAYGROUPS

Playgroups came into being in the 1960s as a response to a lack of nursery school provision in some areas. The aim was, and is, to bring together a group of preschool children from the local community to play under supervision. Each playgroup has a leader and most operate by working a rota of mothers to help. The children must be 3 years old when they start as before this age most will not be ready for social play or able to cope with separation from their parent in strange surroundings. All playgroups must be registered with the social services department. The Preschool Playgroups Association is a national organization which provides training courses for leaders, support for mothers establishing or running playgroups and bulk buy schemes for play materials.

In some areas where there are no facilities for a playgroup, a playbus is used and driven to the community several times a week for the benefit of the children there. This has been particularly useful in new development areas where there may be large numbers of young children but few suitable halls, or in deprived inner city areas where suitable premises may be difficult to find in the area to be served.

In some areas there are specific playgroups for children with special needs. Although these children can join other playgroups, some special playgroups have a physiotherapist who can devise play programmes for individual children. These groups also provide invaluable self-help support for the parents of handicapped children. Many in addition have a toy library which will lend toys to families so that play can continue at home. Toy libraries are organized nationally by the Toy Libraries Association.

DAY NURSERIES

Day nurseries are either provided by the social services department of the local authority, or privately, in which case they must be registered by social services. They are run by trained nursery staff and provide day care for children aged from

6 weeks to school age. In most cities, places in local authority day nurseries are relatively limited, and only the children with the greatest need are admitted. Reasons for admission include known or suspected child abuse, special needs due to a handicapping condition, a handicapped parent, poor housing and so on. Day nurseries usually take no more than 50 children who are divided into small groups of mixed ages with their own nursery nurse to resemble as closely as possible family units. They aim to provide a happy and stimulating environment with emphasis on the emotional and social needs of the child as well as support to the whole family. They work closely with some parents to encourage the development of child-care skills and so enhance the self-esteem of the parent. A report by the DHSS on Services for Under Fives from Ethnic Minority Communities (1974) noted a need in inner city areas for day care provision which reflected the ethnic origin of the child.

NURSERY SCHOOLS/CLASSES

Nursery schools are provided by the education department of the local authority for children aged from 3 to 5 years. They may also be provided by independent schools. Pressure on places ensures that only children with the greatest need are allocated places. Some will be children whose development is delayed because home circumstances do not provide the child with the range of experience needed. The overall aim is to ensure that no child is unnecessarily disadvantaged when starting school.

The Report of the Committee of Enquiry into Education of Handicapped Children and Young People chaired by Mrs Mary Warnock (1978) provided the basis for the Education Act, 1981. It found that up to one in five children require some form of special education provision. The committee recommended

a basic programme of health surveillance for all children. Children with severe, complex or long-term disabilities should have special educational provision based on a detailed profile of their abilities and needs by a multidisciplinary team. These 'statements' begin in the preschool years and also involve the parents. The committee proposed that children with special needs should, whenever possible, be integrated in ordinary schools. Many special schools, for instance those for physically or mentally handicapped children or the profoundly deaf, have nursery classes to ensure that specialist help is given from the earliest possible age. (Many such children will have received specialist help at home before starting at nursery school.)

BEHAVIOURAL AND EMOTIONAL PROBLEMS

The typical behaviour associated with this age includes temper tantrums and night waking. Within many families these episodes will be dealt with successfully and the child will be reassured by the security of the boundaries of her/his world. However, some parents may have neither the confidence nor the skills necessary to deal with this behaviour, and it is recognized that some children are more demanding and difficult to manage than others. Problems can therefore arise at this time which cause the whole family distress, and which may persist into the school years. Richman et al (1982) showed that 61% of such 3-year-olds still showed significant difficulties 5 years later, and significant factors were the relationships within the family, maternal depression and lack of maternal warmth. Intensive health visiting programmes such as the Child Development Programme described in Chapter 3 aim to enhance parenting skills and so reduce behavioural and emotional problems and developmental delay in children.

Table 3. *Non-fatal accidents per 100 000 population in Great Britain.*

Age	Both sexes	Male	Female
0–4	7150	8000	6250
5–14	2150	2350	1900
15–44	1600	1500	1700
45–64	1250	950	1500
65+	1900	1100	2350
All ages	2000	1900	2100

ACCIDENT PREVENTION

The incidence of non-fatal home accidents in the 0 – 4 age group is considerably higher than in any other age group (see Table 3). The number of accidents by type and age and sex for this age group is also shown (see Table 6, p. 131). Firework injuries are especially likely at family or private parties or in the street. In 1985 the number of such accidents jumped 25% to 968, the highest figure since 1973 (RoSPA, 1986). Apart from the official figures many more child victims have minor injuries which are treated by the family without medical attention but which still cause considerable distress. Accidents are essentially preventable and although some risk will always be associated with children because of their need for adventure and experiment, injury can be avoided and accidents reduced.

A survey carried out by Rifat in the city and district of Bath between November 1981 and October 1983 analysed home accidents among children aged 10 years and under. It showed which accidents were most common and at which ages. Falls, burns and scalds were the most common types of accident and the most vulnerable age group was the 1-year-old. Poisons, inhalations and foreign bodies tended to affect the 2-year-olds, and cutting and piercing the 5-year-olds. Of all the injuries the most frequently injured part of the body was the head, and the most common days for accidents to be reported to the A & E department appeared to be Saturday, Sunday and Monday.

There is a great deal which health professionals, particularly health visitors, can do to point out potential dangers to parents as their child approaches a danger time. Around the home children need constant close supervision to protect them from harm. But they must also learn about their environment so that they can master those features which will become essential to their lives whilst treating it with the respect which it merits. This process of careful supervision and education is a major feature of the preschool years. For this parents need a knowledge of child development in order to understand what their youngsters are likely to get up to next and be at least two steps ahead of them. The Health Education booklet *Play it Safe*, which formed the basis of a television series, provides an excellent guide to preventing accidents and some health authorities give it routinely to parents (see Figure 19 for examples of hazardous situations).

Keep dangerous household and garden chemicals in a safe place. A locked cupboard is best, or a very high cupboard – but remember that children climb up to places you would never have thought they could reach.

Figure 19. *Hazardous situations for young children. Adapted from 'Play it Safe', the Health Education Authority. Acknowledgements to RoSPA*

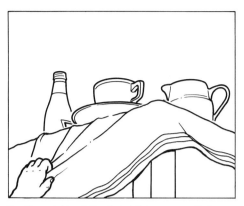

Don't use table cloths that children can pull at.

Keep hot drinks away from the edges of tables. And remember that a mug is safer than a cup with a narrow base.

Never let a child stand on the floor or the seat while the car is moving.

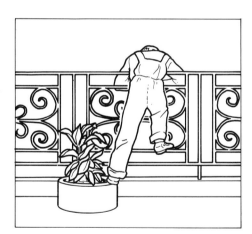

Balconies

Balconies can be dangerous for young children. If you have a private balcony, keep the door to it locked so that your child can't go out onto the balcony alone.

Horizontal balcony railings are very dangerous because they're so easy to climb. Board them up, or fit wire-netting guards.

Never put anything a child can climb on near balcony railings.

When you buy children's night clothes or dressing gowns, try to make sure they are flame-resistant. You can be sure that all children's night dresses made in this country are flame-resistant. For dressing gowns and other clothes, remember that flimsy cotton is the most dangerous material.

Children are also at great risk of accidents on the roads, either as pedestrians or in cars. Children under five playing unsupervised on pavements are inevitably at some risk. Perhaps surprisingly, it may be the quieter streets which are more dangerous because cars there are unexpected. The seat belt law which came into operation in 1983 requires children to be restrained by an adult seat belt whilst travelling in the passenger seat of a car. The compulsory use of seat belts has reduced fatal accidents and serious injuries in all age groups. Although legislation does not cover children being carried in the rear seats, Department of Transport figures show that unrestrained children in these seats are significantly more likely to be killed, seriously injured or slightly injured than restrained children. It is therefore a matter of concern that an observational study carried out by the Automobile Association in the UK found that 30% of 1- to 2-year-olds and 76% of 3- to 5-year-olds were carried unrestrained in rear seats. The evidence clearly suggests that the use of restrainer belts for cots, child safety seats and seat belts for older children would reduce the incidence of injuries to children on the roads.

References and further reading

Altschul, A. & Sinclair, H. C. (1981) *Psychology for Nurses*, 5th edn. London: Baillière Tindall.

Belotti, E. G. (1975) *Little Girls*. London: Writers and Readers Co-operative.

Child Development Programme (1984) University of Bristol: Child Development Project.

Darbyshire, P. (1985) Happiness is an old blanket. *Nursing Times* **81** (10), 40–41.

DHSS (1984) *Services for Under Fives from Ethnic Minority Communities*. London: DHSS.

Douglas, J. & Richman, N. (1984) *Coping with Young Children*. Harmondsworth: Penguin.

Fraiberg, S. (1976) *The Magic Years*. London: Methuen.

The Home Accident Surveillance System: 1982 Presentation. Twelve Months Data (The Sixth Twelve Months (1983) London: Department of Trade and Industry.

Huskisson, J. M. (1988) *Nutrition and Dietetics in Health and Disease*, 2nd edn. London: Baillière Tindall.

Leach,P. (1984) *Baby and Child*. Harmondsworth: Penguin.

Mussen, P. H. et al (1979) *Child Development and Personality*, 5th edn. London: Harper & Row.

Play it Safe, A guide to preventing children's accidents. London: The Health Education Council.

Richman, N. et al (1982) *Pre-School to School. A behavioural study*. London: Academic Press.

Rifat, J. (1985) Home Accidents. A survey among children in the Bath area. *Health Visitor* **58** (2), 38–39.

RoSPA (1984) *Child Safety in the Home* (Home & Leisure Safety Topic Briefing No.8). Birmingham: RoSPA.

RoSPA (Editorial) (1986) Firework injuries worst for 12 years. Birmingham: RoSPA.

Sheridan, M. D. (1983) *From Birth to Five Years. Children's Developmental Progress*. Windsor: NFER-Nelson.

Warnock, M. (chairman) (1978) *Report of the Committee of Enquiry into the Education of Handicapped Children and Young People*. London: HMSO.

Weller, B. F. (1980) *Helping Sick Children Play*. London: Baillière Tindall.

Weller, B. F. & Barlow, S. (1983) *Paediatric Nursing*. London: Baillière Tindall.

Whitehead, N. (1985) Encouraging the use of car restrainer seats for children. *Health Visitor* **58** (2), 39–40.

5

The School Child

At about the age of 5 years the school life of a child begins. Children who have had the opportunity to attend nursery or playgroup will already have learnt to adjust to time away from home and to being part of a group of children in a relatively structured learning environment. Until the age of about 16 years school will, in some ways, dominate a child's life. Home life continues to provide the much needed security, and the relationships within the family, holidays, hobbies, sports, pets and friendships are the cornerstones of a child's world upon which education and experiences at school are built.

When children start school, many mirror the attitudes and ideas of their parents. Gradually, dependence on the family lessens and friends and other adults become increasingly influential. Although the family remains the greatest source of security, new ideas are gained from outside, particularly from teachers, friends, books and television. There will inevitably be times when these conflict with parental attitudes. This conflict can be seen clearly in immigrant families where children are quick to adopt the ways of the host country but the parents retain the ways of their origins. It is important for children to be able to share, and 'check out', new ideas with parents whom they trust, particularly if it is something which confuses or concerns them such as bullying. They also love to be listened to if only to share funny stories (and those terrible jokes!).

DEVELOPMENT

Group learning in class at school is possible because the child is now able to concentrate for longer periods, enjoy the company of special friends, accept discipline, relate to, and place trust in a teacher, and above all derive enormous pleasure from the sheer amazement of learning. Within the group, however, differences between the children can be staggering. Cultural background, size, place in the family, attitudes within the family and so on all lead to considerable variations in development. The acquisition of formal learning is largely judged by intellectual attainment, but other skills and talents such as arts, crafts and sports are equally important. Emotional development is important because early emotional deprivation can impair the capacity to learn.

Cognitive Development: Piaget's Theory

Piaget assumed that knowledge is acquired in order to adapt to the world in which one lives, that it is acquired through active involvement with the world, and that children are constantly active and inventive in trying to understand the world around them. In short he viewed knowledge as a problem-solving activity. Each stage of development is built on experiences, abilities and beliefs from previous stages of development.

Piaget identified four major periods of cognitive development and intellectual

59

growth which arise at about the following ages:

1 sensory motor period — birth to about 2 years;
2 preoperational period — 2–7 years;
3 concrete operational period — 7–11 years;
4 formal operational period — 11+ years.

The preoperational stage is characterized by symbolic actions so that a child at this age will treat a piece of wood as if it were a car or make play bricks form a train. They can match shapes but have no concept of classification. They believe that if the shape of a substance is altered, such as pouring water from a tall beaker into a wide flat one, the amount changes.

During the concrete operational stage children develop the concept of logical groupings. They recognize certain classifications such as that apples are all fruits and that fruits are types of food. They can recognize the constancy of substances so that water or sand, however it is arranged, remains the same in amount.

In the formal operational period children and adolescents are able to consider what might be and are able to comprehend hypothetical situations. They are able to reason.

DIET

There are two basic aims when considering a healthy and nourishing diet for schoolchildren. Firstly it should supply all the necessary nutrients for growth but not in excess, and secondly it should prepare the child for a lifetime of healthy eating. Both of these aims can be fulfilled by a diet which the child finds tasty, attractive and satisfying.

Children require a mixed diet which is well balanced and which contains adequate protein and minerals for rapid growth. The current thinking is that a balanced diet contains less saturated fatty acids, sugar and salt than currently consumed. Cereal and vegetable protein reduce the need for animal sources and will in addition supply fibre. Protein requirement gradually increases as puberty approaches to build the increasing muscle mass, and during the growth spurt calcium is also important for bones. With the onset of menstruation the requirement of iron for girls increases. The added energy requirements of all children at this age demands an increased intake of vitamin B.

In 1907, elementary schools began to provide meals for children who were unable to take full advantage of their education due to poverty and malnutrition. Since that time meals have been provided in state schools and have been free to families on low incomes. However, following the 1981 Education Act schools are no longer required to serve meals of a recommended nutritional standard. Where they are still provided there is a tendency towards cafeteria-type meals offering a choice to children. Some children prefer to have a packed lunch or to go home. A survey (Sharpe, 1984) carried out in four Portsmouth secondary schools in 1984 aimed to discover the source and nutritional value of food taken by children. Its conclusions give cause for concern:

1 All diets (whether from home, school, local shops, etc.) were unsatisfactory in terms of accepted nutritional guidelines for long-term health.
2 In general diets were less healthy when out-of-school sources (e.g. local shops) were used.
3 There was little difference in the rating of food from home and that from the school cafeteria. Both were unsatisfactory. The children's choice tended towards foods high in fat (e.g. chips) and away from fruit, vegetables and unrefined carbohydrates.

It was interesting that all the children were aware of a relationship between diet and health, and most knew what constituted a healthy diet. There was therefore a clear disparity between their knowledge and behaviour.

The appetites of schoolchildren vary enormously. After a hectic day of playing games a child may come home and consume a huge meal but then lose interest in food for a while. Many children need a snack in the afternoon to sustain them until the evening meal. If the child is a reasonable weight for their height it is usually best to allow the child's appetite to dictate meal sizes and snacks needed and not to either force or restrict. Height and weight can be monitored at school by the school nurse using percentile charts (see Figure 15).

The evidence of an association between childhood and adult obesity is conflicting. Myers and Yeung (1979) suggest that about 4 and 5 years of age is a critical time and that if obesity persists beyond this time it may be difficult to control. The National Survey of Health and Development (Stark et al, 1981) suggests that there is no critical time when fat is gained and that excess weight may begin at any time. It suggests that the over-weight child carries a much greater risk of remaining overweight than his or her normal weight contemporaries do of becoming overweight. However, a large national cohort study by Braddon et al (1986) found that childhood obesity was not the major contributor to obesity in 36-year-old adults and that those people who became obese between 11 and 36 years were often not the most overweight in childhood. But they concluded that the result may indicate a long-term effect of eating and exercise habits acquired in childhood.

If the child becomes overweight it is necessary to review the diet and the possible causes. It is helpful if the whole family changes to a more healthy diet so that the child is not singled out as the one with a problem. Often all that is required is to reduce fats and sugar, and reduce treats to once a week. In this way everyone benefits. As puberty approaches children become increasingly aware of their body image. It is unhelpful, and may even be damaging, to focus the child's attention on his or her body shape and size in a negative way. It is much more beneficial to prevent problems of overweight so that the child is not singled out at school and can develop confident self-awareness rather than a poor self-image fringed with embarrassment. A preoccupation with body weight and slim-ming may affect some adolescent girls' sense of body image and with some this may develop into anorexia nervosa (see Chapter 6).

HYGIENE

Social cleanliness is part of a way of life. It is fundamental to health and to social acceptability. The skills involved in caring for one's own body are gradually learned from the earliest age. For younger children evening bathtime is often 'a bore', and having one's hair washed a gross inconvenience. A degree of parental supervision is therefore required. As adolescence approaches the importance and the value of not only being clean but also of looking good begin to be realized.

In some cultural groups cleanliness is linked to religious practices, such as Muslims who ceremoniously cleanse parts of the body prior to prayer, and Hindus who use only one hand for eating and the other for toileting. The dreadlocks of the Rastafarians stem from the Old Testament where Daniel speaking of the fall of Babylon refers to those '. . . of whose head was like unto wool'. All this begins to be learned during childhood.

In parts of the Asian world, girls develop considerable pelvic floor control which brings about long-term benefits in maintaining continence. Shepherd (1980) suggests that this is partly as a conse-quence of squatting to void and partly because in some cultures mothers teach their daughters pelvic floor control for use later in life in sexual stimulation. By learning how to control the flow of urine, by stopping and starting during voiding, girls can begin to develop a life-long habit of strengthening their pelvic floor muscles. They can be encouraged to do this by focusing their attention on the different sounds made by the flow. This gives them the assurity of being able to 'hold on' until a convenient time, and may help to prevent problems of urinary incontinence after childbirth or in later life.

Children with the problem of enuresis, or bed-wetting, may need specialist help to overcome the problem, and will need to give particular care to hygiene. Urine has little odour until it is stale when it gives off a strong smell of ammonia. Classmates are often quick to notice this and find it offensive. This can lead to a child being rejected or even ridiculed at school, and even with the most understanding teacher will almost certainly lead to a degree of social isolation. A reward system or 'star chart' can be helpful for some children. It is essential that the child is involved in the programme by putting the stars on the chart and that the whole issue is discussed with the child in a sensitive way. The 'pad and bell' system is also successful for some children providing they are motivated to use it and are involved in the operation of it.

Hair grooming, apart from making the hair look tidy, has another important function. It seems to combat the activities of the head louse. Until recently, head inspections were a regular occurrence in most schools. They did nothing to reduce the incidence of infected schoolchildren. Today, the main thrust of the campaign against the offending lice, and nits (the eggs) is to educate parents in prevention and early detection with appropriate treatment. Regular brushing or combing of the hair damages the legs of the live louse leaving it unable to lay eggs.

PLAY, HOBBIES AND SPORTS

At some stage during their school years children often become extremely keen on a particular activity. This may sometimes be the current fashion fad, a family activity or something quite different but is likely to reflect the general interests of the cultural or social group and the local community. It may change over time so that complete engrossment in football gives way to fishing then to computers and so on. The intensity of the interest can sometimes be almost to the exclusion of all else and to the despair of parents. It is however important that children develop interests outside school work. Team activity whether it is sport, music or some other interest is typical of this stage of development and reflects the increasing importance of the peer group. Such activities are important for many reasons; they develop skills and talents, provide the opportunity to develop roles within a group, encourage mutual support, and facilitate expression of feelings. They can also give enormous pleasure to those whose abilities are being developed to the full. Individual interests are usual also and include computers, reading, model-making and watching favourite television programmes. Leisure time is an important part of life at any age and skills and interests developed in childhood are often pursued in adult life.

CHILDREN AND DIVORCE (see also Chapter 10)

A third of presently contracted marriages in Britain are likely to end in divorce, and two-thirds of these will involve children. Many children, therefore, live in a single parent family or have step-parents. The response of the child to this dramatic change in their life will depend a great deal on their age and the circumstances although certain reactions are common. This may be the first time they learn that social relations are not eternal. Fears of separation and abandonment may emerge as a protest at being left at school, the need for a night light, or not allowing the remaining parent out of their sight. Anger is another common emotion which is often directed towards both parents, and many children retain a fantasy that some day their parents will be reunited and all will be as it was. Anger may be expressed either directly or indirectly. Feelings can spill over into other situations and the child may become withdrawn or depressed at school, unable to concentrate and less good at work and sport, and pull away from friends. At the time when the child is most vulnerable, the parents may be at their lowest ebb also and least able to offer reassurance. For both there is often a change of house, neighbourhood, friends, and a change in lifestyle and lower income. All these things compound the sense of loss. Ultimately it is the quality of the relationships which matters, and those who remain close to both parents seem to be happiest and suffer least distress.

In recent years self-help groups such as Gingerbread have developed to support parents and children following divorce. Within the school the effects on the child may be more sensitively handled if the school teacher and school nurse know that divorce is pending. The teacher may be more understanding when the child's concentration seems to falter or when the standard of work falls. The child may also need to talk about his feelings and the Educational Welfare Officer may help through counselling the child and working with the whole family. In some cities a conciliation service has been introduced at divorce courts with the aim of helping parents towards the best possible compromise for the sake of the children involved. This seems to have gone some way towards preventing the situation from becoming a battleground with the child as the prize. It allows parents to consider arrangements which are likely to be least disruptive for the children.

INCEST AND SEXUAL ABUSE

Sexual abuse has been defined as 'the involvement of dependent, developmentally immature children and adolescents in sexual activities they do not fully comprehend, to which they are unable to give informed consent and which violate the social taboos of family roles' (Kempe and Kempe, 1978). A *Mori* survey in 1984 found that one in eight girls and one in 12 boys are sexually abused by the age of 16; and that 75% of abusers are known to the child and 25% are strangers. Elliot (1985) states that abusers come from every class, profession, racial and religious background and that approximately 90% of reported offenders are men and most are married with children.

Within the family incest may remain a closely guarded secret for many years. The incidence is therefore not known and may be much higher than criminal statistics suggest. The most common form is father/daughter although other permutations are also possible. The child may have no concept that what is happening is wrong, and is usually persuaded by the abuser, whom they trust, 'not to tell'. The problem may be detected quite by accident by someone like the general practitioner, or school nurse.

Sexual abuse involves anyone not covered by the current incest legislation including adopted and step-children. It may involve sexual intercourse or other forms of sexual activity such as fondling and pornographic activity.

Some junior schools are introducing this subject into the classroom with the aim of instructing children how to cope with such situations. Elliot (1985) describes a prevention programme which includes teaching children the difference between good and bad touches, good and bad secrets, and how to say 'no' assertively. The programme recognizes that children need to learn how to cope with situations which may involve strangers or people who are known to them.

It enables them to understand that they are in control of their own bodies and that they have a say in what happens to them. Children who have been sexually abused need careful counselling to enable them to come to terms with what has happened to them. Unresolved grief may continue to cause anguish through adolescence and into adulthood.

THE SCHOOL HEALTH SERVICE

The aim of the service is to ensure that the child achieves the maximum level of health possible for him or her and so is able to gain the greatest benefit from their education. Particular attention is given to the promotion of health, early detection of a disability so that treatment can be started as early as possible, and the care and treatment of children with known disabilities. As in all aspects of child care the involvement of parents is crucial. It is interesting that in the 1907 legislation regarding school health one of the stated objectives was 'to stimulate a sense of duty in matters affecting health in the homes of people, to enlist the best services and interests of parents . . . It is in the home, in fact, that the seed and fruit of public health are to be found'.

Child Health Records from the pre-school years are forwarded on to the school so that all the new entrants can be discussed by the school nurse and school doctor, any special needs can be identified, and problems appropriately dealt with. In this way an uninterrupted health record is available and the care of the child is continuous.

Medical examinations are carried out in state schools, but their timing may vary between health authorities. The first examination is usually in the second term of infant school. Parents are invited to attend and their permission is always requested. Details of the child's health and medical history and the health of the family may be required to supplement the child's health records. The medical examination includes eyesight and hearing tests, and any problems are referred, with the parents' consent, to a specialist service via the GP.

In some areas all children are seen routinely on school entry, at transfer to senior school and prior to leaving school. Some schools operate a selective medical examinations system in which all children are examined thoroughly on entry and parents then complete a questionnaire on their child's health at 8 and 12 years. A further medical examination is carried out only if indicated by the answers, if the parent, school nurse or teacher requests it, or if there has been a serious illness or repeated absence from school. Children on the Child Abuse and Handicap registers are also likely to be seen more frequently. In this way more time can be given to the children who need it most.

THE SCHOOL DENTAL SERVICE

This is part of the school health service and is concerned with prevention, education and treatment. As with all health care patterns, good dental care established during school days is likely to be continued in adult life. The District Dental Officer will take careful note of the standard of dental health within the health authority, and in areas where children have a large number of dental caries there may be a special health promotion programme. Preventive measures include regular brushing with fluoride toothpaste, avoidance of sweet foods (especially sticky or sucked sweets), and regular dental checks which may include fluoride treatments in areas with naturally low levels. Dental care is free to children under 16 years and dental checks in schools are routine. However the parent may elect to send the child to the family dentist for treatment or use the school dentist. Dental care of handicapped children is particularly important because they may have difficulty brushing their teeth, and certain drugs, e.g. tetracycline, may discolour teeth. A survey by Todd (1975) in England and Wales found that 78% of 8-year-olds had active tooth decay.

CHILD AND FAMILY GUIDANCE

This is a multidisciplinary service made up of child psychiatrists, social workers and educational psychologists. They will assess and see children of any age with behavioural or emotional problems. The problem may arise at home or at school, or both. They use various methods of therapy including counselling and family therapy depending on the needs of the needs of the child and the family. Because the child can never be viewed as an isolated individual the family is virtually always included and their motivation and willingness to be part of the therapy is crucial. A typical problem which may be dealt with by this department is 'school phobia'. Family therapy views the family as a unit in which the relationships between the various members all play a part in the problem which the child manifests. This is represented diagrammatically in Figure 20 (see also Social and Emotional Needs later).

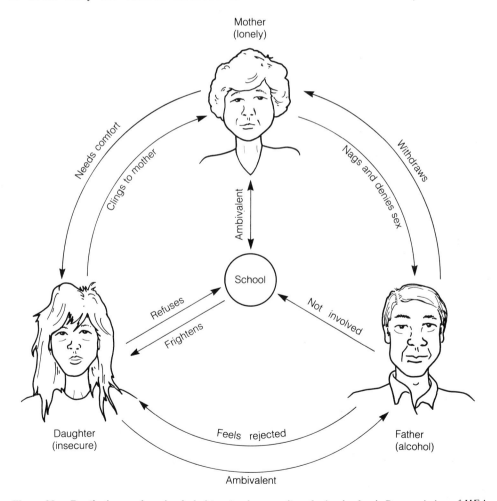

Figure 20.   *Family therapy for school phobia: circular causality of school refusal. By permission of HEA.*

Table 4. *Inclusion and exclusion periods for the commoner communicable diseases.*

Disease	Normal incubation period (days)	Period of communicability	Minimal period of exclusion	
			Cases (subject to clinical recovery)	Contacts
Bacillary dysentery	1–7	Whilst organism is present in stools	Until clinically fit and, when necessary, bacteriological examination is clear	Siblings from primary or nursery schools should be excluded until bacteriological examination is clear
Chickenpox	14–21	From 1 day before to 6 days after appearance of rash	6 days from onset of rash	None
Diphtheria	2–5	Whilst the organism is present in nose or throat	Until bacteriological examination is clear	Until bacteriological examination is clear
Food poisoning (including salmonellosis)	2–48 hours according to cause	Varies according to cause	Until clinically fit and, when necessary, bacteriological examination is clear	None
German measles (rubella)	14–21	From a few days before to 4 days after onset of rash	4 days from onset of rash	None
Hepatitis A	15–50 (commonly 28)	From 1–2 weeks before to 1 week after onset	7 days from onset of jaundice	None
Measles	10–15 (commonly 12 to onset of illness and 16 to appearance of rash)	From a few days before to 7 days after onset of rash	7 days from onset of rash	None
Meningococcal infection (meningitis)	2–10 (commonly 2–5)	Whilst organism is present in nasopharynx	Until clinical recovery	None

THE EDUCATION WELFARE OFFICER

EWOs grew out of the need to enforce school attendance where children were frequently absent from school. Much of their work still revolves around truancy and the court proceedings which may result, but they are also involved with the child's progress at school as well as the social care of families. They can help with claims for financial assistance from DHSS and with transport. They may be involved in the supervision of children under care orders, and will almost certainly be involved when an incident of child abuse is noticed at school.

INFECTIOUS DISEASE

It is the responsibility of the school health service to prevent, investigate and control outbreaks of infectious disease at school. This includes immunization against certain infectious diseases (see Figure 16). Rubella immunization is offered to all girls at about the age of 12 years as protection against complications in pregnancy later in life. Prevention against disease can to some extent be achieved by ensuring a clean environment, especially where food is being handled or where pets are being kept, and by teaching children the basic principles of hygiene such as washing their hands. A well

Table 4. *cont'd*

Disease	Normal incubation period (days)	Period of communicability	Minimal period of exclusion	
			Cases (subject to clinical recovery)	Contacts
Mumps	18–21	From 7 days before onset of symptoms to subsidence of swelling	Until swelling has subsided (7 days minimum)	None
Poliomyelitis	3–21	Whilst virus is present in stools	At the discretion of the Medical Officer for Environmental Health	At the discretion of the Medical Officer for Environmental Health
Smallpox	10–16 (commonly 12)	From first symptoms to disappearance of all scabs	At the discretion of the Medical Officer for Environmental Health	At the discretion of the Medical Officer for Environmental Health
Steptococcal infection	2–5	Whilst organism is present in nasopharynx	Until clinical recovery	None
Tuberculosis (primary)	4–6 weeks		At the discretion of the physician	
Tuberculosis (secondary)	variable	Whilst organism is present in sputum	Until declared to be non-infectious	None
Typhoid fever	7–21 (usually 14)	Whilst organism is present in stools or urine	Until bacteriological examination is clear	None except for home contact
Paratyphoid fever	1–10	Whilst organism is present in stools or urine	Until bacteriological examination is clear	None except for home contact
Whooping cough (pertussis)	7–10	From 7 days after exposure to 21 days after onset of paroxysmal cough	21 days from onset of paroxysmal cough	None

From DHSS and Welsh Office (1977) *Control of Communicable Diseases in Schools.*

ventilated environment is important for the prevention of diseases spread by droplet, such as colds, influenza and meningitis. Table 4 shows the inclusion and exclusion periods for the commoner communicable diseases.

HEALTH PROMOTION

Many infant, junior and secondary schools have health promotion programmes which span the school years so that a wide range of health issues are covered. These are carefully designed so that the material is presented in a suitable and attractive way for children at a particular stage of development. The *My Body* project (1983) has been evaluated and found to be useful for children aged 8 – 12 years and is particularly good on the subject of smoking. Others include *All About Me* (1977), *Think Well* (1977), *Fit for Life* (1983) and *Life Skills Teaching Programme* (1982). Health promotion usually involves the teacher, school nurse and clinical medical officer.

CHILDREN WITH SPECIAL NEEDS

Some handicapping conditions such as spina bifida are apparent from birth, some may only come to be recognized later during infancy, for instance a hearing loss, and others are actually acquired during childhood as a consequence of either illness or accident. Some handicapping conditions are life-threatening, for instance muscular dystrophy and cystic fibrosis, and others, such as visual or hearing loss, may remain throughout a natural lifespan. The nature of the condition and its likely outcome will have a considerable effect on the way in which the child, and the whole family, adjusts to the limitations imposed.

The diagnosis of a handicapping condition is likely to be a devastating time for parents. Some react with disbelief and stunned shock. They may express anger towards the doctor in an irrational attempt to apportion blame for something so terrible that they cannot immediately accept it. Others may have suspected for some time that something was wrong but had considerable difficulty convincing health professionals; many mothers have been labelled 'over-anxious' only to have their worst fears confirmed at a later date. Such parents may express relief that the period of uncertainty is over. Whatever the nature of the condition the parent is likely to suffer additional stress, an increased financial burden, and many hours in hospital outpatients departments.

Explaining to the child that he has an illness, is unable to live life as others, or will have to spend long periods in hospital sometimes in great discomfort is a major problem. In general it is always best to be truthful and honest and wherever possible prepare the child in advance for what is to happen. Half truths may be confusing and there is always the risk that the child will find out something accidentally. When discussing limitations and helping the child to accept these it is always possible to focus the child's mind on the parts of his body which do work well and which he can take pride in. Even the most skilled nurses can find this difficult. It is extremely hard listening to a child with a life-threatening condition

describing what he wants to do when he grows up.

The Report of the Committee of Enquiry into the Education of Handicapped Children and Young People (Warnock, 1978) stated that children should no longer be categorized according to a specific handicap but rather considered according to their individual educational needs. This takes into account not only children with mental or physical disorders but also those with learning difficulties and emotional or behavioural disorders. Children with complex and long-term disabilities are assessed by a multidisciplinary team of professionals, who, in conjunction with the parents, decide on the best form of provision. Disabilities do not always fit into neat categories; for instance, some children are multiply handicapped by conditions such as cerebral palsy and spina bifida, and a child with a physical disability may develop emotional difficulties during adolescence. It further recommended that as far as possible special classes and units should be attached to ordinary schools so that children have the opportunity to integrate as much as possible.

Visual Loss

Not all of these children will be blind, indeed only about 10% of people registered as blind have no sight at all. The rest are partially sighted to varying degrees. A great deal of help can be offered by the Royal National Institute for the Blind who have a team of advisors to help the parent at home. Blind children are likely to remain relatively inactive and resist change and they may even seem backward. The parent needs to be a determined educator from the child's earliest age if he is to reach his full potential. Learning involves using other senses, especially touch, and it is salutary to recall the words of Helen Keller who was both blind and deaf, 'Remember that you, dependent on your sight, do not realize how many things are tangible'.

Blind children are educated at special schools or at normal school using the special school as a resource. Many universities and colleges of further education are equipped for blind students.

Hearing Loss

Children who cannot hear what other people are saying are unable to imitate sounds, and without speech they have difficulty making relationships. In the past deaf children were sometimes mistakenly assumed to be mentally backward. In 1984 The National Deaf Children's Society estimated that about 10% of 5-year-olds were educationally at risk as a result of hearing difficulties. This will range from a mild hearing loss to profound deafness. A number of these will be undiagnosed at school entry. Children with a serious impairment will be offered specialist help in the home from a peripatetic teacher of the deaf or nursery provision. It is crucial that the child learns communication skills at an early age and does not become isolated. In recent years through advances in technology hearing aids have become much improved giving many severely affected children the benefits and joys of sound.

Mentally Handicapped Children

It was not so many years ago that many of these children were admitted to long-stay hospitals for the mentally handicapped where they would spend most of their lives. The trend today is for them to remain at home with their families and for extra support to be offered. This is likely to start soon after birth and will include the midwife, paediatric team, health visitor, and voluntary and self-help groups. Later the support may include home care assistants, respite care, and specialist learning packages such as the Portage scheme for the parents to use to develop their child's skills. The aim is for these children to develop and

maximize their potential. All will receive an education, usually in a special school. It is the duty of the education department to provide transport if the most appropriate school is some distance from the child's home.

The whole family must be considered. Butler et al (1978) found that 50% of mothers with mentally and physically handicapped children found their own social activities severely restricted because of their child's handicap, and many were extremely worried about the prospects for their child's future. Care and support of the parents is a primary concern, and includes not only practical arrangements such as foster parents to provide the much needed respite care, or the therapeutic care offered by a developmental paediatrician or speech therapist, but also someone to simply be there to listen to their joys and woes.

Physically Handicapped Children

These children and their families are also likely to have received help in the preschool years with home support and nursery provision. Voluntary organizations such as the Muscular Dystrophy Group and the Spastics Society provide support and practical help. Some special schools have intensive physiotherapy programmes to develop the child's physical capabilities to their maximum. It is important that the child has the opportunity for play which will enable him or her to develop spatial concepts as well as all the other skills relevant to their age. In such schools it is now less common to see children in wheelchairs.

SOCIAL AND EMOTIONAL NEEDS

Slack (1978) states that 'learning to manage successfully one's own personal difficulties is part of the preparation for becoming a well adjusted and healthy adult, and achieving this is an important responsibility of the school's educational aims'. Children's emotional responses to the difficulties which they experience will differ according to their age and vary from child to child. Sometimes counselling and support from the teacher, school nurse or educational welfare officer is all that is required but sometimes psychiatric referral is warranted in which case they are usually seen by the Child and Family Guidance Service. Mental health problems arising in schools are now far greater than those of a physical nature. The Isle of Wight survey (Rutter et al, 1970) found that in a primary school of 250 pupils there are likely to be 6–7 children with a physical problem and about 17 children with a psychiatric problem. In general these problems are more common in urban than in rural areas, and in boys rather than girls. An important role of the school nurse, working in a team of teaching and other support staff, is to prevent, recognize and manage these problems. The main types of problems experienced are as follows:

1   antisocial and conduct disorders (truancy, lying, stealing, destructive behaviour, violence, petty theft);
2   neurotic disorders (anxiety and phobias, school refusal, depression, obsessional neurosis, hysterics); children often show a mixed pattern of both antisocial and neurotic behaviour;
3   specific delays and disorders (poor speech and language, slow learning, clumsiness, tics, toilet problems, enuresis, encopresis, eating and sleeping difficulties);
4   psychosis.

Behaviour disturbances are common in most children at some time. They are only a problem if they persist and start to interfere with the child's learning and development. The disturbances listed above are more likely to occur in certain types of children:

1   children who have spent long periods of time in foster care or separated from the home in early childhood;
2   children who have had repeated hospital admissions before the age of 5 years;
3   handicapped children, particularly severely mentally handicapped and those with epilepsy and conditions involving brain pathology;
4   children of families with long-standing social, marital or health problems.

A survey carried out by the London-based National Campaign against Solvent Abuse in 1986 found that nearly one in four fourth-year school children had experimented with solvent abuse. It also found that girls were more likely than boys to abuse solvents and that most learnt it from their friends and not the media. The survey also found that more than 120 deaths in 1985 were associated with solvent abuse (although the official figure from OPCS is 81). Clearly this is a major health problem in schools. Solvent and drug abuse and smoking are considered more fully in Chapter 6.

VIDEO VIOLENCE

Videos are rapidly becoming a major source of home entertainment. The censorship which operates in cinemas and on television to protect children cannot be applied to videos in the same way. The ease with which violent and obscene videos can be obtained and the access which some children appear to have to them gives considerable cause for concern. Barlow and Hill (1985) draw together research evidence which strongly suggests that such experiences have an adverse effect on children's health, especially their emotional health. A report by Pearl et al (1982) in the USA estimated that from the ages of 7–17 45% of children will see an obscene video. A National Viewers Survey (Nelson, 1984) in Britain found that 57% of children aged 7–16 had seen at least one X-rated film and 29% had seen four or more. Many videos combine violence with obscenity and are particularly demeaning of women. For some children this may be their first experience of sex, and some are greatly disturbed by what they see for some time afterwards. A survey of psychiatrists cited in Barlow and Hill (1985) concluded that video violence is generally harmful in its effects. There does appear to be a direct causal relationship between video (or television) violence and real-life violence.

GIFTED CHILDREN

Children may be disadvantaged from exceptionally high intelligence. Gifted children are defined as those who have an exceptional all round capacity to learn as opposed to talented children who have a special aptitude in one particular sphere. They may seem disruptive at school, difficult at home and become bored very easily. They may have little in common with peers and prefer the company of older children. If their needs are left unfulfilled they may become withdrawn, anxious and sarcastic. They can therefore be either a pain or a pleasure to parents, and eventually either an asset or a threat to society. There may be a temptation to concentrate on intellectual development although most teachers recognize the need for the whole child to be developed. A child whose emotional and recreational needs are not met may become anxious, unhappy or lonely and may have difficulties in relating to people in adult life.

All children are gifted in some way and all have special talents to develop and a unique contribution to make. It is the duty of those involved with children to enable these skills to reach their maximum potential principally for the sake of the child's health and happiness, but also because the patterns of health laid down in childhood will influence

health in later life and so it is essential that the basis for a healthy life is established at this stage. Ultimately the health of the community is greatly influenced by the games which the adults played when they were children.

References and further reading

Altschul, A. & Sinclair, H. G. (1981) *Psychology for Nurses*, 5th edn. London: Baillière Tindall.

Axline, V. (1971) *Dibs: In Search of Self (A Disturbed Child)*. Harmondsworth: Penguin.

Barlow, G. & Hill, A. (1985) *Video Violence and Children*. Sevenoaks: Hodder and Stoughton.

Bond, S. (1986) *Eat and Be Fit*. London: Ladybird Books.

Braddon et al (1986) Onset of obesity in a 36 year birth cohort study. *British Medical Journal* **293**, 299–303.

Butler, N. et al (1978) *Handicapped Children — Their Homes and Lifestyles. A Study in Avon*. Department of Child Health, University of Bristol.

DHSS and the Welsh Office (1977) *Control of Communicable Disease in Schools*. London: HMSO.

Elliot, M. (1985) *Preventing Child Sexual Assault. A practical guide to talking with children*. London: Bedford Square Press/ NCVO.

Field, F. (1974) *Unequal Britain. A Report on the Cycle of Inequality*. London: Arrow Books.

Fraser, G. R. (1977) *The Causes of Profound Deafness in Children*. London: Baillière Tindall.

Huskisson, J. M. (1985) *Nutrition and Dietetics in Health and Disease*, 2nd edn. London: Baillière Tindall.

Kempe, R. S. & Kempe, C. H. (1978) *Child Abuse*. London: Fontana.

Lansdown, R. (1980) *More than Sympathy: The everyday needs of sick and handicapped children and their families*. London: Tavistock Publications.

Lusk, A. (1983) One of the family: short-term relief care for handicapped children. In: Harbert, W. & Rogers, P., eds. *Community Based Social Care*, London: Bedford Square Press/NCVO.

Macfarlane, J. A. (ed.) (1984) *Progress in Child Health*, Vol. 1. Edinburgh: Churchill Livingstone.

Myers, A. W. & Yeung, D. L. (1979) Obesity in infants: significant aetiology and prevention. *Canadian Journal of Public Health* **70** (2), 113–119.

National Campaign Against Solvent Abuse (1986) *School Survey 1985–86*. London: National Campaign Against Solvent Abuse.

Nelson, G. K. (1985) The findings of the National Viewers Survey. In: Barlow, G. & Hill, A., eds., *Video Violence and Children*, Chapter 2. London: Hodder & Stoughton.

Pearl, D. et al (1982) *Television and Behaviour: Ten Years of Scientific Progress and Implications for the Eighties*, Vols. 1 & 2. Washington, DC: US Government Printing Office.

Rutter, M. et al (1970) *Education, Health and Behaviour*. Harlow, Essex: Longman.

Sharpe, K. (1984) *Schoolchildren and What They Eat: A survey of 11–16 year olds in Portsmouth and SE Hants Health District*. Health Education Department, Portsmouth and SE Hants Health Authority.

Shepherd, A. M. (1986) In: *Incontinence and its Management*, 2nd edn., Mandelstam, D., ed. London: Croom Helm.

Slack, P. A. (1978) *School Nursing*. London: Baillière Tindall.

Stark, O. et al (1981) Longitudinal study of obesity in the national survey of health and development. *British Medical Journal* **283**, 13–17.

Todd, J. E. (1975) *Children's Dental Health in England and Wales*. London: HMSO.

Warnock, M. (chairman) (1978) *Report of the Committee of Enquiry into the Education of Handicapped Children and Young People*. London: HMSO.

Wedge, P. & Prosser, H. (1973) *Born to Fail? (Striking differences in the lives of British children)*. London: Arrow Books in association with The National Children's Bureau.

6

Adolescence

There is no precise definition of adolescence, the stage of life which makes the transition from childhood to adulthood. There are wide individual differences in when it begins and ends but for the sake of convenience it is generally recognized that adolescence begins at puberty usually at about 12 years and ends at maturity which in Britain is taken to be 18 when young people are entitled to vote.

'Passionate. . . and apt to be carried away by their impulses' said Aristotle of adolescents. This is an age of intense emotions and rapid change, but also of contradictions. A time of absolute self-confidence but terrible self-doubt, irrepressible joy but inconsolable sadness, high idealism but total despair, ruthless condemnation of some but hero worship of others. In many ways it is an age destined to be misunderstood as characteristically the only people who can truly understand adolescents are their own peers. Even the term 'adolescent' is often used in a derogatory way, synonymous with immaturity, naïvety and waywardness. Perhaps 'youth' is a more descriptive word. Conger (1979) states that for most of us adolescence will be remembered as the time 'when our identities began to crystallize, when our potentialities were at their height; when, whatever the pain, we lived most intensely. And if we are old and unsatisfied, perhaps some of us also resent the adolescents about us as the enviably uncaring inheritors enjoying "what we never had"'.

PHYSICAL DEVELOPMENT

During adolescence there are a number of physical changes within the body which consequently have a profound effect on emotional and mental health and on self-image. Puberty is a time of rapid physical change accompanied by changes in the reproductive system and in the development of secondary sexual characteristics. One of the many physical changes is the 'growth spurt', an accelerated rate of increase in height and weight which in boys occurs usually at about the age of 13, and in girls at about the age of 12, although in both sexes there are wide individual differences. Height increases faster than at any other time in extra-uterine life. Height velocities of typical boys and girls are shown in Figure 21. Growth comes to an end when the epiphyses of the bones fuse under the influence of the sex hormones.

Associated with this growth spurt are other bodily changes. There is a decline in basal metabolism and a rapid increase in the size and weight of the heart, an accelerated growth of the lungs, and an increase in the number of red blood cells. There is also a marked increase in muscle mass and in physical strength and endurance together with an increase in systolic blood pressure which is greater in boys than in girls. Physical growth may be erratic. Changes in the proportions of the body may make the person feel and appear rather ungainly. Other changes

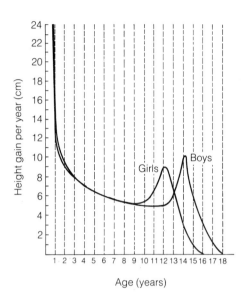

Figure 21.   *Typical velocity curves for supine length or height in boys or girls, representing the growth velocity at any given instant. From Tanner, J. M. Whitehouse, R. H. & Takaishi, M. (1966)* Archives of Disease in Childhood **41**.

which occur are increased activity of the sebaceous glands, which may produce acne, increased perspiration and instability of the vasomotor system which can cause blushing.

The physiological changes are regulated by the action of the pituitary gland. Hormones are released which in turn stimulate other endocrine glands to release their own growth-related hormones. Thyroxine from the thyroid gland and cortisol from the adrenal glands activate the growth of bone and muscle leading to the growth spurt. Also stimulated are the sex hormones, including testosterone in boys and oestrogen in girls which stimulate the growth of mature sperm and ova. Sexual maturation occurs approximately 18–24 months earlier for girls than for boys. There will inevitably be individual, and perfectly normal, variations but the typical sequence of events is as follows.

Girls

In a girl the growth spurt is followed by development of the breasts and rounding of the hips which brings about a noticeable change in body shape. This is followed by the growth of pubic and axillary hair, and then by the growth of the uterus and the vagina. Menarche occurs after the peak rate of growth in height has occurred. It is a relatively late event (mean age in the UK is approximately 13.0 years), and is triggered by a critical body weight. To begin with the menstrual periods may be rather irregular but for most girls it gradually settles into a cycle of about 28 days. It is important that a girl is prepared for the menarche and recognizes that it is an integral part of womanhood. Taboos about menstruation exist in many cultures and there may be rules about what she is unable to do at that time. There may also be 'old wives' tales' of not being able to wash her hair or being 'unwell'. A common euphemism in Britain is 'the curse'. It is a great pity that girls should grow up with these attitudes. Anne Frank, in her diary published in 1947, had this to say about the beginning of her periods: 'I think what is happening to me is so wonderful, and not only what can be seen on my body but all that is taking place inside . . . in spite of all the pain, unpleasantness and nastiness, I have a sweet secret'.

Boys

In a boy the first sign of puberty is an increase in the size of the testes, scrotum and penis followed by the growth of pubic hair and then by facial, axillary and chest hair. His body changes shape becoming broader around the chest and shoulders. Usually sometime later than this his voice breaks which may be abrupt or gradual. The larynx (Adam's apple) grows larger and the vocal chords virtually double in length. As a result his voice can drop about an octave in tone and may alternate between a high squeak and a deep bass.

Seminal emissions, the loss of seminal fluid during sleep, begin. A boy's first ejaculation is likely to occur within a year of the onset of the growth spurt which may be as early as 11 or as late as 16. It may take place as a result of masturbation or nocturnal emission (ejaculation during sleep, the 'wet dream') or of spontaneous waking orgasm. If a boy is unprepared for this he may feel anxious or ashamed of his developing sexuality whereas a boy who is able to discuss this with his parents and perhaps has had health education at school will recognize this as part of his developing manhood.

MENTAL DEVELOPMENT

The dramatic physical development of adolescence is accompanied by equally impressive, if less obvious, gains in mental achievement. Mental ability, cleverness or brightness manifests itself in many different ways and most people are better at some things than at others. Overall mental ability increases quite rapidly through the years of childhood and adolescence and then slows down during adulthood. These years are very important to intellectual development because it is at this time that the capacity to acquire and utilize knowledge approaches its peak.

At about the age of 12 (although there are marked individual variations) young people reach what Piaget describes as the period of formal operational thinking. The world is no longer dominated by what is but by what might be. This involves the ability to consider a variety of possibilities, thoroughly and objectively, in abstract terms and vastly increases the capacity to deal with issues and problems relating to self, the family and the world. Suddenly the young person begins to question social, political and moral values. Parents whose word and values were once absolute are now found to have 'feet of clay'.

Intense questioning and criticism together with radical proposals for the way things ought to be is likely to create turbulence within a family. Most families will survive this difficult time and will probably benefit from heated discussions on topics such as the Campaign for Nuclear Disarmament. It is important for adolescents to have such intellectual adventures even if they do nothing practical about them. Unfortunately, some may have their ideas and views ridiculed or may be discouraged from having such dreams. They may become disillusioned through being urged to accept things as they are and told that nothing can be changed.

The most important 'task' of adolescence is to develop a self-concept; a sense of feeling comfortable with how one appears, of one's own self-worth and what one expects from life. Personality development is often described as 'a search for identity; the eternal question of "Who am I?"'. Many people at this stage become more introspective and analytical in their thoughts and behaviour. At first, when their body is going through a period of rapid change young people are often preoccupied with their physical appearance and most, at some stage, will have a negative self-image. They may agonize over being either too tall or too short, over- or under-developed, too fat or too thin. Participation in sport or dance can to a great extent enhance physical and mental development because it usually leads to better coordination of movement and greater confidence in physical ability and appearance.

At a later stage the intellectual and social aspects of their personality gain in importance. In industrialized countries intellectual ability is bound up in academic achievement as most countries plan major examinations at the end of the school years. They can place the young person under a great deal of pressure as their future career may depend on their performance at this time. But the intellectual powers of adolescence are not only to do with examinations. This is a time of intellectual adventure, of believing that anything is possible and that the world can be changed. It is a time of unparalleled creativity and, as Conger (1979) says, 'many adolescent dreams will never be fulfilled, but just having had them can make the remainder of a person's life richer and fuller'.

The adolescent will try out a number of different roles before feeling comfortable in both his/her own and other people's eyes. Typically there is imitation of and identification with a number of different key people. In some countries the media may present an image of youth which is difficult for most young people to achieve. The rock star image, the lithe gymnast or the super-sports personality may be admired but impossible to emulate. Hero worship is normal and healthy and the associated trappings of records, fashionable clothes and sports equipment is part of the market economy. However, the persistent portrayal of 'beautiful' young people in fast cars and nice clothes may be particularly difficult to reconcile if one lives in a decaying inner city area with little prospect of even getting a job.

FRIENDS AND PEERS

Friends and peers play an especially important role in adolescence. There is at this time a gradual disengagement from the parents and family. The emotional gap which is left is filled by the support and understanding of friends. The bonds of friendship are strengthened by the fact that difficulties at home and the anxieties which are commonly experienced at this time can be shared by people who are having the same experiences themselves. Close friends are particularly important because of the feelings of vulnerability and lack of self-confidence which are commonly experienced. The peer group is also a place where people with like interests can revel in the enjoyment of spending time with others who are just

as keen on a particular sport or type of music as they are. There will probably be no other time in one's life when one is surrounded by people who share in one's own interests so intensely.

Not surprisingly this leads to a need to conform to the fads and fashions of the peer group. A particular hair style or type of clothing, a love of a particular television programme or music group becomes acceptable just as certain other styles become totally unacceptable. Some may seem trivial to the outsider, for instance one particular brand of jeans instead of another, but to the adolescent they serve as a badge of belonging. They also create a clear line of demarcation between their own world and that of all the others; in effect their own culture. To the outsider this is a closed and strange place, to the insider it is a place where, amidst the security of friends, one's own personality can be allowed to grow. No matter how much adolescents identify with the peer group, they are always seeking identities which are individual to themselves.

Relationships at this time tend to be particularly intimate, honest, intense and open. In order for this to be possible there has to be absolute trust in each other. Within the wider boundaries of 'the crowd' there is usually a smaller group and within this there are especially close friendships. However, there may be feelings of jealousy and insecurity associated with fears of being abandoned or betrayed. Adolescents generally want friends to be loyal, trustworthy and a reliable source of support in an emotional crisis. The demands made on a friendship are very high but then so are the rewards. This loyalty may be tested by requests or dares which are difficult to comply with and may conflict with the values of parents. Peer group pressure is a major factor in experimentation with smoking, alcohol and drug taking. The intensity of these relationships is such that inevitably some will founder amidst feelings of hurt and recriminations. Young people who have the greatest personal problems and who have problematic relationships with their parents may be the least able to sustain friendships because of feelings of suspicion and fear of hurt. Those who are unable to make friends may become 'loners' and continue to experience difficulty in developing relationships.

ADOLESCENTS AND THEIR PARENTS

It is not only adolescents who face an 'identity crisis'; their parents often do too. They may feel ambivalent about their child's growing independence, looking forward to a time when they have settled into a job and a family of their own whilst at the same time wanting to hold on to the close and dependent relationship of childhood. They may find it hard to reconcile their expectations of what they wanted for their child and what he/she actually is. Parents are sometimes heard to say, 'I just want what's right for her' and perhaps this is the key. Through encouraging discussion, by showing understanding and tolerance, by simply being there and demonstrating that they care, parents may find the fine balance between giving guidance and allowing freedom. Independence is not built in a day, indeed some dependence continues to exist. Perhaps only the nature of the relationship changes, seeing each other as equals with separate identities and, on some issues, differing opinions. In this way it may be possible to prevent explosive rebellion or inappropriate, continued dependence.

The notion that adolescents reject the values of their parents out of hand seems to be unfounded. It is noteworthy that in several surveys (Bandura, 1972; Rutter, 1976; Farrell, 1978) adolescents have been found to show a great deal of respect for their parents' views and a large majority of parents feel no increase in alienation at this time. Farrell's study showed that adolescents would prefer to learn about matters relating to sexuality from their parents rather than from teachers or friends. Moreover, in general adolescents select friends from a similar social group who are largely approved of by parents. Most adolescents get to know their friends' parents so that a network is built up which knits together family and friends.

ADOLESCENTS IN ASIAN FAMILIES

In school Asian children learn the ways of the host culture and its language. They seem able to cope with the expectations of the two cultures providing conflicting demands are not made on them. Problems may develop if they are subjected to stereotyped and inaccurate images of their own culture and so come to reject the values of their parents and the influence exerted by their extended family in Asia. Conversely they may experience problems if the family is very restrictive and fails to recognize their need to share a social life with friends. This can cause great problems especially for adolescent girls who are expected to be chaste and so their relationships and movements are normally severely restricted. A bad reputation will not only affect a girl's marriage prospects but can bring shame on the whole family. Olowu (1983) identified a need for counselling amongst Asian girls especially in relation to their relationships with teachers and family and their social confidence. Children in schools where there was a relatively small ethnic minority population had greatest difficulties. Weinreich (1979) also found that immigrant girls especially those from Pakistani families had high levels of anxiety and uncertainty. In general Asian families have high expectations of their children and want them to do well. In professional families, and increasingly in other families, girls have equal opportunities for career development.

DIET

Diet in adolescence is influenced by many things. Increasing independence means that more responsibility is assumed for selecting appropriate meals when away from the family. Peers are likely to influence which snacks are chosen, and going down to the local shop for a pie with friends becomes more important than staying at school or going home for a balanced meal on one's own. Perhaps most important of all is how the person sees him/herself and the confidence they have in their own self-image. Excessive over- or undereating can be a symptom of deep-seated unhappiness. Adolescents on special diets for diseases such as diabetes or coeliac disease may start to rebel against the restrictions imposed and careful counselling from a nurse may be helpful to enable the young person to come to terms with the illness and all the other changes which are taking place.

Nutritional requirements alter during adolescence due to the growth spurt. An increase in protein is needed, especially by boys, to build the increasing muscle mass. Requirements for vitamins A, C and B complex increase in both sexes as well as requirements for calcium because of the growth of bone. Iron is important especially for girls because of the onset of menstruation. Some young people develop a voracious appetite at this time especially if they are taking a lot of physical exercise. These added energy needs may be met by increased quantities of wholewheat bread and whole grains. The general principles of a healthy diet are the same as at any other time of life: adequate fibre, and low sugar, salt and fat.

ANOREXIA NERVOSA

Anorexia nervosa is a condition of severe undereating which can lead to extreme malnourishment or even death. Typically it begins during the adolescent years although it may start later; the average age of onset is about 18 years. It is a condition which mainly affects girls; only about one in ten anorexics are boys. Crisp et al (1976) estimated that one in every 100 girls over the age of 16 years in private education would have severe anorexia nervosa. The prevalence was significantly lower in girls in comprehensive schools, indicating that the condition is more likely to affect girls in social classes 1 and 2 than those in families in other social classes. It has been described as the 'slimmers' disease' as a slimming diet is often the trigger which starts it. However, the causes of anorexia are far more complex and, although there are many theories, the condition is still not fully understood. Lawrence (1984) states that anorexia occurs at a particular stage of a woman's development when she can find no other means of expressing how she feels about herself or other people. Minuchin et al (1978) suggests that it is the result of family interaction and that families with an anorexic member have an intense atmosphere, tend to be overinvolved with each other and tend to be overprotective.

Parents are often surprised when they realize that their child has anorexia as they had always seemed so quiet, obedient, eager to please and 'good'. This struggle to be perfect in their parents' eyes can prevent them from leading their own lives and developing their own identity. Perhaps as a reaction they display an obsessional need to be in control of this aspect of their life. Their self-image becomes distorted so that they are totally convinced that they are fat even when their weight may be as low as 30 kg. In Britain there are several specialist units where a multidisciplinary team works with the young person and her family. A self-help group, Anorexic Aid, is also very useful. The aim is to enable her to reach a reasonable weight for her height, to feel comfortable with this, to lose her obsession with food and to develop a realistic self-image. It may take months or even years before this is achieved.

SEXUALITY

Of all the dramatic changes which take place during adolescence none has as much impact as the increase in sexuality, and probably none lead to as much confusion. Surrounding young people are films, magazines and pop groups all extolling the thrills of sex. Yet at the same time come warnings from parents and teachers of the terrible things which can befall those who dare to experiment: unwanted pregnancy, sexually transmitted disease, and a ruined life. In the midst of this conflict the adolescent is experiencing feelings of almost uncontrollable desire at the same time as abject fear.

Sexuality involves a conscious awareness of sexual impulses intertwined with other needs such as love, self-esteem, reassurance and affection. Sexual fulfilment becomes important to boys and girls and is partly a search for love and approval. There comes a need to express concerns about sexual feelings and to ask about such practical matters as masturbation, contraception, sexual intercourse, homosexuality and conception. They will also start questioning moral values and begin to develop their own ideas about the expression of sexuality within their relationships. Farrell (1978) in her survey into attitudes of 16- to 19-year-olds found that they would most like to discuss these issues with their parents (with teachers as a second best choice). In reality, however, this tended not to happen and they were most likely to find out about such things from friends.

Much has been said about the 'new sexual morality', and the inference that young people are 'free and easy'. Certainly amongst adults extramarital sexual relationships have become more usual. Coleman (1980) states that this has influenced the sexual attitudes of young people. He notes some important differences between adolescents today and those of 20 years ago. Firstly, he states, they are more open about sexual matters, and they need greater opportunity for discussing sexual problems with adults because of this. Secondly, they see sexual behaviour more as a matter of private rather than public morality. Instead of looking for guidelines set by society they do what they feel is right for them. This makes their decisions less simple and straightforward. Thirdly, far from believing in 'free and easy sex' there appears to be a growing sense of the importance of sex being associated with stable, long-term relationships. Coleman concludes, 'Perhaps in this they have been influenced to some extent by the sight of their elders experiencing so much unhappiness in their own search for sexual fulfilment'.

Some adolescents may at some stage wonder if they are homosexual. In early adolescence there is usually close contact between members of the same sex. Intense interest in the changes which are taking place may lead to sexual experimentation such as comparison of genitalia, and masturbation in each other's presence, or to cuddles and holding hands. This is quite usual and is probably experienced by at least half of all boys and a third of all girls. Most people later adopt a heterosexual lifestyle; a minority become homosexual. Why people differ in this respect is not clear and attempts to find a physiological basis have been unproductive. Until relatively recently homosexuality was viewed by society as abnormal and gay people were subjected to hostility and discrimination. Some gay people still prefer to keep their sexuality secret. It may be very difficult for these young people to discuss their feelings with their parents. It is helpful if a counsellor (perhaps a school nurse) is available for them to discuss their feelings and fears so that their sexuality can be fully expressed. Hopefully they will come to realize that it is the quality of the relationship which is important and that all feelings which are warm, thoughtful and giving are to be valued.

ADOLESCENTS WITH SPECIAL NEEDS

During adolescence young people gradually lessen the dependence on their family. Those who are physically or mentally handicapped are likely to experience particular difficulties. In many ways handicap is more manageable in childhood. Those requiring physical care are easier to care for when they are small, and problems such as incontinence are relatively acceptable in childhood. Also, of course, parents are younger and perhaps more patient and able. Relationships within the family may become more difficult as the child matures. Education caters for their needs and is often in special schools which attract enthusiastic and caring staff who devise individual programmes for the children which are based on hard work and fun. Outings to all sorts of exciting places are an additional bonus. Some teachers argue that the problems really start when a child leaves school.

Physical Handicap

As an adolescent becomes more self-aware the difficulties associated with a physical handicap become more pronounced. Life at home and at school is relatively easy to organize compared with cinemas and entertainment centres. Although there is now a great deal more provision for handicapped people in public places it is difficult initially to sort out the practicalities of arranging a night out with friends. Attitudes of other people change too. Handicapped children attract special affection even from strangers whereas, although attitudes are changing, handicapped adults may still experience a negative public reaction. There may also be problems in finding places in further education as there are few universities or polytechnics which have suitable facilities. To succeed requires considerable determination. Whatever the person's particular talents it is important that they develop their potential to the maximum. In this way the feelings of 'handicap', and of being restricted, may lessen and the feeling of living life to the full may emerge.

During adolescence accelerated growth and weight gain may cause additional strain on weak muscles and a child who was able to walk with aids may become confined to a wheelchair. Parents who were once able to carry a child upstairs to bed find that they are no longer able to manage. Arrangements may have to be made for the adolescent to sleep downstairs in the living area and this may cause disruption in the household. Sexual feelings develop as in all other adolescents yet for some strange reason it is easy to ignore their sexuality. All young people have a need to feel attractive and to develop particularly close relationships with members of both their own and the opposite sex. Physically handicapped young people need careful counselling on matters such as menstruation, masturbation and sexual intercourse. For instance, young people with an indwelling catheter may suppose, wrongly, that they will never be able to have sexual intercourse.

SOLVENT AND DRUG ABUSE

Solvent abuse is not new (inhalation of volatile substances to alter psychological states has been in evidence for hundreds of years), but recently it has become a habit amongst some children and adolescents. Petrol and glue sniffing began in the United States in the 1950s, and during the 1970s solvent abuse 'caught on' in Britain. Glue is the most common substance which is 'sniffed' although a wide range of substances are used. These include dry-cleaning fluid, Tipp-Ex, hair lacquer, paint thinners and many aerosol products. All of these substances are readily, cheaply and legally available. The purpose initially is experimentation; after that it is intoxication. The substance may be inhaled through the nose or the mouth. Glue is often inhaled from a crisp bag, and solvents sniffed either directly from the bottle or from a saturated rag.

Experimentation is a normal part of adolescence, as is allegiance to the peer group. Many youngsters will 'try things out' when they are with friends and in many ways it can be argued that such experimentation is a normal part of development. However, this practice is associated with health risks. Acute poisoning can result which may present as similar to acute alcohol poisoning, and renal damage, transient liver upset, and status epilepticus have been observed. Behavioural problems may also result, as may family problems. Accidents, especially physical harm and inhalation of vomit, sometimes occur as out-of-the-way sites such as canal banks and railway sidings are often chosen. In general this is usually a passing fad, but there is some suggestion that 'sniffers' are more likely to go on to drug or alcohol abuse. Young people who sniff alone may also present a particular problem because of their difficulty in establishing relationships and the greater risk of accident with nobody to help.

Since the mid 1960s there has been a dramatic increase in the number of adolescents abusing illegal drugs. A survey by Caplin and Woodward (1986) found that 15 was the average age when heroin addicts first started taking drugs. Drug abuse is a nationwide problem affecting rural as well as urban areas, and it affects people of all social groups and from all sorts of backgrounds. They found that young people usually started taking drugs 'to be like everyone else' so that they would not be the odd one out and feel 'stupid'. Three-quarters of them first received drugs from friends. Adolescents seem to be much less able to cope and control their drug taking and are more likely than older people to go on to take harder drugs. Probably most young people will be offered drugs before the age of 20.

In 1985 a major health education campaign aimed to show young people the true picture of drug addiction and to encourage them to 'Just say no!' (see Figure 22). In the United States parent peer groups have formed which provide an opportunity for parents to get together to talk about their anxieties regarding drug abuse, to warn other parents of the dangers of drugs and to share with them ways of keeping their children away from drugs. Caplin and Woodward conclude that the campaign to prevent drug abuse should start when children are 11 or 12 years old and that it should fight the problem on all fronts; at school, in the family, through the media, using community organizations, by informed opinion, and with the help of trained doctors, nurses, police, social workers and teachers, but above all by informed young people — those who will have to make the choice.

Of all the young people who come into contact with drugs some will not try them, some will try them and leave them and some will try them and go on to abuse them. It is the latter group that causes concern. For them drugs may seem an easy way to numb their bleak inner lives or to make problems temporarily seem to go away. But in reality they may only alleviate the symptoms of the real problems which are loneliness, anxiety, frustration and fear of failure. What is more, dependence on drugs may prevent that person from developing the skills necessary to deal with problems effectively. Failure, although painful, teaches us about ourselves and enables us to gain a measure of ourselves. Escape through drugs eliminates this learning experience. The real solution therefore lies in enabling adolescents to face life's challenges, to support them through the difficult times, to help them to set realistic goals for themselves, to encourage them to develop interests and activities which will stimulate and challenge, and perhaps most of all to listen when they agonize over life's injustices. Drug problems appear to be more common amongst adolescents who have parents who are

HOW LOW
CAN YOU GET
ON HEROIN?

Mental Problems

Skin Infections

Aching Limbs

Blood Diseases

Wasted Muscles

Liver Complaints

Constipation

Take heroin and before long you'll start looking ill, losing weight and feeling like death.
So, if you're offered heroin, you know what to say.

HEROIN SCREWS YOU UP

Figure 22. *'Just say no!' to drugs. An example of material used in the drugs campaign by the DHSS.*

neglectful, overly permissive, or conversely autocratic or hostile.

SMOKING

Smoking is a major health problem amongst young people. The associated health problems are listed in Chapter 2. Although smoking has an immediate effect on fitness, most of the associated diseases are more likely to develop in later life. It is therefore difficult to convince a young person of the benefits of not smoking or of stopping when the important thing for them is to join in with their friends and to look sophisticated. Dobbs and Marsh (1983) carried out a survey of smoking amongst secondary school children. They found that in England and Wales 27% of fifth formers were regular smokers and that there was little difference between boys and girls although in general boys started earlier. There was a clear increase in prevalence with age. In England and Wales 73% of the first-year pupils had never smoked but this was the case for only 26% of fifth-year pupils. Most said that they started smoking with friends and that they smoked more at the weekends when they were out socializing.

HEALTH EDUCATION IN SCHOOL

By the time adolescence is reached most schools promoting health education will have prepared adolescents for the physical and emotional changes which are taking place. By this age group discussion can be used to allow frank and open sharing of experiences. Issues which might be covered include reaching decisions, family patterns, minority groups, the needs of children, parenting and sexuality. Guided discussions allow adolescents to reach their own conclusions and form their own judgements on sensitive issues. The greatest influence on behaviour, including smoking and drug taking, is the peer group and so group work is particularly effective at this age. In order to discuss an issue one needs to have the necessary vocabulary. In her book, *The Ostrich Position*, Carol Lee describes how she overcomes the basic problem which many people have when talking about sex: language. She manages to break down some of the barriers by using word games to provide words and phrases which can be used to ask questions or express feelings. It is also important for parents to be informed of the content of health education programmes and to have the opportunity to comment on these. Many parents agonize over such things as the possibility of their child becoming pregnant or taking drugs. Discussion groups for parents where they can confront these issues and share ways in which they have approached them might also be helpful.

ACCIDENT PREVENTION

Accidents are the most common form of death in the adolescent age group. Road accidents account for the highest percentage, especially motor cycle accidents. Risk taking is a feature of adolescence but when it involves driving, and possibly alcohol and drugs as well, it can transport the young person into extreme danger. In Britain the Health Education Authority often mounts a campaign at Christmas aimed specifically at discouraging young people from drinking and driving. In Britain the wearing of crash helmets for motor cycle drivers (and pillion riders) and seat belts for drivers and front seat passengers is compulsory by law. This has considerably reduced deaths and serious injuries.

Sports injuries can also be serious amongst young people. Because of the naturally reckless nature of youth it is vital that adequate instruction be given before dangerous sports are attempted.

Organizations such as Venture Scouts and the Duke of Edinburgh Award scheme encourage safe adventure. Even seemingly 'safe' sports can be harmful. In the USA tennis players under the age of 16 years are restricted in the number of competitions in which they may play because of the injuries which have been incurred from intensive playing.

EMPLOYMENT AND UNEMPLOYMENT

One of the features of adolescence is that it prepares the way for future life and therefore, for many people, work. For some, natural talents and interests emerge and develop into an occupation; others follow in their father's (or mother's) footsteps; and some take what they can get. Some young people go straight to work from school whereas others go on to further education before finding employment. In recent years there has been a gradual increase in the number of young people leaving school with formal qualifications and those going on to further education. However, since 1960 there has also been a steady rise in the number of young people unemployed. In 1985 about 35% of people aged 18 – 24 years in the UK reported some unemployment (figures from the *Employment Gazette*). In some cities this can be as high as 50%. Added to this, young people are remaining unemployed for longer periods and it is now recognized that some young people leaving school may never gain employment. The effects of this can lead to despair, depression, feelings of worthlessness, and for some a life on supplementary benefit living in cheap, temporary accommodation.

In response to this the government has introduced Youth Training Schemes which are organized by the Manpower Services Commission. YTS is open to all 16-year-old school leavers, both employed and unemployed, to some 17-year-olds who are unemployed and to some disabled young people up to the age of 21. It aims to help them in their work during YTS and afterwards, in finding jobs, in doing another course, or in going on to further education. In short it offers a year of vocational training between school and work. Trainees gain work experience in settings such as training workshops, community projects, companies or factory floors. There is a certificate at the end of the year which can help towards further employment. However for many the prospects of permanent employment at the end of this experience are slim.

ALIENATION

Rebellion is part of adolescence and sometimes this may result in young people adopting an appearance which appears alien to those outside the group. The shaved heads of the 'skinheads' and the weird and wonderful styles of the 'punks' seem threatening and hostile. 'Gang' behaviour sometimes leads to disturbances such as those witnessed at soccer matches although it is inaccurate and unfair to put all antisocial behaviour down to adolescents. Most of these youngsters will eventually grow into reasonably happy, effective and conforming adults. But there will be some who may find difficulty in finding a way back into the mainstream of society because they feel dissatisfied with either themselves or society or both. If they are poor they may resent the wealth they see around them; if they are black they may respond to the attitudes of discrimination which they often sense.

LOOKING TO THE FUTURE

What adolescents seek above all else is a clear and confident sense of their own self-worth. For most people these are difficult and testing times which finally settle down into the rather less intense and more self-assured years of adulthood. 'The young of today' are destined to be a much maligned group in any generation. But without them life would be very dull, and without those adolescent dreams adult life would surely lack purpose.

References and further reading

Altschul, A. & Sinclair, H.C. (1981) *Psychology for Nurses*, 5th edn. London: Baillière Tindall.

Bandura, A. (1972) The stormy decade. Fact or fiction? In: Rogers, D., ed., *Issues in Adolescent Psychology*, 2nd edn. New York: Appleton-Century-Crofts.

Caplin, S. & Woodward, S. (1986) *Drugwatch: Just Say No*. London: Corgi Books.

Coleman, J. C. (1980) *The Nature of Adolescence*. London: Methuen.

Conger, J. (1979) *Adolescence. Generation under Pressure*. London: Harper & Row.

Crisp, A. H. et al (1976) How common is anorexia nervosa? A prevalence study. *British Journal of Psychiatry* **128**, 549–554.

Dobbs, J. & Marsh, A. (1983) *Smoking among Secondary Children*. London: HMSO.

Farrell, C. (1978) *My Mother Said . . . .* London: Routledge & Kegan Paul.

Frank, A. (1953) *The Diary of Anne Frank*. London: Vallentine, Mitchell & Co. Ltd.

Huskisson, J. M. (1985) *Nutrition and Dietetics in Health and Disease*, 2nd edn. London: Baillière Tindall.

Lawrence, M. (1984) *The Anorexic Experience*. London: The Women's Press.

Lee, C. (1983) *The Ostrich Position: Sex, Schooling and Mystification*. London: Writers and Readers.

McAlhone, B., ed. (1983) *Where on Drugs. A Parent's Handbook*. Cambridge: Advisory Centre for Education.

Minuchin, S. et al (1978) *Psychosomatic Families*. London: Harvard University Press.

National Advisory Committee on Nutrition Education (1983) *Proposals for Nutritional Guidelines for Health Education in Britain*. London: Health Education Council.

Olowu (1983) Counselling needs of immigrant children. *New Commonwealth* **10** (3), 410–420.

Rutter, M. et al (1976) Adolescent turmoil. Fact or fiction? *Journal of Child Psychology and Psychiatry* **17**, 35–56.

Watson, J. M. (1984) Solvent abuse and adolescents. *Practitioner* **228**, 487–490.

Weinreich, P. (1979) Ethnicity and adolescent identity conflicts. In: Khan, S., ed., *Minority Families in Britain*. London: Macmillan.

7

Parenthood

In the not too distant past parenthood was viewed as the duty of all married adults. Outside wedlock it was considered shameful. Those who did not fit into this pattern of expectations became slightly detached from the mainstream of society. Today, more than at any other time in our past, parenthood can be a matter of choice. It is possible to have a heterosexual relationship and choose not to become a parent at all, or to defer it until one feels the time is right. An increasing number of women become parents in their thirties and forties. It is also becoming more usual for single people to choose to have children. But the choice of parenthood is more unpredictable than most others that we will make. It can never be an informed choice because nobody knows what it will be like to be a parent. The decision is predominantly emotional, based on a feeling or a desire which is difficult to rationalize and once made is irrevocable. For women the decision not to have children is also irrevocable once the years in which pregnancy is possible have passed.

Some parents comment that it is difficult for them to believe that their child has not always been with them. The birth of a baby has an enormous impact on the way in which one sees oneself as well as the way in which one is regarded by others. Until this time life is largely dominated by concern with oneself. Loving relationships involve concern for others but do not match the intensely intimate relationship with one's own child. A child is entirely dependent on its parent(s) and this creates a switch of primary interests away from oneself. The freedom which one had before is severely curtailed, especially in western countries where children are barred from many places and activities. The feelings of responsibility in parenthood can create doubt about one's abilities to cope and to be a 'good parent'; fears for the future which can be overwhelming. Parenthood is essentially a two-fold experience; it involves the growth and development of the child through the love and care of the parent, and it also provides the parent with the opportunity to grow and to experience a new dimension of emotions and ultimately to learn about oneself.

The birth of a child leads to the formation of a family whether this is a two-parent, one-parent, foster, or other type of family. It is within the family that the child will learn about relationships, the nature of love, the feeling of being cared for and later of caring for others. It is the place where the foundations of all life's experiences and expectations are laid. The family therefore carries a heavy responsibility to ensure that the needs of both child and parents are met (see also Chapter 11).

FAMILY PLANNING

Contraceptive methods allow prospective parents to choose when to start a family, and established families the opportunity to dictate the space between babies and the eventual size of their family. For couples who experience a delay in conception, a greater awareness of the factors involved in fertility, and medical advances in techniques such as artificial insemination and 'in vitro' fertilization can make parenthood a possibility.

The aims of the Family Planning Association are:

1 to preserve and protect the good health, both mental and physical, of parents, young people and children, and to prevent the poverty, hardship and distress caused by unwanted conception;

2 to educate the public in the field of procreation, contraception and health with particular reference to personal responsibility in sexual relationships and to the consequences of population growth;

3 to give medical advice and assistance in cases of involuntary sterility or of difficulties connected with the partnership or sexual problems for which medical advice or treatment is appropriate.

In order to achieve these aims the general health of the women and men must be considered. Health care available includes:

1 Contraceptive advice and care to women and men irrespective of marital status. This is usually clinic based but may also include a domiciliary service to people in rural areas or to those immobilized by physical disability. It may also involve specialist care to people on long-term drug therapy, diabetics, epileptics, mentally handicapped people, and so on.

2 Screening — cervical cytology, screening for hypertension, the teaching of self-examination of breasts (in some areas mammography), screening for sickle cell anaemia and thalassaemia, detection and referral for treatment of women with pelvic infection.

3 Advice and treatment for couples with reduced fertility which now affects an estimated one in seven couples in Britain.

4 Youth Advisory Service. This may be provided by the Brook Advisory Service which specializes in the needs of young people. Health education is also provided in many schools.

5 Psychosexual counselling.

6 Well Women's Clinic. This may include screening and counselling and treatment for menopaused-related health problems and premenstrual syndrome.

Contraception

Conception depends on live healthy sperm reaching a mature healthy living egg in a conducive environment. Contraception (see Figure 23) aims to prevent this from occurring. Several methods are available and only the couple involved can decide which is best for them at that particular stage of their relationship. The method chosen should be unobtrusive, reliable and free from side-effects.

Natural Family Planning

All natural methods depend on a woman being able reliably to detect the time of ovulation, and the couple then avoiding intercourse around that time. The symptothermal method combines observations of several signs which signal ovulation which usually occurs about 14 days before a menstrual period. Sperm live for about 3–5 days, the ovum 1–2 days and it is therefore possible using a calender to gain some idea of the 'safe period' (see Figure 24). Other indicators are the body temperature which rises immediately after ovulation, the condition of the cervical mucus which tends to be dry on the infertile days gradually becoming thicker and then clear, thin and stretchy around the time of ovulation, and personal signs such as mood swings, breast

THE COMBINED PILL
Oral contraceptive
Triphasic and biphasic pills }
Everyday/ED pill
Almost 100% effective

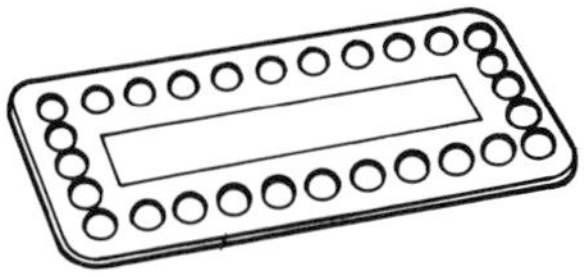

MINI-PILL
Progestogen-only pill
98% effective

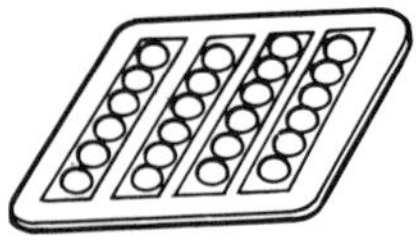

INJECTABLE CONTRACEPTIVE
Depo-Provera }
The jab
Almost 100% effective

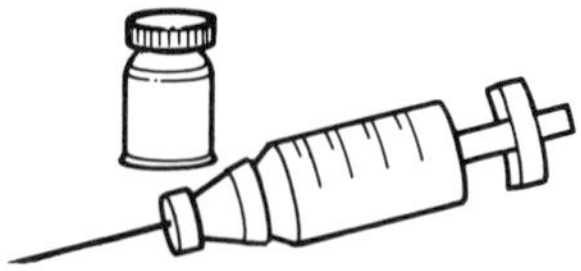

INTRAUTERINE DEVICE
IUD, IUCD }
Coil
96–98% effective

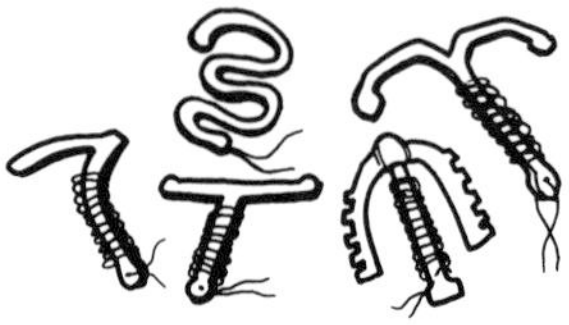

DIAPHRAGM OR CAP + SPERMICIDE
97% effective, with careful use

CONDOM
Sheath, Protective }
Rubber, Johnny
97% effective, with careful use

NATURAL FAMILY PLANNING (NFP)
where the couple are motivated and
trained by a recognized NFP teacher,
this method can be as effective as the
oral contraceptive pill

FEMALE STERILIZATION
Occasional failures occur

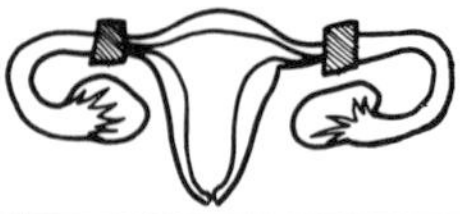

MALE STERILIZATION
Vasectomy
Occasional failures occur

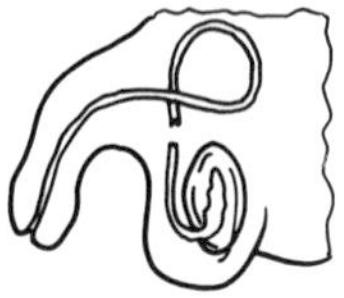

Figure 23.   *Contraception methods and failure rates. From Tanner, J. M. et al. (1966)* Archives of Disease in Childhood, **41**.

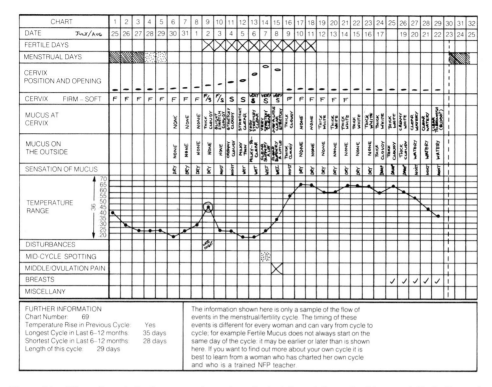

Figure 24. *The safe period—the symptothermal method. Adopted from the Menstrual Cycle Poster by Bristol Women's Health Group.*

tenderness or mid-cycle pain. The couple can use this method either as contraception or to plan conception. The advantages of this method include freedom from medical intervention, and some claim a greater closeness between the couple because of the commitment which is needed from both partners. An additional benefit is that the woman becomes intimately aware of her own fertility and body functioning. It is also acceptable to the Catholic Church.

Coitus Interruptus (withdrawal)

The earliest reference to contraception is in the Book of Genesis where it states that Onan spilt his seed upon the ground to prevent fertilization of his brother's wife. The method depends on the with-

drawal of the penis from the vagina just before ejaculation so that the semen is deposited away from the vagina and vulva. It is difficult to estimate how many couples use it today but Peel and Potts (1969) noted that 44% of couples had used it at some time and that for 21% it was their current method. Many people refer to it as 'being careful'. There has been no scientific study of this method but it is generally regarded as unreliable with an estimated pregnancy rate of 20–30%. This is because drops of fluid on the penis prior to ejaculation contain some sperm and may cause pregnancy. Also it is a method which demands a considerable degree of self-control by both partners.

Greer (1984) challenged the rejection of coitus interruptus as a method. She found that in parts of Italy it is the preferred method of contraception even though it is regarded by the church as a grave sin. The method is used during engagements (which may be for several years), and to space children after marriage. The men feel that it is their duty to prevent conception and in addition take pride in their capacity to prolong sexual intercourse for the pleasure of the woman. Greer suggests that coitus interruptus will be an unsatisfactory method if it is used as a substitute for 'normal' sex when withdrawal takes place at the moment before the involuntary reflex takes over. However, for some couples mutual sexual stimulation, which avoids the possibility of sperm reaching the vagina, may be a perfectly satisfactory expression of sexuality.

Barrier Methods

The condom is a thin rubber sheath worn over the erect penis to contain sperm and so prevent them being deposited in the vagina. The condom should be put on before genital contact begins because some sperm may be present at the tip of the urethra before ejaculation and if deposited at the entrance to the vagina may still reach the cervix. The penis should be withdrawn carefully whilst still erect so that no semen escapes into the vagina. When used with a spermicide, which may be in the form of a cream, jelly, pessary or aerosol foam, it is a reliable method of contraception. Condoms are readily available and no medical supervision is required. They remain the most popular method of contraception in Britain. They also give some protection against sexually transmitted diseases and for this reason are being promoted in some countries such as Sweden. Their use, with spermicide, is now being advocated as one way of reducing the spread of human immune deficiency virus (HIV) and AIDS.

Several different types of cervical cap are available (see Figure 24). Each type covers the cervix and provides a barrier against the entry of sperm into the uterus. The type most commonly used is the diaphragm. The correct size and shape for the individual patient is determined by pelvic examination by a specially trained doctor or nurse. It is inserted before intercourse and left in position for at least 6 hours afterwards. It must be used in conjunction with a spermicide, and its reliability depends on correct and continuous use. The use of the cap must be carefully taught. It is a popular method with couples who have a regular pattern of intercourse, but is less easy to use when this pattern is unpredictable or when there is little privacy. Contraceptive sponges are also now available although they are less reliable.

The Pill

The combined pill, when taken according to the instructions, is almost 100% reliable. The action of the combined pill is to prevent the ovary from producing an ovum. It contains synthetic hormones; oestrogen which inhibits the feedback mechanism to the hypothalamus which in turn prevents the anterior pituitary from producing follicle stimulating hormone; and progestogen which causes the cervical mucus to become dense and difficult for the sperm to penetrate. Pills are taken over a 28-day cycle with a 7 day break. The biphasic and triphasic pills have varying levels of hormones and so mirror more closely the normal menstrual pattern. It is suitable for most women under the age of 35 years although there are increased risks for the very overweight, smokers and women with high blood pressure. Absolute contraindications to its use are oestrogen-dependent carcinoma, history of thrombosis, and recent liver disease. There are other conditions producing risk factors and for this reason it may only be prescribed by a doctor. A woman taking the pill should have her health monitored six monthly.

The progestogen-only pill (the mini-pill) is used as an alternative for women for whom oestrogen-containing pills are unsuitable. It is especially useful for breast-feeding mothers, women over 35 years and women who are not able to tolerate the combined pill or are developing hypertension. Its action is three-fold; it alters the cervical mucus making it impenetrable to sperm, it affects the endometrium reducing its ability to receive a fertilized ovum, and it affects the motility of the uterine tubes so that transport of the ovum is slowed. The pill must be taken very regularly. If missed for longer than 3 hours extra precautions should be taken. Its main disadvantage is its effect on the menstrual cycle, which may become irregular in spacing, and menstrual loss.

The injectable contraceptive acts in a similar way to the mini-pill and also stops ovulation. The hormone progestogen is injected into a muscle and is released slowly into the body. Each injection is usually effective for 2–3 months. However, the woman may experience irregular bleeding and a delay in returning to her normal menstrual pattern. Because its action is not reversible for 3 months, clear informed consent is needed. It has advantages for women who tend to forget to take the pill but is not a commonly used method.

The post-coital or 'morning after' pill is available as an emergency measure following unprotected intercourse. Treatment must start within 3 days of intercourse.

Intrauterine Contraceptive Devices

The intrauterine contraceptive device (IUCD or coil) acts by preventing implantation of the fertilized ovum. It is a small, flexible device made of plastic and sometimes bound with copper which is inserted into the uterus by a doctor (see Figure 24). It has a direct action on the endometrium and creates an unfavourable environment for the implantation of the ovum. A strand of thread projects from the cervix and the woman is taught

to check it regularly to ensure that the IUCD has not been expelled. IUCDs with copper are usually changed every 3 – 5 years; plastic devices may remain longer. Although they can be used by women who have not been pregnant, they are usually chosen by women with children as insertion is generally easier. There is a small risk of ectopic pregnancy and pelvic infection which should be clearly explained to the woman before she finally decides. It is a method which requires very little attention by the woman. A yearly check by the doctor is recommended.

The IUCD can also be used as an emergency post-coital method following unprotected intercourse. It must be inserted within 5 days and left until the next menstrual period.

Sterilization

Sterilization of the man or the woman must be considered irreversible and permanent. It therefore requires very careful consideration by both partners who should ideally be offered counselling prior to making a decision. This method can give great peace of mind to couples who have completed their families, but it may cause anguish to those who later desire another child. In male sterilization, or vasectomy, the vas deferens through which sperm travel from the testes to the penis are cut so that they can no longer enter the ejaculate. The two tubes are reached by a small incision either in the middle of on each side of the scrotum. The operation is usually carried out under local anaesthetic and takes about 10 minutes. Vasectomy has no effect on sexual activity or desire. It normally takes several weeks for the semen to become clear of sperm, and two consecutive sperm-free samples of semen are required.

In female sterilization the uterine tubes are either cut or clipped so that the ovum cannot travel down to reach the sperm. The uterine tubes can be reached either through a small incision in the abdominal wall or by laparoscopy. Sterilization can be carried out under local anaesthetic, but is more usually done under general anaesthetic with a hospital stay of at least a day. It is effective after the next normal menstrual period. This operation is usually carried out not less than 6 months following the birth of a baby as the mother may find the two events together emotionally overwhelming.

Termination of Pregnancy

Although this is not a method of contraception, nor an alternative for it, it is in many countries a legal option. In Britain termination of pregnancy is governed by the 1967 Abortion Act. It is justified if the circumstances fit into one of the following categories:

1 The continuance of the pregnancy would involve risk to the life of the pregnant woman greater than if the pregnancy were terminated.
2 The continuance of the pregnancy would involve risk of injury to the physical or mental health of the pregnant woman greater than if the pregnancy were terminated.
3 The continuance of the pregnancy would involve risk of injury to the physical or mental health of the existing child(ren) of the family of the pregnant woman greater than if the pregnancy were terminated.
4 There is substantial risk that if the child were born it would suffer from such physical or mental abnormalities as to be seriously handicapped.

The final decision of whether to have a termination must rest with the woman concerned. In order to reach this decision expert counselling is important. She must also have the agreement of two doctors who have seen and examined her and are satisfied that it is justified. Facilities exist in most National Health Service hospitals as well as in private clinics some of which

are run by charities. One of the best known is the British Pregnancy Advisory Service (BPAS), a non-profit-making trust which provides an abortion counselling and referral service.

PRE-CONCEPTION CARE

For those who elect for parenthood there are advantages to commencing health care prior to conception. Pre-conception care aims to promote the health of the unborn child and prevent abnormalities, as well as to promote the health of the parents. Fear and apprehension during pregnancy may be allayed because both parents know that they have done as much as they can to create a healthy pregnancy. Guidance on pre-conception care is offered at some Family Planning Clinics. The general guidelines are as follows:

1 *Stopping contraception*. It is advisable for the woman to wait for 3 months and to have at least one normal menstrual period between stopping the pill and attempting to conceive. This will allow her body time to expel the excess hormones, and will also enable the expected date of delivery to be more accurately calculated. Women using the coil should have it removed at the end of a period. There is no need to wait before trying to conceive. Women using the symptothermal method may be able to detect their most fertile time with some accuracy.
2 *Rubella immunity*. Rubella (German measles) during early pregnancy can lead to congenital abnormalities. A blood test will indicate immunity. Women who are not immune should be vaccinated and advised to wait for at least 3 months before becoming pregnant. A susceptible woman who comes into contact with rubella during pregnancy may be offered passive immunity. The immune status of a woman during pregnancy should be

noted so that she can be offered vaccination after pregnancy if necessary.

3 *Diet.* A healthy diet depends on a variety of foods being eaten at regular times. This should include raw fruit and vegetables to ensure adequate vitamin and mineral intake. Foods high in sugar, salt and fat should be reduced and foods high in fibres such as wholemeal bread and pulses increased. Folic acid is necessary for the baby's development and is probably especially important pre-conceptually and in the early weeks. Foods containing folic acid are meat, green leafy vegetables, peanuts and brown rice. An extra 500 ml of milk (which can be skimmed) will ensure an adequate intake of protein and calcium. Supplementation of trace elements and vitamins is not usually necessary, but ferrous iron may be prescribed if iron deficiency anaemia develops during pregnancy.

4 *General fitness.* Prior to becoming pregnant, women excessively under- or overweight will need to pay particular attention to their diet and lifestyle in order to bring their weight to within normal limits. Very low body weight may diminish fertility. Dietary regimens designed to alter body weight radically in a short period of time should be avoided, and a reducing diet should not be undertaken during pregnancy. Intensive and prolonged physical exercise may lead to menstrual irregularities, but regular exercise which results in reasonable increases in cardiovascular function will promote health both before and during pregnancy. Periods of rest and relaxation are also important to promote health and a feeling of wellbeing.

5 *Smoking.* Apart from the general risks to health, especially cardiovascular disease and lung disease, nicotine passes into the bloodstream of the unborn baby. There is a higher risk of prematurity, the baby is more likely to be of low birth weight, and perinatal mortality is significantly increased. Men who are heavy smokers have a higher incidence of abnormal sperm. Ideally, both partners should stop smoking prior to conception, and during pregnancy the mother should avoid prolonged periods in a smoky atmosphere.

6 *Alcohol.* Alcohol passes into the baby's bloodstream and heavy drinking during pregnancy can affect its development and may lead to fetal alcohol syndrome. It is now generally accepted that alcohol may be teratogenic and that even moderate or light drinking may affect the baby although less severely. It is best to eliminate alcohol completely about the time of conception and during pregnancy, or at most to have only the occasional drink.

7 *Pills and medicines.* Any medication, even that bought from a chemist, is best avoided immediately before and throughout pregnancy. This is because of the potential teratogenic effect of drugs, even those believed to be 'safe'.

8 *Hazards at work.* Anyone working with chemicals, radiation, lead or toxic substances should seek guidance from their employer. If there is a risk, a move away from that particular work environment may be necessary.

9 *Genetic counselling.* A couple who have previously had a child with a congenital abnormality, or who have a family history of an inherited disorder, may benefit from genetic counselling. The likelihood of a similar problem arising can be calculated and they can be informed of the risks and the specialized tests available. They can then make an informed decision on whether to go ahead with a further pregnancy.

10 *Medical conditions.* Pre-conception care should take account of infectious diseases and other medical conditions which may affect the developing embryo. Maternal infections such as syphilis, rubella, cytomegalovirus, toxoplasmosis and herpes simplex may cause congenital abnormalities. Protection against rubella is available (see above) but there is no immunization for cytomegalovirus. Nurses planning a pregnancy should not care for infants with cytomegalovirus, or patients with Acquired Immune Deficiency Syndrome because they frequently carry this virus.

Prospective parents with chronic health disorders usually need specialist care. There is, for instance, a relatively high incidence of congenital abnormalities in babies born to insulin-dependent diabetics and it is important that the condition is well controlled before and during the pregnancy. Diabetes and coeliac disease may adversely affect male reproduction function and sperm counts may be necessary. Other conditions which may require specialist medical attention at this time include epilepsy, endocrine or metabolic disorders, cardiovascular or haemolytic disorders such as haemophilia, sickle cell disease and thalassaemia, renal disease, pre-malignancy and malignancy, long-term drug therapy and handicap in the parents. Pregnancy is recognized as a co-factor in the development of Acquired Immune Deficiency Syndrome, and babies born to mothers who are positive for HIV antibodies are also at high risk of developing the disease. For this reason the HIV antibody test is indicated in women in the high-risk groups (see Chapter 16).

ANTENATAL CARE

The aims of antenatal care are:

1   to promote and maintain good physical and mental health during pregnancy;
2   to ensure a mature, live healthy infant;
3   to prepare the woman for labour, lactation and the subsequent care of her child, physically, psychologically, socially and educationally;
4   to detect early and treat appropriately 'high-risk' conditions, medical and obstetrical, that would endanger the life or impair the health of mother or baby.

The success in achieving these aims can be seen by the reduction in infant and maternal mortality rates (see Figure 25). However, there remain marked differences in the perinatal mortality rate in relation to the occupational status of the parent. *Fit for the Future: The Report of the Committee on Child Health Services* (Court Report, 1976) noted that between 1950 and 1973 the perinatal mortality rate declined by 45% for those of professional and 49% for those of managerial class, but only 34% for those of the unskilled manual class. In 1986 babies born to unskilled manual workers are twice as likely to die in their first year of life as babies born to professionals. Also, the House of Commons Social Services Committee (1980) chaired by Rene Short drew attention to the relatively high perinatal mortality rate amongst Asians in Britain. There is a clearly identified need for health care to be directed towards the most vulnerable groups of prospective parents.

The first sign of pregnancy is likely to be a missed menstrual period. The woman may also experience around this time nausea, frequency of micturition, tenderness and fullness in the breasts and fatigue. Pregnancy may be confirmed by immunological testing either by a chemist, general practitioner or Family Planning Clinic. Many women will have a pregnancy confirmed within 6 – 8 weeks of conception.

Following confirmation of pregnancy a decision will be reached between parent and GP on where the baby will be born. Women in Britain are encouraged to have their babies in hospital, although a small number have home deliveries. This will only be possible if both home conditions and the previous obstetric history are satisfactory. Responsibility for antenatal care is shared between the midwife, general practitioner and obstetrician.

At the first antenatal visit a full medical and obstetric history is taken to assess the health of the woman and the health

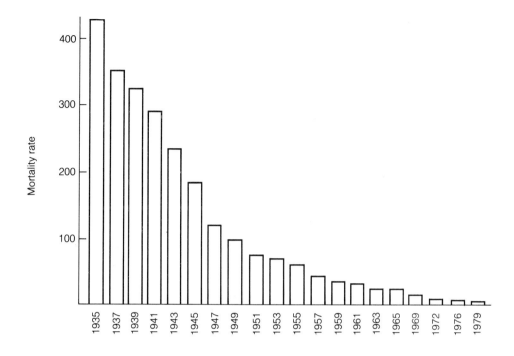

Figure 25. *Maternal mortality rates in England and Wales, 1935–1979.*

of her and her partner's family, and to detect any condition which could affect pregnancy and labour. Routine investigations which are carried out at the beginning of pregnancy include haemoglobin level to exclude anaemia, blood grouping, screening for the presence of antibodies which may cause haemolytic disease of the newborn, rubella antibody titre and screening for syphilis. Women of Afro-Caribbean or mediterranean descent should also be screened for sickle cell disease and thalassaemia. A particular note should be taken of the presence of genital herpes as this may require treatment and may preclude a vaginal delivery. A urine specimen for bacteriological examination is taken to exclude any hidden urinary infection which is symptom free and may develop into pyelonephritis if untreated. Urine is also

examined for the presence of sugar and to exclude albumin. Blood pressure is recorded. These provide a baseline against which any changes during pregnancy may be compared.

The expected date of delivery, which is normally 283 days from the first day of the last menstrual period, is estimated. If there is doubt over this, for instance if the woman had an irregular menstrual cycle or had recently stopped taking the oral contraceptive pill, tests using ultrasonic scanning of the fetus may be necessary to more accurately determine its maturity. (This test may also reveal a multiple pregnancy or fetal abnormality and give information on the placental site and the volume of amniotic fluid.) In many hospitals ultrasonic scanning is available to all on request. The expected date of delivery is inevitably approximate and the arrival of the baby 2 weeks either side of this date can be anticipated.

Throughout pregnancy the woman will have regular examinations from the midwife and doctor in order to continually monitor her health and the progress of the pregnancy. She may be offered specialized tests to exclude specific abnormalities of the fetus. At 16 weeks' gestation a blood test for alpha-fetoproteins may be made to exclude open neural tube defects such as spina bifida. The likelihood of having a Down's syndrome baby rises steeply after 35 years of age. Therefore women in this age group or with a family history of Down's syndrome will be offered amniocentesis to detect chromosomal abnormalities in the fetus. The woman will then be offered termination of pregnancy.

If there are no complications subsequent antenatal visits will be arranged at four weekly intervals until the 28th week of pregnancy, fortnightly until the 36th week and weekly thereafter. At each visit the woman will be asked about her general health and any changes which she has noticed, such as fetal movement. Weight and blood pressure are recorded, urine is tested and the presence of oedema is noted to detect onset of pre-eclampsia. Abdominal examination will reveal the height of the fundus, size and shape of the uterus, the position of the fetus, the presence of fetal movement and the fetal heart beat, and later in pregnancy the engagement of the fetal head. If there is any question about the growth of the fetus after the 34th week, collections of urine may be taken to measure levels of oestriol which will indicate the efficiency of the placenta. This will, in any event, become less efficient after the 42nd week of pregnancy.

Good dental hygiene is always important and this should be continued throughout pregnancy. In Britain dental care is free during pregnancy and for a year afterwards. It is important to remember also that the diet of a woman before and during her pregnancy will influence the future dental health of the child.

Preparation for Parenthood

Antenatal care should enable prospective parent(s) to adjust to their forthcoming change of role, to gain knowledge and insight, and to build in confidence so that from the beginning parenthood is rewarding, pleasurable and fun. This will include home visits by the midwife and health visitor to discuss specific health issues and to monitor health. In addition Preparation for Parenthood Groups are held where prospective parent(s) can learn together and share their feelings and thoughts. The 'facilitators' will be the midwife, health visitor and obstetric physiotherapist and the groups are usually held in the health centre, health clinic or maternity hospital. Classes are also provided by other groups such as the National Childbirth Trust.

Topics which are likely to be covered are:

- health in pregnancy,
- sexual relations during pregnancy and afterwards, and family planning,
- rights and benefits,
- fetal development,
- exercises, control of breathing and relaxation,
- labour and birth,
- care of the baby (including feeding),
- obstetric practice, including a visit to the maternity hospital,
- adjustment to parenthood.

Dress

It is important for a woman to feel comfortable throughout her pregnancy. Many women feel warmer than usual, especially during the summer, and so loose clothes and cotton underwear tend to be more comfortable. Nylon tights may need to be left off because they can cause excess sweating around the vulva and may precipitate a thrush infection. Women with aching legs or varicose veins will gain some relief from support stockings. The breasts enlarge during pregnancy, and so a well fitting support bra during the day and a sleep bra at night will aid comfort as well as helping to preserve breats shape when the pregnancy is over.

Posture

From the early months of pregnancy until about 6 months after the birth there is some relaxation of the ligaments which support the spine. This may lead to backache and therefore posture is especially important. Shoes should be of the same heel height as those usually worn although very high heels may increase the

strain on the curve of the spine, and will increase the likelihood of overbalancing (see Figure 26).

Exercise, rest and relaxation

For most women a certain amount of exercise is part of daily life and there is no reason to restrict this. Women accustomed to sports and physical exercise can continue provided the pregnancy is progressing normally and does not involve undue tiredness and exhaustion. Extra physical activity should not be started for the first time during pregnancy. Ideally a woman should aim to have 8 hours sleep and 2 hours rest in the afternoon. This is not always possible, but she should try to rest before becoming excessively tired. Relaxation exercises will relax the body and the mind more completely and will help to reduce fatigue and stress.

Sexual Relations

There is no reason why sexual intercourse should not continue throughout pregnancy. The uterus is effectively sealed by a plug of cervical mucus. However, later in pregnancy, orgasm may cause contractions of the uterine muscles which can be uncomfortable, and can occasionally initiate labour. Women who have had a previous miscarriage should seek advice from their doctor and certainly avoid intercourse in the early months. Some couples prefer not to have intercourse during pregnancy, and for some there may be cultural or religious taboos against it. These couples will find other ways of sexual expression.

CHILDBIRTH

Kitzinger describes childbirth as a normal life crisis. For many people it will be the most emotional and significant event in their life. It is however associated with risks to health for both mother and child,

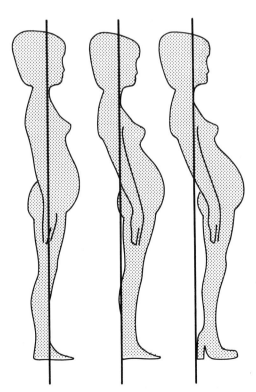

Figure 26. *Posture in pregnancy. By permission of Bristol Women's Health Group.*

and the event therefore requires access to essential medical equipment if required whilst at the same time preserving the intimate and individual nature of the experience. Within the boundaries dictated by safety, the couple can choose the style of childbirth they prefer.

In recent years attitudes to childbirth have been greatly influenced by two obstetricians; Leboyer and Odent. They both advocate techniques aimed at minimizing the birth trauma. Leboyer (1975) in his book, *Birth Without Violence*, describes birth from the viewpoint of the baby. He suggests that the baby is supersensitive to all that is going on around it. The bright lights, loud noises and harsh fabrics in which it is wrapped are an assault on its senses. Birth is unnecessarily physically and emotionally traumatic. However, if carried out in an environment designed to harmonize with the baby's experiences in the womb birth can be a gentle transition into the world. He suggests dim lighting, hushed sounds, skin to skin contact with the mother, and a bath of water at body temperature for the baby to relax in. The photographs in his book are convincing evidence of an alert yet peaceful baby. Some maternity hospitals have birthing rooms where this style of birth can be carried out if requested by the parents.

Whatever the style of birth the father is encouraged to be present. This can provide considerable practical and emotional support for the mother. Contact between the mother, father and baby immediately after delivery is important for emotional bonding, and it is likely that this has a considerable effect on subsequent relationships not only between mother and child but within the whole family. Contact may be very brief if the baby is of low birthweight or ill and requires immediate transfer to a special care baby unit. However, it is important that as much contact as possible between parent(s) and child is encouraged especially in the period immediately after delivery. This is also important if the baby is born handicapped or dead. It seems to be far more distressing for parent(s) if the child is taken away and they are not allowed to see it. Care of the family at this time requires extreme sensitivity.

POSTNATAL CARE

The 3 months after birth are sometimes referred to as the 'fourth trimester' of pregnancy. It is a time of physical, social and emotional adjustment, and the start of a new role as parent.

The process of bonding begins at birth. Some parents experience an immediate surge of emotion and affection whilst others find that their relationship with their child develops slowly and gradually and they may be disappointed at first that it was not love at first sight. The feelings of elation and relief which a mother often feels at the time of the birth are often followed after 3 or 4 days by 'baby blues'. She may have spells of crying, have frightening dreams or fantasies, or feel scared by her lack of maternal feelings and feel that she will never be able to cope. It is probably partly due to the sudden hormonal change, partly physical tiredness, but also a feeling of apprehension as she becomes aware of the tremendous responsibility of caring for this new person. A few mothers experience postnatal depression and require expert medical help as well as constant support from their husband, health visitor and, if possible, a self-help support group.

For general health and fitness a mother should continue the nourishing diet and regular meals she took during pregnancy. Sleep at night may be disturbed by the baby requiring feeds. If this is the case a rest and relaxation session in the day is particularly helpful. Moderate exercise can be resumed as soon as the mother feels able, but it is probably best to wait until after the postnatal examination at 6 weeks before resuming any strenuous exercise.

Most women want to regain their pre-pregnancy body shape, and postnatal exercises can help to achieve this. Probably the most important aim is to regain muscle tone in the pelvic floor which will have been stretched during delivery. Pelvic floor (Kegel) exercises involve alternately contracting and releasing the muscles around the perineum and should be done daily. They can be associated with a particular daily task such as washing up. Another part of the exercises is to stop and start the flow of urine midstream. Practised regularly they can help to prevent urinary incontinence as well as increase pleasure during sexual intercourse.

Sexual relations can be resumed as soon as both partners feel comfortable to do so and this will take longer for some than for others. This is a difficult time for many couples. The physical discomfort of perineal sutures added to the emotional turmoil of parenthood, disrupted nights and physical fatigue all combine to prevent the couple from resuming the sexual relationship which they previously had. For some, sexual difficulties begin at this time and it is important therefore that feelings are discussed. Contraception should be considered before resumption of sexual activity.

ETHNIC MINORITY GROUPS

Contraception needs vary between people of different cultural groups. An understanding of the cultural background is important if individual needs are to be met sensitively. For instance, amongst Muslim women menstruation is a curse because it excludes them from prayers and Ramadan. Contraception which causes heavy or irregular menstrual bleeding will not be acceptable. Amongst Hindus contraception will be influenced by their children—if they have sons contraception will be used but not if they have daughters. A major problem is

lack of understanding between the health services, which may know little about the cultural customs and religious beliefs of minority groups, and the women, who may have limited use of the host language and so not be able to make their needs known. In some city areas Health Advocates or link workers are employed by non-health service agencies to speak on behalf of women and to represent their interests. They enable the woman to obtain the health care she needs and can also influence health authorities to adapt their services to meet the local need.

Attitudes to childbirth differ according to the cultural group. For instance, in Asian cultures pregnancy and childbirth are regarded solely as the domain of women. Husbands are virtually excluded from discussion and preparations and would usually not consider attending Preparation for Parenthood groups in Britain nor being present at the birth. Experienced mothers within the extended family offer considerable support, guidance, advice and practical help. In Asia, women seek obstetric care from female doctors although those in rural areas where antenatal care is limited may rely even more on the family. A woman will frequently go to her family for the childbirth and return to the husband's family when the lying in period is over (usually 40 days). In Britain this can be misinterpreted as marital discord.

The relatively high perinatal mortality rate for Asian babies makes it especially important that Asian women have access to antenatal care. Link workers can be very helpful. Some health authorities, as well as some non-health service agencies, are employing women who speak the languages of the local ethnic groups to act as health aides or interpreters. The main qualification is that they have the trust and respect of the local community. They work closely with midwives and health visitors who teach them about relevant aspects of antenatal care and they then act as health educators for the local women. They may also accompany them to clinics, interpret for them and explain the various procedures.

TEENAGE PREGNANCY AND PARENTHOOD

Sexual activity amongst young people under the age of 16 is an emotive issue. From the research evidence, notably the Kinsey Report (Kinsey et al, 1948; 1953), Schofield (1965) and Farrell (1978), it appears that the age at which people become sexually active is becoming younger. Farrell (1978) estimated that one in eight girls and one in three boys are sexually active before 16. Most of the relationships were of 6 months or more and most young people had given serious thought to the consequences of their actions although many were still ill-informed about the risks involved. Contraceptive help is available to young single people at Family Planning Clinics and from GPs. In some cities there is a Youth Advisory service. In Britain doctors may prescribe contraceptives to girls under 16 without their parents' consent if the following criteria are satisfied:

1 The girl, although under 16, would understand his advice.
2 He could not persuade her to inform her parents or allow him to inform the parents that she was seeking contraceptive advice.
3 She was very likely to have sexual intercourse with or without contraceptive treatment.
4 Unless she received contraceptive advice or treatment her physical or mental health, or both, were likely to suffer.
5 Her best interests required him to give her contraceptive advice, treatment, or both without parental consent.

Conceptions in the 11–15 age group in Britain rose slowly from 1969 to 1975 and then slightly dropped. This coincided with the first DHSS recommendations in 1974 that contraceptive advice could be given to under 16s without parental consent in exceptional circumstances. The incidence of unplanned teenage pregnancies is particularly high in the USA and relatively high in Britain whereas it is relatively low in the Netherlands and Japan. The highest rates appear to be in countries with the least open attitudes to sexuality. An attitude still exists in Britain and the USA that seeking contraceptive advice is immoral but unprotected intercourse is excusable.

In 1979 a joint working party report on schoolgirl mothers made several recommendations relating to health care. It recommended appropriate teaching about responsible sexual behaviour in the first year of secondary school and information about contraception. It also suggested that girls who become pregnant whilst at school and continue with their pregnancies may remain disadvantaged for the rest of their lives. They need prompt help from the health services and immediate contact with one person who can undertake a counselling role and help with important decisions. Girls under the age of 15 have the greatest health problems. They have a higher rate of pregnancy morbidity and congenital abnormalities than women in the optimum childbearing years. This may be partly attributable to adverse circumstances which are typical, notably low socioeconomic group, heavy smoking and malnourishment.

Adolescence is a difficult age in which to adopt the role of parent. It is hard to consider the needs of someone else when one has not yet sorted out one's own needs. The influence of friends and the desire to be out with them doing the things which adolescents normally do conflicts strongly with the restrictions imposed by a demanding infant. Early infancy however may be easier to cope with than the toddler stage when the child becomes more independent and in some ways more demanding. Support from the family is important throughout these years. Where this is not available schemes such as Home-Start have been found to help young parents to come to terms with their new role, learning parenting skills and increase self-esteem.

The place of the teenage father may easily be forgotten but work carried out in the USA found that fathers were eager to help their partner and child. A project coordinated by New York City's Bank Street College of Education reported in *Time* (1985) offered vocational services, counselling and prenatal and parenting classes to nearly 400 teenage fathers and prospective fathers in eight US cities. At the end of the 2-year programme, 82% reported having daily contact with their children; 74% said that they contributed to the child's financial support; and almost 90% maintained a relationship with the mother whom they had known for an average of 2 years. The project concluded that many teenage fathers are anxious to participate in the parenting of their children but need a lot of support to help them assume a responsible father role.

PARENTHOOD IN LATER YEARS

In Britain, as in many western countries, a trend has developed for some women to delay starting a family until their thirties or later. These are usually women who choose to develop a professional career first. In Britain in 1984 29% of first time mothers in social classes 1 and 2 were over 30 compared to 15% in 1974. In health terms there seem to be benefits as well as potential problems. On the positive side these women are usually well informed about pre-conception and antenatal care and are keen to attend clinics for regular health checks and parentcraft groups, they are usually fit and well

nourished, and have relatively secure home circumstances. There are several drawbacks which need to be considered. Difficulties in conception are more likely as fertility begins to wane after the age of 30, obstetric problems which necessitate the use of forceps and caesarian section are more likely to occur in this age group and, finally, abnormalities, especially Down's syndrome are more common. Amniocentesis, which is carried out at about the 16th week of pregnancy, can detect about 40 possible abnormalities but about 1% of pregnancies miscarry as a direct result of the test and the psychological strain of possibly facing a termination is considerable.

Adjustment to life as a parent can also be fraught. The structured work environment of the past may contrast strongly with the unpredictable demands of a new baby. A mother may find difficulty adjusting to the responsibilities of the role in which she feels uncertain after a job which she was trained for and where she felt in control. Some women choose to combine the role of mother with career and so have to establish a balance between the demands of home, family and work and come to terms with the compromises which may have to be made. Many women feel physically tired especially if they do not have a partner with whom they can share the chores and their concerns. Almost always however they have no regrets and many comment that they feel that their maturity and understanding enables them to enjoy their children more than they might had they opted for parenthood at a younger age. Many feel extremely privileged to be able to 'have it all'.

DISABILITY AND PARENTHOOD

Disability may have a profound effect on parenthood but should not preclude it. Children of parents who are deaf or blind may benefit from nursery placements to ensure that they have access to a full range of sounds and experiences. Physically disabled people may have particular difficulties. A paralysed woman is no more likely to have an abnormal child than an able-bodied one but she may experience practical difficulties in caring for the child. Support services such as Home Help and home adaptations can overcome many of these difficulties. However, paraplegic and tetraplegic men are unlikely to father a child. Most can get an erection but it is less likely that they will be able to ejaculate. Even if they can, the sperm count is usually low although it is worth seeking specialist help to check the sperm count and viability. For couples where the man is paralysed, artificial insemination by donor may be an option. Adoption is also a possibility although rather remote with so few babies now being available for adoption.

The situation regarding mentally handicapped people is very different. Those living in hostels often develop loving relationships and some marry. Couples who have children are likely to need a considerable amount of support, practical help and education in child care skills. They will learn new skills very slowly and so may require someone such as a nursery nurse working very closely with them. As the child gets older a nursery placement may be appropriate to ensure that he/she has the full range of experiences. As with any new parents it is important not to undermine their confidence or usurp their role of the main care giver.

Whatever the circumstances, age of the parent, cultural group or the religious background certain features of parenthood are universal. Inevitably the arrival of a baby brings changes to the way in which one sees oneself, the status one has, one's place within the family and within one's role and relationships. It may also bring joy, pride, care, concern and an intense feeling of responsibility. Mutual understanding and the sharing of feelings within the family is important if it is to strengthen and grow together as the months and years pass.

References and further reading

Bromwich, P.& Parsons, T. (1984) *Contraception. The Facts*. Oxford: Oxford University Press.

Court Report (1976) *Fit for the Future: The Report of The Committee on Child Health Services*. London: HMSO.

Cowper, A. & Young, C. (1983) *Family Planning. Fundamentals for Health Professionals*. London: Croom Helm.

Dowling, S. (1983) *Health for a Change. The Provision of Preventive Health Care in Pregnancy and Early Childhood*. London: Child Poverty Action Group.

Farrell, C. (1978) *My Mother Said . . . .* London: Routledge & Kegan Paul.

Greer, G. (1984) *Sex and Destiny: The Politics of Human Fertility*. London: Picador.

Guillebaud, J. (1984) *The Pill*. Oxford: Oxford University Press.

Health Education Council (1984) *Pregnancy Book*. London: HEC.

Huskisson, J. M. (1985) *Nutrition and Dietetics in Health and Disease*, 2nd edn. London: Baillière Tindall.

Joint Working Party on Pregnant School Girls and School Girl Mothers (1979) *Pregnant at School*. London: National Council for One Parent Families and the Community Development Trust.

Kinsey, A. C. et al (1948) *Sexual Behavior in the Human Male*. Philadelphia: W. B. Saunders.

Kinsey, A. C. et al (1953) *Sexual Behavior in the Human Female*. Philadelphia: W. B. Saunders.

Kitzinger, S. (1977) *Education and Counselling for Childbirth*. London: Baillière Tindall.

Kitzinger, S. (1982) *Birth over Thirty*. London: Sheldon Press.

Leboyer, F. (1975) *Birth Without Violence*. New York: Alfred A. Knopf.

Milunsky, A. (1980) *Know Your Genes*. Harmondsworth: Penguin.

Myles, M. F. (1981) *Textbook for Midwives*, 9th edn. Edinburgh: Churchill Livingstone.

Peel, J. & Potts, M. (1969) *Textbook of*

Contraceptive Practice. London: Cambridge University Press.

Phillips, A. & Rakusen, J. eds. (1978) *Our Bodies Ourselves*. Harmondsworth: Penguin.

Schofield, M. (1965) *The Sexual Behaviour of Young People*. London: Longman.

Stengel, R. (1985). The missing father myth. Reported in *Time* December 9, 37.

Van der Eyken, W. (1982) *Home-start. A Four Year Evaluation*. Leicester: Home Start Consultancy.

8

Adulthood

Health care tends to be directed, in the main, towards the young and the old. Adults are generally expected to be able to care for themselves except at times of ill-health or disability. Indeed they are expected to be the carers of the young and the old and any others who are dependent due to frailty or sickness. The developing years of adolescence are over; in adulthood the personality is developed and strength and ability reach their peak. Adults are the workers, the wealth earners, and therefore hold most of the power in society. In undeveloped countries this division is less rigid. It is more usual for children to share the care of others, especially the daily care of younger siblings, and also for the 'elders' to be respected for their wisdom and experience and to take a principal role in decision making. The expectation of adulthood as the age of peak performance and independence is misleading because it suggests that adults are not dependent on anyone else and have no health needs of their own. It can also lead to older and younger people being denied the right to make decisions about their own lives. Adulthood is essentially a time of continued growth, development and change when many people do reach the peak of their achievements in life and gain self-assurance.

GENERAL HEALTH

General health measures are outlined in Chapter 2 and all are relevant in the adult years. A state of wellness involves physical and emotional health as well as the capacity to enjoy life and to face its challenges. Many different theories have been put forward in an attempt to understand the development of 'self'. The main ones are as follows:

1 *The trait approach*. A trait is any characteristic in which a person differs from another in a relatively consistent way. A person can be described by their position on a number of continuous dimensions (Figure 27). This theory describes behaviour but does not explain the reason for it. Moreover, by looking for the stable dimensions of the personality it infers that people cannot significantly change their behaviour.
2 *The psychoanalytic approach* (see Chapter 3).
3 *The social learning approach* (see Chapter 4).
4 *The humanistic approach*. This includes a number of theories (especially those of Carl Rogers and Abraham Maslow) which concentrate on man's potential for self-direction and freedom of choice. They reject the notion that man is primarily influenced by internal instincts and external stimuli and argue that it is the person's perception of himself, immediate experiences and his personal

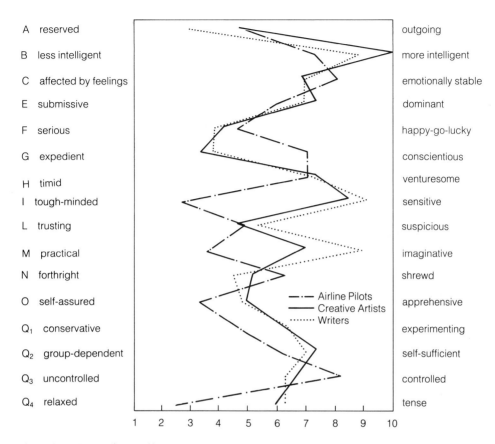

			outgoing
A	reserved		
B	less intelligent		more intelligent
C	affected by feelings		emotionally stable
E	submissive		dominant
F	serious		happy-go-lucky
G	expedient		conscientious
H	timid		venturesome
I	tough-minded		sensitive
L	trusting		suspicious
M	practical		imaginative
N	forthright		shrewd
O	self-assured		apprehensive
Q_1	conservative		experimenting
Q_2	group-dependent		self-sufficient
Q_3	uncontrolled		controlled
Q_4	relaxed		tense

Figure 27.   *Personality profiles. From Cattrell, R. B. Personality Profiles, 1973. Illinois: Champaign.*

view of the world which are of prime importance. The emphasis is on what is happening 'here and now' rather than what happened in the past. They also stress the positive nature of man; that each person has the motivation and ability to change and will push towards growth and 'self-actualization'. Self-actualization is the development of full individuality with all parts of the personality in harmony. Maslow (1954) hypothesized a hierarchy of needs and argued that the lower needs must be at least partially satisfied before the higher ones can become important sources of motivation (see Figure 28). Very few people will

achieve true self-actualization although some will experience transient moments or peak experiences which give unique feelings of fulfilment and happiness.

MENTAL HEALTH

Mental health is as variable as physical health. Most people experience peaks of happiness and troughs of despair when nothing seems to go right. Rowe (1983) begins her book, *Depression*, with the words, 'Depression is as old as the human race and rare is the person who has not felt its touch'. Feelings of sadness,

Figure 28. *Maslow's hierarchy of needs.*

loneliness, anxiety and fear are all common at certain times in life, and the need to share feelings and concerns is always present. A word which is in constant use by health professionals is, 'coping'. We say that a widow is coping with her bereavement, or that a teenager is coping with exams. One of the essential factors in adult health is the ability to cope with life's stressors; to deal with them appropriately, to learn from them and to move on.

In 1965 Elliot Jacques coined the phrase 'mid-life crisis'. He noted that the energy and creativity of artists tended to alter around the age of 35. There seemed to be three different patterns: firstly, loss of creativity; secondly, a new release of energy and creativity; and, thirdly, a change in the quality and style of creative work. He hypothesized that this existed throughout the general population. It is now reasonably well documented that men and women can at about this time experience a need to reflect on their lives and perhaps do something different. They may question the relevance of what they have spent their working time doing to date. These feelings may be compounded by changes within the family as parents face their children's growing independence and accept that they will eventually leave home. A woman may decide after raising a family that she now wants a career. The term 'mid-life crisis' infers that this is a problem stage. This need not be so as it can be an exciting stage of new challenges and intellectual growth.

Stress can be present at any stage of life (see Chapter 2). It has been linked to a number of illnesses including diverticulitis and coronary heart disease. Holmes and Rahe (1967) devised an

Table 5. *The Holmes–Rahe Life Events Scale.*

Changes in lifestyle	Scale
Death of husband or wife	100
Divorce	73
Marital separation	65
Jail sentence or being institutionalized	63
Death of close member of family	63
Illness or injury	53
Marriage	50
Loss of job	47
Reconciliation with marriage partner	45
Retirement	45
Health problem of close member of family	44
Pregnancy	40
Sex problems	39
Addition to family	39
Major change at work	39
Change of financial status	39
Death of friend	37
Change in line of work	36
Change in number of marital arguments	35
Large mortgage taken out	31
Mortgage or loan foreclosed	30
Responsibility change	29
Child leaves home	29
In-law problems	29
Personal achievement realized	28
Wife starts or stops work	26
Starting at new school	26
Leaving school	26
Change in living conditions	25
Change in personal habits	24
Trouble with employer	23
Change in working hours	20
Change in residence	20
Change in recreation	19
Change in church activities	19
Change in social activities	18
Small mortgage taken out	17
Change in sleeping habits	16
Change in number of family get-togethers	15
Major change in eating pattern	15
Holiday	13
Christmas	12
Minor violation of law	11

inventory in which typical life events were ascribed a rating. By noting the value of each event which had occurred during the past year a stress rating could be ascertained, and this could indicate the chance of a major breakdown in the next two years (see Table 5).

A particular health problem is drug abuse. This can include cigarettes, excessive coffee, alcohol, prescribed drugs, retail drugs or illegal drugs. A habit can develop with any of these substances so that the person increasingly comes to rely on them and as a consequence there is a detrimental effect on health. Self-help support groups exist in many areas for people who want to break their habit. During the 1970s there was a tendency for minor tranquillizing drugs to be prescribed for stress. Many people later found that they were dependent on these drugs and self-help groups, such as Tranx, and advice centres now exist in many large towns specifically for people trying to stop this form of medication.

The Health Education Authority's health package *Look After Yourself* details a comprehensive plan for health and wellness. The course runs for 10 weeks and each two hourly session has three parts: exercise and health including an individualized fitness programme, stress and relaxation including relaxation techniques, and healthy eating and other health topics which may include smoking, alcohol or how to manage stress at work. The Health Education booklet gives details of the course and the practical hints on how to stay healthy are easy to follow and adopt even for those who do not take the course.

SEXUALITY

Attitudes to sexuality develop throughout childhood and adolescence and sexual expression is an important aspect of life throughout the years of adolescence and adulthood including old age. Sexuality is not only important for the procreation of children. It is also an expression of love. For most people a deepening long-term relationship in which sex is an expression of love is of great importance. It is not only a matter of physical pleasure and satisfaction but also a way in which we confirm our commitment to a relationship and share affection. It is also an important means by which we develop personal feelings of esteem and self-worth.

In western societies sex is often viewed as the prerogative of the young, although sexual activity is enjoyed by people of all ages. Both Kinsey et al (1948, 1953) and Masters and Johnson (1970) found that postmenopausal women and older men were fully capable of sexual response. In general terms both men and women retain a normal capacity for arousal, responsiveness and the experience of pleasure. However their bodies operate in a slower and less intense manner. It seems that if the quality of the relationship is maintained there need be no diminution of either desire or performance.

Kinsey (1953), from his extensive research, found that the labels 'homosexual' and 'heterosexual' were artificial and that there was a continuum of sexual preference. Sexuality involves not only the outward overt behaviour of mannerisms and sexual partners but also covert behaviour of daydreams and fantasies. This leads to a self-image which may be comfortable or confused. It is often a painful time for young people when they realize their sexual preference. Social attitudes, especially ignorance, ridicule and derogatory comments made about gay people in their presence, may initially make them feel 'abnormal' and lead to low self-esteem. Many gay people still choose to pass for heterosexuals in daily social activities because they fear hostility and social stigma. Some use marriage as a disguise and as a way of maintaining social credibility. Others may not realize their true preference until some time later or may remain bisexual.

Homosexuality may trap people in a style of life which can never be entirely free or allow them full personal expression. For some people it means living a secret life, constantly wondering if other people will find out, and many gay people have been victimized for their style of life. This may be a particular problem if, within the couple, one is more open than the other. For lesbians life can be especially difficult because they have perhaps not yet gained the degree of social acceptability which gay men have. It may lead to stress and social isolation. In terms of physical health, however, lesbians do not have problems, such as cervical cancer, AIDS and sexually transmitted diseases, which affect gay men and heterosexuals. The gay liberation movement has done a great deal to change hostile attitudes towards homosexuality and there can now be much greater openness amongst gay people with increasing numbers choosing to 'come out'. Gay magazines, gay clubs, special interest groups for gay people as well as advice centres are becoming commonplace, especially in large cities.

Tiefer (1979) states that some of the standard 'crises' of adult life can be expected to have an impact on sexuality. These include developing an intimate relationship with and commitment to a particular life partner, adjusting one's sexual needs to those of another person on a regular and continuing basis, adjusting sexual relations during pregnancy, reacting to feelings of boredom and monotony in sexual relations with one lifelong partner, changes in self-esteem related to occupational, financial and status changes, intermittent physical and mental illness, and physical limitations from ageing. Most sexual problems can be overcome with expert help. Sex therapy was pioneered by Masters and Johnson whose methods are still widely used by therapists. The Marriage Guidance Service offers expert counselling to couples, including gay couples.

WOMEN'S HEALTH

Health care for women is usually directed towards physical health although emotional, social and mental health are equally important. The health status of a woman is dependent on many things such as her role within the family, the demands on her as a carer and her relationship with partners, but especially the value which she places on her health and the extent to which she can make choices on those factors which influence it. The role of women in western societies has changed considerably over the past 20 years. The feminist movement reshaped the position of the woman in society. Franks (1981) argues that women in the past tended to become slaves and martyrs, placing the welfare of husband and children above themselves. At the same time, perhaps because of the social climate, little attention was given by health professionals to women's health issues; the premenstrual syndrome and menopause-related problems simply did not exist in medical terms until relatively recently. Women were prepared to struggle along with dribbling incontinence or depression because they believed that this was the way things must be. In terms of health care one of the most important changes has been greater assertiveness by women who now demand better health care for themselves (Davies, 1915).

Specific health issues of relevance to women are the following.

Premenstrual Syndrome

In the late 1930s, Dr R. T. Frank used the term 'premenstrual tension' to describe a collection of symptoms and bodily changes associated with menstruation. Premenstrual syndrome (PMS) occurs regularly from a few days to 2 weeks before the menstrual period and ceases, or reduces significantly, with its arrival. Katz (1984) states that 95% of the female population experience moderate symptoms, only 2.5% experience nothing at all and 2.5% suffer intolerable symptoms. Whilst some days of the menstrual cycle can be incapacitating others can be relatively happy and creative. Reactions to these symptoms may in part be affected by the way in which girls are brought up to regard menstruation as a curse. Many different symptoms have been described and the commonest tend to be grouped together as follows:

- nervous tension, mood swings, irritability, anxiety;
- weight gain, swelling of extremities, breast tenderness, abdominal bloating;
- headache, craving for sweets, increased appetite, heart pounding, fatigue, dizziness, fainting;
- depression, confusion, forgetfulness, crying, insomnia.

Stewart (1984) of the Premenstrual Tension Advisory Service states that 30–40% of women of childbearing age suffer significant premenstrual symptoms, and Wood et al (1979) found that the age group when it most commonly occurred was 30–39 years. Dalton (1984) suggests that the cause is a hormonal imbalance in which there is too little progesterone in relation to oestrogen. Dalton pioneered progesterone therapy which is a very successful form of treatment for some women. Stewart (1984) states that women with PMS usually have either an imbalanced diet or existing deficiencies which are not being corrected by their diet. Symptoms may become worse if extra demands are made on the body, for instance after childbirth, during prolonged breast feeding, or after any major stressful situation. The Premenstrual Tension Advisory service make the following general recommendations (but suggest additional nutritional supplements in individual cases):

1   Reduce intake of sugar and 'junk' foods.
2   Reduce intake of salt.
3   Reduce intake of tea and coffee.

4 Eat green vegetables or salad daily.
5 Limit intake of dairy products.
6 Limit use of alcohol and tobacco.
7 Use good vegetable oils, e.g. sun-flower oil.
8 Eat plenty of whole foods.
9 Have regular exercise.
10 In moments of pure desperation, take a walk.

One of the conclusions of their research was that an individualized dietary, supplement and exercise programme was highly effective in severe-to-moderate premenstrual tension. They found an overall 85% reduction of symptoms.

Breasts: Preventative Care

The female breast begins to develop during puberty and its size depends on the amount of fatty and fibrous tissue. Most women have one breast which differs slightly in size and shape to the other. The breast tissue is attached to the underlying pectoral muscles and the overlying skin by fine ligaments called Cooper's ligaments. The breast is basically hemispherical in shape with a tongue-like extension, the axillary tail, leading into the armpit. The breast is surrounded by lymph glands.

Breast problems include engorgement and tenderness especially during the premenstrual phase, benign breast lumps and, of course, breast cancer, the most common form of cancer in women. For women aged 35–54 breast cancer is the leading cause of death in Britain; one woman in 17 will develop the disease and one woman in 30 can expect to die of it. Some women are at a greater risk of developing this disease than others. High-risk factors include:

- early menarche (before 13 years) and late menopause (after 50 years). Women who have no children or had their first baby after the age of 35 years are at greater risk.
- racial type and country of residence.

North American and West European women are more prone than Asian or Black African women.

- age. Risk begins to increase during the late thirties and early forties.
- family history. Women whose mothers or close relatives on the female side had the disease.

The relationship between the oral contraceptive pill and breast cancer remains controversial. Research by Pike et al (1983) suggested that there was a link. Stadel et al (1985) found no relationship between the use of oral contraception by young women and their risk of breast cancer before 45 years of age.

There are long-term studies investigating the feasibility and sensitivity of mammography as a screening procedure and some health authorities are now introducing this for women in the high-risk groups. However, self-examination is still recommended in order to detect the problem at an early stage. This examination is best undertaken on a regular monthly basis after menstruation when the breasts are at their softest and preferably on the same day each month. The stages are illustrated in Figure 29. Approximately eight out of every ten breast lumps are harmless but every breast lump should be investigated by a doctor.

Most women fear the thought of mastectomy (surgical removal of a breast) as much as they fear the disease. The breast is an important sexual characteristic and to some extent determines the way a woman sees herself. Loss of a breast will therefore lead to a period of grief (see Chapter 10). Many hospitals have a nurse counsellor who sees patients prior to surgery and over a period of time afterwards. She can also help with practical considerations such as the fitting of a prosthesis. Support groups offer help and encouragement and are usually actively involved in the care plan both in hospital and when the woman returns home. Because of the emotional trauma, many surgeons now elect to remove only the

LOOKING

When you examine your breasts you're looking for anything that's unusual. For this, looking is just as important as feeling.

Undress to the waist and sit or stand in front of a mirror in a good light. When you look at your breasts, remember that no two are the same – not even your own two. One will probably be slightly larger than the other, and one a little lower on the chest.

Here's what to look for:

☐ any change in the size of either breast

☐ any change in either nipple

☐ bleeding or discharge from either nipple

☐ any unusual dimple or puckering on the breast or nipple

☐ veins standing out more than is usual for you.

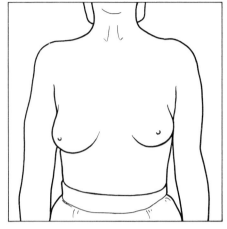

1. First let your arms hang loosely by your sides and look at your breasts in the mirror.

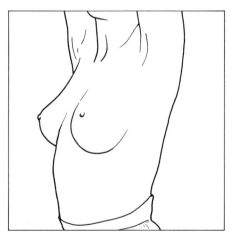

2. Next raise your arms above your head. Watch in the mirror as you turn from side to side to see your breasts from different angles.

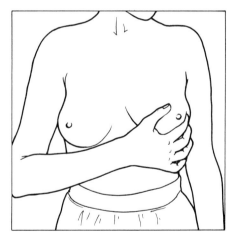

3. Now look down at your breasts and squeeze each nipple gently to check for any bleeding or discharge that's unusual for you.

Figure 29. *Breast self-examination.*

FEELING

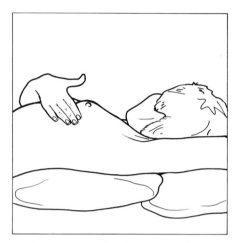

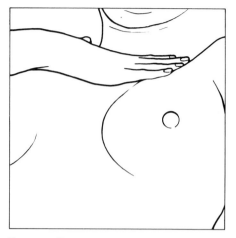

Lie down on your bed and make yourself comfortable with your head on a pillow.

Examine one breast at a time.

Put a folded towel under your shoulder-blade on the side you are examining. This helps to spread the breast tissue so that it is easier to examine.

Use your right hand to examine your left breast and vice versa. Put the hand you're not using under your head.

Keep your fingers together and use the flat of the fingers, not the tips.

Start from the collarbone above your breast.

Figure 29.   *cont'd*

lump rather than the whole breast. Other methods of treatment include radio-therapy and chemotherapy.

Cervical Cytology

During puberty the cervix undergoes several changes under the influence of hormones. Columnar cells from the cervical canal begin to migrate outwards replacing some of the original squamous epithelium. The squamocolumnar junction which borders the transformation zone is visible on examination and appears bright pink. This is sometimes termed, rather misleadingly, an 'erosion'. Cervical cancer is a preventable disease which can be detected in its precancerous stage by

taking a scrape, or smear, of these cells. Normally only superficial desquamated or intermediate cells are seen on microscopic examination. The presence of parabasal or basal cells might indicate atrophy and would warrant a further smear being taken and possibly further examination and biopsy by colposcopy.

In Britain about 2000 women die each year from cervical cancer, the majority of whom have never had a smear test, and the incidence is increasing. The test is offered to all women over the age of 35 (in some health authorities over the age of 20) every 3–5 years, and to all women attending family planning clinics. Women most at risk are those who become sexually active at an early age,

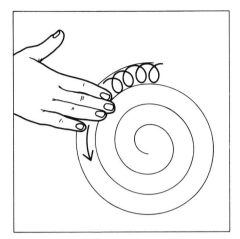

Trace a continuous spiral round your breast moving your fingers in small circles. Feel gently but firmly for any unusual lump or thickening.

Work right round the outside of your breast first. When you get back to your starting point, work round again in a slightly smaller circle, and so on. Keep on doing this until you have worked right up to the nipple. Make sure you cover every part of your breast.

You may find a ridge of firm tissue in a half-moon shape under your breast. This is quite normal. It is tissue that develops to help support your breast.

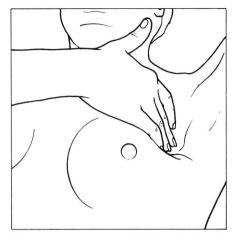

Finally, examine your armpit. Still use the flat of your fingers and the same small circular movements to feel for any lumps.

Start right up in the hollow of your armpit and gradually work your way down towards your breast.

It's important not to forget this last part of the examination.

Figure 29. *cont'd*

who have had frequent sexual partners, those whose partners have had frequent sexual partners, and those whose partners have genital warts. There is also a well-established association between human papillomavirus type 16 DNA and cervical cancer, and so the treatment of both sexual partners may be indicated. It is also more common amongst women of socioeconomic group 5 and amongst women who work (or whose husbands work) in certain occupations such as mining or quarrying (probably due to irritant dust). There continues to be controversy about the relationship between the oral contraceptive pill and cervical cancer although no causative link has been found and the risk factors

mentioned above are thought to be more important.

The Menopause

The menopause means 'final menstruation', but has come to encompass all the other related changes which occur at this time, which is usually at about the age of 50. During the childbearing years about 400 ova mature and are released. When these have been used up fertility is over and the production of oestrogen and progesterone declines. The result is an irregular menstrual pattern and after a variable length of time (up to 5 years) an end to the monthly cycle. Other bodily changes include atrophy of the ovaries and the lining of the uterus, thinning of the vaginal wall making it more vulnerable to infection, narrowing of the vagina and thinning of the external skin making it less sexually responsive, thinning of the bladder neck contributing to urinary frequency and urgency, loss of subcutaneous fat causing wrinkling, absence of oestrogen causing the breasts to lose their firmness, and a rise in bone reabsorption which may lead to osteoporosis.

Some women produce extra oestrogen from the adrenal glands and so avoid any problems at this time. However about 85% of women experience symptoms which include 'hot flushes', tiredness, nervousness, sweating, headaches, insomnia, depression, irritability, joint and muscle pains, dizziness, palpitations, and tingling or crawling sensations. In recent years hormone replacement therapy has been avilable to women with particular problems. Specific problems may be treated as they occur, such as oestrogen cream for vaginitis and lubricant gels for sexual dysfunction. As at any other age, attention to diet and exercise is important (see Chapter 2).

Well women's clinics are run in many health authorities and offer comprehensive health care including weighing, blood pressure measurement, urinalysis, cervical smear and breast examination. They also provide information and advice on other problems which affect health such as diet, smoking, alcohol, stress, role as carer for a disabled or elderly person, and so on. Health education can be offered on subjects such as diet, breast self-examination and the maintenance of continence. Specific health needs can be identified and appropriate support given, or referral made to specialist services or self-help groups.

Women as Carers

The health of many women is greatly influenced by their role as carer for others. Longfield (1984), when considering the care of frail, elderly people, concludes '. . . too often the carers, especially women, are forced to give up their job, jeopardize their family life and even damage their own health because there are no acceptable alternatives'. Health problems include stress, fatigue, emotional disturbances and physical ill-health such as back injury.

A study commission on the family (1983) found that more than 50% of women with dependent children were in paid employment. The practical and social pressures of combining the two roles can be considerable. Some mothers who would choose to go out to work may not have the opportunity if there are not enough child care facilities or jobs with flexible hours available. Women who remain at home to care for their children are also subject to certain stresses. Gavron (1966) identifies a considerable amount of social isolation amongst women at home, especially amongst 'working class' women. She noted that women were not fully prepared for the responsibilities of motherhood and many were acutely aware of the restrictions it imposed on their lives. A woman with several children may be particularly isolated because of the practical difficulties in getting out. Also she may become immersed in the needs of her children and their wellbeing to the exclusion of her own needs for fulfilment.

MEN'S HEALTH

In recent years a number of 'Well Man' clinics have been offered. The aim is to improve the health of men, focusing on the middle years, and to prevent specific health problems, such as coronary heart disease. The target group may include men aged 40–60 years and who are offered health screening which can include weighing, urinalysis, blood pressure measurement, and teaching testicular self-examination.

Testicular cancer affects approximately one man in 500 before the age of 50.

It is more common in men who had undescended testes after the age of six. Trauma and infection may also be contributory factors. As with any cancer it is important that the disease is recognized and treated as early as possible. A monthly self-examination is recommended. The best time is after a warm bath or shower when the scrotal skin is relaxed. Each testicle should be rolled gently between thumb and fingers of each hand feeling for any changes from normal especially any small, hard lumps. The epididymous and spermatic cords should also be examined (see Figure 30).

Discussion on other matters which affect health such as stress, diet, alcohol consumption and leisure activities is also relevant. The Health Education Authority's, *Look After Yourself* course originated as a health programme for young men who had had a heart attack. Self-help groups can be established for specific needs such as 'Stop Smoking'.

WORK

Work is usually taken to mean paid employment. There are however many other types of work which are equally useful although unpaid. Financial reward is usually the primary motivation for work although it also serves a number of other functions:

- It provides social contacts outside the family.
- It provides a clearly defined role within society.
- It affords an identity and status within the community.

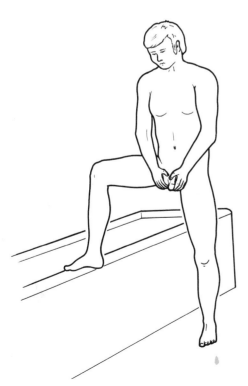
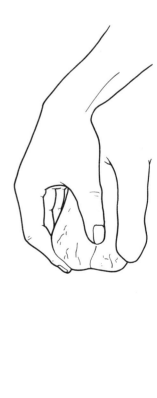

Figure 30. *Testicular self-examination. Adapted with kind permission from Stanford, J. (1986)* The Professional Nurse **1**(5), 132–133.

- It structures psychological time.
- It can facilitate personal growth and development; intellectual, physical and emotional.
- It affords feelings of self-worth and self-confidence.

A place within the 'workforce' is therefore an expectation of most adolescents and a need for most adults. The rising trend of unemployment in western countries in the 1970s and 1980s led to the realization that some people would spend long periods unemployed and that some young people may never gain employment. For many, therefore, it is necessary to come to terms with being unemployed and to find ways outside work of developing a useful and satisfying life. This involves preparing adolescents for the possibility of short or long periods of unemployment, finding outlets in community or voluntary work and taking advantage of educational and leisure facilities which offer special rates for unemployed people.

CARE IN THE COMMUNITY

The increasing emphasis on community care is dependent on large numbers of people, mostly women, being prepared to take work of a caring nature. The aim of keeping frail elderly people in their own homes rather than being admitted to residential care has been largely dependent on Community Nursing, the Home Care Service, Meals on Wheels and so on. Moreover, plans to prevent children from being admitted to Children's Homes has been dependent on the availability of adequate numbers of suitably motivated foster parents, and the care of mentally handicapped children and adults within their own family depends on respite care being available with other families. Care in the community is primarily dependent, however, on family care and neighbourliness which is unpaid work, apart from certain benefits for some. Longfield

(1984) found that despite the increase in numbers of over-65s, the vast majority of elderly people still live in the community and if they need care it is almost always the family who will provide it. The Equal Opportunities Commission (1980) estimated that there were more than one and a quarter million people, mostly women, caring for an ill or disabled person. There is also 'neighbourliness' or 'natural caring networks' where people outside the family give their time and energy to supplement care. Most frail and dependent people (young, adult and elderly) are therefore cared for by adults outside the official workforce.

OCCUPATIONAL HEALTH

The workplace has always been associated with health hazards. The Health and Safety at Work, etc., Act, 1974 detailed ways in which health and safety could be protected in the work place. It placed an obligation on management to write a health and safety policy as well as a detailed policy manual for specific procedures. These are drafted by management and trade unions working in collaboration. It incorporates any statutory regulations regarding the health maintenance of workers in particular trades which could bring them into contact with hazardous substances such as lead and toxic gases. No one knows how much ill-health is attributable to occupation as official figures can cover only sickness absence, industrial accidents and proscribed diseases. Certain diseases are notifiable by law in the UK and include lead poisoning, toxic jaundice and mercurial poisoning. In addition to the diseases reportable to the Health and Safety Executive for the purposes of prevention, there are other occupational diseases prescribed by the Department of Health and Social Security for the purposes of compensating workers who have contracted them. The objectives of an occupational health service as stated by the Royal College of Nursing are concerned with:

- the effects of work on health,
- monitoring of the environment and development of control methods,
- identification and advice on hazards,
- periodic examinations related to identified risk,
- provision of emergency care for casualties,
- interpretation of the law, e.g. factory, commercial, and professional,
- health supervision of welfare facilities,
- health education — health advice,
- epidemiology, sickness absence,
- disaster planning,
- the effects of health on work,
- examinations relative to job demands, e.g. pre-employment, special hazards,
- assessment of capacity after sickness and advice on fitness for task,
- rehabilitation and resettlement,
- care for special groups, e.g. the disabled, the young, pregnant women,
- health advice to employees/clients.

The role of the occupational health nurse involves the identification of health needs amongst the workforce, planning health care for individual workers in complete confidence, and care for specific groups of workers.

REHABILITATION AND RESETTLEMENT

Harrison (1984) states that 'rehabilitation is the combined and coordinated use of all the available services from the onset of the disabling illness or injury until the individual is returned to normal activity or, failing this, to the highest possible level of functional ability'. This will require a systematic and individualized care plan. Care by the nurse will usually include home visits to assess, plan and evaluate the care given and to coordinate the work of the occupational health team.

In this way the nurse can sensitively initiate care to suit both patient and family.

If that person is unable to return to their former job, resettlement will be necessary. This may involve the Disablement Resettlement Officer or the Blind Persons Resettlement Officer. Their aims are two-fold; to help employers recruit disabled people and to use their skills most effectively, and to help disabled people to find the job best suited to their aptitude and ability and to help them settle into work. Counselling helps to ensure that the person has come to terms with the need for a change of work as feelings of grief for the job which has been lost are likely. It is also important to ensure that the necessary training is given. The Government involvement in employee rehabilitation and resettlement is through the Manpower Services Commission who operate the Job Centres. The Employment Medical Advisory Service has an advisory role to assist in this. Also, information should be given on the relevant support services which are available, particularly social services, as well as the social security benefits.

PRE-RETIREMENT

One of the more recent developments in occupational health has been pre-retirement courses which, in some workplaces, are offered to workers usually 2 years before their retirement date. This allows time to make preparations for retirement, both practical and emotional. Details of pensions, benefits and clubs for retired people can be given so that the transition from work to leisure is as gradual as possible. This reduces the stress which may develop due to the sudden and radical change in lifestyle. For people whose workplace does not offer these courses they are sometimes held by health visitors in health centres or in adult education centres.

PHYSICALLY DISABLED ADULTS

Physical disability in adulthood may be either congenital or acquired and it may be a static or progressive condition. The nature of the disability will clearly have a considerable effect on the way in which the person and their family come to terms with the problem. Meredith Davies (1982) offers the following definitions:

- Impairment — a physical or psychological abnormality.
- Disability — interference of function.
- Handicap — disability × reaction.

The extent to which a person is handicapped therefore depends on the extent to which they overcome their impairment and the emotional reaction which they have to their functioning level. Someone with considerable physical impairment might develop a lifestyle which allows them to be completely fulfilled whereas an active sportsperson might feel considerably handicapped with a much less severe physical impairment. In general, however, the typical consequences of disability are low expectations, a doubtful sense of purpose, great uncertainty about the future, and the problem of work or how to live a useful and satisfying life without work. The remarkable book *Joey* by Deacon (1974) illustrates how rich the life of a severely handicapped person can be.

The most common causes of disability in adults are multiple sclerosis, rheumatoid arthritis, spondylitis, accidental paraplegia, strokes, angina, blindness and deafness. Whatever the nature of the disability it is never entirely an individual experience. It affects the whole family, as well as friendships and workmates. Typical emotional reactions to a disabled person are overprotection, pity, rejection, prejudice and fear. It is extremely important for the partner to be involved in rehabilitation and to be given opportunity to express their feelings. The partner will grieve for the 'whole' person who they have lost and adjustment to the change will take time. Feelings of anger, fear and depression if shared may strengthen the relationship whereas feelings which are not communicated may lead to emotional coldness and erosion of the relationship. The partner may need to assume different responsibilities within the relationship such as becoming the main wage earner or the car driver. This will involve readjustment for both people. PHAB clubs (Physically Handicapped and Able Bodied) are very supportive to all family members and offer practical help and advice as well as social activities. (See also Chapter 10.)

Society, for reasons which are difficult to understand, tends to project the message that serious physical or mental impairment condemns a person to asexuality. Someone who becomes disabled in adulthood may take some time to reassert their sexuality. Intimacy involves more than sexual intercourse. It includes physical closeness, affection, comfort and caressing and can be pleasing and satisfying without intercourse. Sexual intercourse may be more difficult to achieve although with help it is usually possible however severe the disability. Help may be necessary, for instance, on finding positions which are comfortable for someone with arthritis or on the management of a catheter. Contraception also needs careful consideration as some methods may be impractical. Fallon (1975) gives clear practical information. SPOD (Committee on Sexual and Personal Relationships of the Disabled) offers expert advice.

MENTALLY HANDICAPPED ADULTS

Until relatively recently many mentally handicapped people lived in hospitals and spent a large part of their lives there. They were treated either as patients with a defect or as children with no rights or opinions of their own. In the 1970s a radical change in thinking came about when it was decided that these people should live in their own homes and enjoy the lifestyle which all people expect. This would include work and household chores as well as the pleasures of leisure, friendships and sexual relationships. They would have the freedom to make their own choices in their lives although because of their relative vulnerability most would require some guidance and supervision, especially the more profoundly handicapped. This is provided, in the main, by community mental handicap nurses and social workers. Mentally handicapped children and adolescents are no longer being admitted to long-stay hospitals and many people have moved from hospitals to hostels. For some this has meant a considerable upheaval and some have grieved for the friends and familiar places which they have left behind. However, on the whole, it has led to a great improvement in the quality of life of these people. Health care services are the same as for anyone else; general practitioner for medical care, family planning service for contraception, district nursing for nursing care in the home and so on. Normalization and humanization are the essential aims of all the services involved.

References and further reading

Altschul, A. & Sinclair, H. C. (1981) *Psychology for Nurses*, 5th edn. London: Baillière Tindall.

Berger, R. M. (1983) What is a homosexual? A definition model. *Social Work* **28** (2), 132–135.

Cahn, A. (1984) Communicating sexual needs and wants. *Maternal and Child Health* **9** (3), 92–94.

Cooper, W. (1983) *No Change*, 2nd edn. London: Arrow Books.

Dalton, K. (1984) *The Premenstrual Syndrome and Progesterone Therapy* 2nd edn. London: Heinemann Medical.

Davies, M. L., ed. (1915) *Maternity. Letters from Working Women*. London: Virago, 1978.

Deacon, J. J. (1974) *Joey*. New York: Charles Scribner.

Equal Opportunities Commission (1980) *The Experience of Caring for Elderly and Handicapped Dependents*. Manchester: Equal Opportunities Commission.

Fagin, L. & Little, M. (1984) *The Forsaken Families*. Harmondsworth: Penguin.

Fallon, B. (1975) *So You're Paralysed*. London: Spinal Injuries Association.

Faulder, C. (1982) *Breast Cancer. A Guide to its Early Detection and Treatment*. London: Virago.

Fogarty, M. (1975) *Forty to Sixty. How we Waste the Middle Aged*. London: Bedford Square Press.

Franks, H. (1981) *Prime Time*. London: Pan Books.

Gavron, H. (1966) *The Captive Wife*. Harmondsworth: Penguin.

Harrington, J. M. & Gill, F. S. (1983) *Occupational Health*. Oxford: Blackwell Scientific Publications.

Harrison, B. M. (1984) *Essentials of Occupational Health Nursing*. Oxford: Blackwell Scientific Publications.

Health Education Council (1979) *Look After Yourself* (booklet).

Hilgard, E. R. et al (1979) *Introduction to Psychology*, 7th edn. New York: Harcourt Brace Jovanovich.

Holmes, T. H. & Rahe, R. H. (1967) The social readjustment rating scale. *Journal of Psychosomatic Research* **11**, 213–218.

Katz, M. (1984) *The Premenstrual Syndrome*. London: Update Publications.

Kinsey, A. C. et al (1948) *Sexual Behavior in the Human Male*. Philadelphia: W. B. Saunders.

Kinsey, A. C. et al (1953) *Sexual Behavior in the Human Female*. Philadelphia: W. B. Saunders.

Longfield, J. (1984) *Ask the Family*. London: Bedford Square Press/NCVO.

Males, J. (1985) The challenge of mental handicap care. *Professional Nurse* **1** (2), 35–37.

Maslow, A. (1954) *Motivation and Personality*. New York: Harper & Row.

Masters, W. H. & Johnson, V. E. (1970) *Human Sexual Inadequacy*. London: Churchill.

Meredith Davies, B. (1982) *The Disabled Child and Adult*. London: Baillière Tindall.

Open University (1980) *The Good Health Guide*. London: Pan Books.

Orbach, S. (1978) *Fat is a Feminist Issue*. London: Hamlyn.

Phillips, A. & Rakusen, J. (1978) *Our Bodies Ourselves*. Harmondsworth: Penguin.

Pike, M. C. et al (1983) Breast cancer in young women and use of oral contraceptives: possible modifying effect of formulation and age at use. *Lancet* **ii**, 926–930.

Rowe, D. (1983) *Depression. The Way Out of Your Prison*. London: Routledge & Kegan Paul.

Stadel, B. V. et al (1985) Oral contraceptives and breast cancer in young women. *Lancet* **ii**, 970–973.

Stanford, J. (1986) Testicular self-examination. *The Professional Nurse* **1** (5), 132–133.

Stewart, M. (1984) *Pre-menstrual Tension. Nutritional Recommendations*. Brighton: Ideal Press.

Practitioner (1983) Health of women. *Practitioner* **227**.

Tiefer, L. (1979) *Human Sexuality. Feelings and Functions*. London: Harper & Row.

Women as providers of health care (1983) *WHO Chronicle* **37** (4), 134–138.

Wood, C. et al (1979) Social and psychological factors in relation to premenstrual tension and menstrual pain. *Australia and New Zealand Journal of Obstetrics and Gynaecology* **19** (2) 111–115.

9

Old Age

Throughout the life cycle there is one common factor; ageing. At each stage a certain quality of health can be enjoyed and, at the same time, threats to health must be negotiated. The preceding years have a considerable influence, therefore the degree of health which accompanies old age will, to a great extent, be influenced by the lifestyle which has gone before. It will also be influenced by many other factors such as sex, social class, family history, culture, advances in health care, and the overall life expectancy of the age in which one lives. Equally important are the attitudes which surround old age. Ageing is a natural process which occurs in all people of all cultures; 'growing old' however is a personal reaction which influences the way in which one sees oneself and is largely determined by how one is seen by others.

WHO ARE 'THE ELDERLY'?

The elderly are the oldest people living in a society but the point at which one becomes 'elderly' is difficult to define. In Western cultures it usually means those past the normal retirement age, which can be as low as 55 years or over 75 years. In Britain retirement age is usually 60 years for women (although they can now work until they are 65) and 65 years for men. Such a system is useful for statistical purposes but takes no account of people's health or functional capacity.

There are wide individual differences in relation to ageing so that one person might be running in the London marathon at 76 years of age whereas someone else might be virtually housebound.

Britain, in common with other developed countries, has an ageing population. This means that whereas the overall population is levelling off, the proportion of elderly people within it is rising and is expected to continue to rise for some years. The proportion of the population who were of pensionable age in 1981 was 18%, double what it was 50 years ago (see Figure 31). Moreover, the number of very elderly people (those over 85 years) is expected to continue to rise after the number of younger elderly has levelled off around 1991. There are also sex differences. Women tend to live longer than men so that in the 74–84 age group there are almost two women for every man, and in the 85 and over age group about four women for every man.

The question 'who are the elderly' must take account of their role and status in society. In pre-industrial societies it is usual for people to continue to work until they are no longer physically able and then to assume another role. The 'elders' have traditionally been respected for their experience and wisdom and accordingly they become the decision makers. The 'wise old man/woman' was perhaps the ultimate honour, and a key position within the social group. In industrial societies where work revolves around the

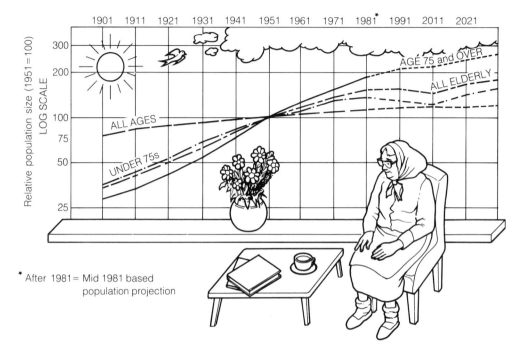

Figure 31.   *Relative size of the elderly population of Great Britain from 1901–2021 (1951=100). From OPCS and the Central Office of Information (1984).*

young and the fit, the role and status of the elderly has both diminished and become ambiguous. The way in which they are viewed has become distorted so that they are easily seen as people with no valid opinion to offer, as a 'problem group', or as inevitably ill and infirm. Their primary role may be seen as a group of people who need looking after. In reality this is both inaccurate and unfair. Outside the traditional work situation elderly people continue to offer a great deal of help and support within families; there is still a deep understanding between grandparents and grandchildren on important life issues, and they contribute to voluntary organizations and neighbourhood matters although their contribution can easily be overlooked in a society which revolves around wage earning.

RETIREMENT

In many societies there is an acccepted age at which people retire from work. Retirement may be viewed in three ways; firstly that after a lifetime of work one deserves a rest, secondly that elderly people need to make way for school leavers coming onto the employment market, and thirdly that beyond a certain time a person cannot be relied upon to do a job efficiently. The latter cannot be justified because in certain privileged occupations such as politics there is no 'cut off' point. Whatever the reason, retirement will form a substantial part of most people's lives; perhaps 20–30 years. Moreover, in times of high unemployment many workers face redundancy and men and women still in middle age have to accept the fact that they are unlikely to find work again. In Britain in 1983 in the 5 years before the state retirement age only 60% of men and 50% of women were working. It is important therefore that retirement is an enjoyable, enriching and healthy time.

However good the preparation for retirement, adjustment to the change in lifestyle will take time and there will inevitably be feelings of loss. The absence of a pay packet will mean a lowering of living standards for most people even if they have retirement pensions, supplementary pensions, insurance premiums or savings. The benefits conveyed through work such as status, daily routine, social contacts and so on need to be found elsewhere. It is difficult for some people to develop a meaningful life after retirement and some employers have developed a system of flexible retirement whereby people can, within limits, choose the time when they cease working. Some employers, such as the National Westminster Bank, second workers near retirement to voluntary organizations so that they can slowly ease out of work but continue to make a useful contribution to society. Some actively encourage the workers to maintain contact with their workplace afterwards through social clubs.

Retirement brings gains as well as losses. The pressures of work stop; those with other interests find their spare time rapidly consumed, and those who 'lived for their work' find a vacuum which gradually fills. Some people choose to participate in voluntary work, continue another type of work, develop interests or hobbies, or take Open University degrees. Some may simply maintain their interest in community life and offer the benefits of their experience and knowledge to those around them. But first and foremost, most continue to offer a considerable amount of practical help and support to their families. These years can bring expanding interests, deepening friendships, strengthened family ties, travel, and all those other things which one

always wanted to do but never had the time for. Time is no longer structured from outside; there is no 'boss' determining one's moves, one is free to do as one chooses.

Relationships also change. Some partners may not have spent so much time together before. Wives may complain that they cannot get on with their housework with their husband around all the time, and husbands may feel at a loss to know what to do (although with changes in the traditional sex roles this is less so). Retirement may renew the closeness in the relationship of earlier years. Conversely, if the relationship has never been close it may come under increased stress; a wife whose husband regularly 'drank the housekeeping money' or who was violent towards her may test her resolve if he becomes infirm in later life and needs her to care for him.

THE AGEING PROCESS

The natural process of ageing, senescence, will inevitably bring some degenerative changes. However, there are many myths surrounding ageing, particularly that infirmity is the norm. Fit, active and interested elderly people are generally regarded as exceptional instead of as living proof of the degree of health which can be enjoyed, and perhaps expected, in old age. Age is relative, and it is both a cliché and a truism that 'you are only as old as you feel'. There is tremendous variation from one person to another. People can sometimes pinpoint a certain time or event when they began to feel old; perhaps when they were invited to join the Golden Oldies club or offered a seat on a crowded bus. There may be times when they realize that they are not able to do those things which they used to, such as managing an allotment or doing the painting and decorating. Illness may take on a different significance; whereas it was once seen as a temporary inconvenience it may seem to herald a taste of things to come and bring with it fears of infirmity and dependence; it may serve as a reminder that life is not forever. The personal acceptance of becoming old is gradual and extends throughout adult life. Each episode brings with it adaptation, acceptance and a readiness for the future.

Physical Changes

The immune response declines with age so that resistance to infection changes. For instance tuberculosis which developed earlier in life may recur.

The musculoskeletal system undergoes changes. The intervertebral discs thin causing shortening of the trunk and an overall height reduction of on average two inches. This may cause a stoop, kyphosis, which in turn leads to compensation in the posture tipping the head backwards and bending the knees. Bone fragility due to osteoporosis can occur, especially in women as a result of the lack of oestrogen. Voluntary movement becomes slower and there is often a decrease in the strength of the grip.

The size of the kidneys reduces and nephrons are lost leading to reduced blood flow and glomerular filtration. There is also decreased bladder capacity and weakening of the pelvic floor muscles. In practical terms this means more frequent micturition, especially at night, and a shorter warning time. Enlargement of the prostate gland in men, and prolapse of the uterus in women, can lead to urinary difficulties and incontinence. It is therefore important that women continue to exercise and strengthen the pelvic floor muscles throughout life. In addition it is helpful if the toilet, or commode, is easily accessible, especially at night.

It is relatively uncommon for an elderly person to have all their own teeth and so many rely on dentures. The gums tend to recede with age and this may lead to dentures becoming loose and the need for a new set. The production of saliva

is reduced and the gag reflex becomes less efficient. Throughout the gastrointestinal tract motility is generally more sluggish and there is a lack of muscle tone which causes slower oesophageal and gastric emptying. Absorption is reduced due to changes in gastric secretion, fewer cells on the surface of the small bowel, and reduced intestinal blood flow. The liver becomes smaller leading to delay of fat absorption, and carbohydrate metabolism may be affected by decreased insulin production and utilization. It is generally thought that elderly people are especially prone to constipation. In developed countries this is a common problem amongst adults of all ages, although elderly people may be more distressed by it.

The cardiovascular system becomes less efficient and cardiac output drops. Blood vessel walls generally become less elastic and, in Western countries, a degree of atherosclerosis is regarded as normal. This causes blood pressure to rise with age. It also takes significantly longer for the blood pressure to return to its normal state following exertion or stress.

The lungs become more rigid and less elastic, and the bronchioles and alveoli enlarge creating wasteful space. The vital capacity may be reduced by up to 25%. Weaker respiratory muscles and decreased ciliary action may make expectoration more difficult.

In the nervous system, brain weight decreases with age as neurones are lost. Reduced conduction velocity along the axones causes response and reaction time to be slower. This is apparent in sport when a person sees the ball but delays in moving towards it. More seriously, it may mean that an elderly person sees a car coming but is unable to get out of its way in time.

The senses gradually become somewhat dulled because sensory receptors become less efficient. Gradually a higher threshold of stimulation is required. Taste buds reduce and the sense of smell becomes less acute so that food needs to be especially tasty and appealing. External temperature or pressure is less easily detectable and may lead to burns from sitting too close to a fire, or from hot water bottles, or corns from poorly fitting shoes. Hearing acuity decreases, particularly to high-pitched frequencies, due to rigidity of the ossicles, atrophy of the eighth cranial nerve and perhaps deposition of wax in the external auditory meatus. Visual changes occur as the pupils become smaller and less responsive to light. The lacrimal glands function less well which may cause the eyes to be dry and irritating. The lens becomes more opaque and less elastic leading to reduced accommodation. Many people over the age of 40–50 years need reading glasses. Peripheral vision generally becomes narrower and colour perception is decreased.

The skin wrinkles because of loss of tissue elasticity and reduction of subcutaneous tissue. This loss together with reduced peripheral circulation causes an increased sensitivity to cold. It also contributes to the prominence of tendons, veins and knuckles which are characteristic of the limbs of elderly people. The epidermis thins and becomes more dry. Surface blood vessels become more fragile, sometimes breaking, causing tiny haemorrhages or purpura. Sweat glands in the dermis atrophy causing a reduction in perspiration; one reason why elderly people may not be able to tolerate intense heat. Hair becomes grey from loss of pigment and thins, sometimes leading to baldness. Bodily hair regresses, except hair on the face (an increase in facial hair can be embarrassing to women). Nails thicken and may be difficult to cut.

Sexuality

In the reproductive system, in women, the ovaries thicken and become smaller, the uterine tubes shorten, and the uterus and cervix shrink. There is a loss of elastic tissue in the vaginal walls and the mucosa lessens and becomes more alkaline. Breasts tend to droop and become smaller and less firm. In men, the number of viable sperm decreases and the time taken to achieve an erection increases. There are however many myths surrounding sexuality in old age particularly that it does not exist. The work of Kinsey et al (1948, 1953) and Masters and Johnson (1966) showed that sexual interest and activity continue throughout life although there is a gradual decline with age. By their late seventies about 25% of men are still sexually active and they can still become fathers, e.g. Charlie Chaplin. Women similarly remain sexually active and most attribute cessation to their husband, due to lack of interest, illness or impotence. In general terms active young lovers are more likely to become active old lovers. In the context of an intimate and loving relationship frequency of intercourse becomes less relevant. In old age, men and women retain their identity as sexual beings although this is often thwarted by the attitudes prevalent in society that old people are not (or should not be) interested in sex. At any age sexuality involves the need for affection, the desire to love and to be loved, and the right to be treated respectfully by others. The survival of sensual awareness gives vitality to one's personality and one's relationships with others.

Mental and Emotional Changes

There is no personality change, and as at any other stage there will be further growth and development. Without the constraints previously imposed by family or work, the personality may be allowed freer expression. For the naturally introspective person this may lead to a more quiet life of withdrawal from social contacts, enjoyment of one's own company and of reflection. More outgoing and sociable people may seize this time as an opportunity for increased social activity, new friendships, new interests and voluntary work. Expression of emotions may also be less inhibited and tears of happiness and sorrow are more readily shed. All elderly people retain the capacity for change but perhaps not the enthusiasm for it. After a lifetime of experience bringing a mixture of both happiness and disappointment, they may elect to stay with the things they know, trust and feel secure with.

Memory is affected with ageing, especially short-term memory retrieval. Most elderly people can astound both themselves and others with detailed accounts of events which happened years before. These apparently forgotten memories seem to rise to the surface as the person reflects on and reviews the events of the past. A recent event may trigger recollection of a similar incident in the past and warrant the telling of the tale. Recent events seem much more difficult to remember, even things which happened in the past few days. However, when reminded, recollection seems to be unimpaired, demonstrating that coding and storage of the memory is satisfactory.

There is still debate over the preservation of intelligence in old age. The results of testing indicate that intelligence slowly declines with age but this could reflect the type of tests being used which do not take account of changing life experiences. Many people now believe that it is relatively constant providing that the person continues to live a stimulating life. Learning new information remains possible as is demonstrated by the many elderly people who do evening classes and Open University degrees. They may however learn at a slower pace than younger fellow students, but then perhaps their ultimate understanding of an issue is more complete. Creativity may change in the nature of its expression but the capacity remains. There are many writers and artists who remain creative into very old age, and although they may lack the originality of their earlier work they continue to stimulate and impress.

An essential feature of old age seems to be a 'review of life'. Reminiscences form a part of this, but it has a greater significance than simply recalling and telling interesting or funny stories from the past. There seems to be a need to return to the consciousness of past events and grapple once more with unresolved conflicts and to place these, and other important events, into perspective. To the outsider, even a family member, this may be difficult to understand or share. If they are not privy to the details it may seem to them as if the person is 'worrying over nothing'.

DIET AND NUTRITION

Eating habits are usually established early in life but ideas about food and what is believed to constitute a healthy diet change over time. In the post-war years there was a considerable increase in the consumption of refined and sweet foods which had previously been unavailable. Protein foods, especially meat, became cheaper and came to be regarded as the basis of a 'good diet'. The present trend for unrefined foods based on cereals, pulses, vegetables and fruit, with a reduction in foods high in fat, protein and sugar, probably represents a 'poor' diet in the eyes of many elderly people.

Nutritional requirements differ little throughout adulthood and old age except that the total energy requirement will decline as activity declines. At any age, size of appetite varies from person to person and this seems to stay relatively constant throughout life, and is not affected by age alone. However, *A Longitudinal Study of the Dietary of Elderly Women* (Stanton and Exton-Smith, 1970) found that during the eighth decade there was a remarkable decline in the dietary intake amounting to as much as to 30% in the case of some nutrients. A later study, *Nutrition and Health in Old Age* (DHSS, 1979) also found malnutrition to be twice as common amongst the over 80s, and those most at risk were people housebound and over 70. Davies (1981) found that elderly people at home tended to be deficient in certain nutrients:

1 *Vitamin C*. Reasons given for not eating foods rich in this vitamin included sources too expensive, oranges were believed to be 'too acid', greens caused flatulence, and many fruits and vegetables were too difficult to eat. Meals on Wheels were found to be low in this vitamin because of the long time between cooking and eating. Solutions proposed included microwave cooking of the Meals on Wheels and ascorbic acid sweets after meals.

2 *Vitamin D*. Low intake was largely due to a lack of sunlight and a dislike of vitamin D-rich foods such as eggs (binding), oily fish (boney), and liver ('too strong'). Associated problems were osteoporosis and a predisposition to fractures of the femur. Solutions proposed included teaching Home Helps actively to encourage elderly people to sit by an open window or outside in the shade and to suggest margarine rather than butter as it has a more constant supply of fat-soluble vitamins.

3 *Potassium*. Elderly people, especially women, tend to select a diet low in potassium and this may be worsened by the oral diuretics. Associated health problems include muscle weakness, poor grip, mental confusion and depression. Possible solutions proposed included the encouragement of milky drinks and 'nightcaps', and potassium-rich foods such as bananas and custard.

There was a drop in the intake of protein although this rarely caused a deficiency unless the energy intake was very low. Protein came largely from milk and cereal sources. Meat being too expensive for many people, it was particularly appreciated from the Meals on Wheels service.

Adequate amounts of fibre are important to provide bulk to the stool and to stimulate motility of the gut so preventing constipation. Water is also important for digestion, and to prevent urine from becoming overly concentrated in the bladder so leading to irritation and urgency. Eight to ten cups of water, tea, etc., daily is sufficient.

The main factors which have been identified as leading to malnutrition include insufficient money, inadequate cooking facilities, lack of help, poor dentition, drugs affecting appetite (such as indomethacin), physical illness, loneliness, bereavement, and mental and emotional changes. It is interesting to note, however, that a study by Bilderbeck et al (1981) demonstrated that elderly men and women were capable of making dietary changes when they were informed that it could improve their health. It would seem therefore that a considerable amount can be done to improve the diet of the very elderly by tackling the predisposing factors, offering health education and providing Meals on Wheels. The Meals on Wheels service can, in some areas, offer special diets to people of ethnic minority groups such as halal and kosher.

FAMILY AND SOCIAL LIFE

One often seems to hear the statement that 'families today don't look after their elderly'. However, there is no reason to believe that people have become any less caring over recent years. The overall situation however has altered and it is worth considering the changes in the family life of elderly people and some of the reasons why family care is limited. For example, in recent years there has been a substantial increase in the numbers of elderly people living alone.

The study by Young and Willmott (1957), *Family and Kinship in East London*, describes the family life of a community in Bethnal Green highlighting the intricate network of care and mutual support which existed within families and within the community. Many such communities were broken up with the post-war rehousing policies which moved people from inner city areas to suburbs and new towns. Some people believed that the extended family would not survive this disturbance and that the family of the future would be the nuclear family, of only two generations living together. In reality the extended family appears to have survived remarkably well. The Study Commission on the Family (1982) found that over half the elderly people were visited by their relatives at least once a week. However, the 1976 Elderly at Home Study (Hunt, 1978) found that whereas 33% of all elderly people received visits from relatives several times a week, this was true for only 26% of those bedfast and housebound, 20% of those living in retirement areas, 16% of the divorced and separated, and 14% of the single.

It is estimated that over three-quarters of people over the age of 65 are in reasonably good health. Contrary to popular opinion most are not helpless nor do they need looking after. However when the time comes that they do need caring for, it is still usually the family who offer most support. The percentage of elderly people living in institutions has remained relatively constant throughout this century even though there are many more elderly people living to a greater age. Family care usually centres on one person, either the spouse or a daughter. They sometimes continue as carer for many years, with little help, and may themselves be elderly. For some elderly people, family care is limited, or nonexistent. This may be due to a number of factors; childlessness, children who have moved away from the area perhaps for work, emigration, parents who have outlived their children, discord within the family and so on. (See also Chapter 11.)

The attitude of elderly people to attention, or lack of it, from other family members may seem unreasonable at times. Time seems to take on a different meaning with increasing age. Paradoxically it seems to pass more quickly with age and so becomes more precious yet between family visits time may seem interminable. This time scale may be very different from that of a young working adult with a busy family and working life, or to a child or adolescent for whom time passes relatively slowly. An older person cannot easily wait months or years for gratification but looks only to the present, or the immediate future. This may create friction within the family until an understanding of each other's needs is reached and compromises made. Tensions which have simmered for years may finally boil over and this may lead either to family rifts or to reconciliation and renewed closeness.

Outside the family, social activities are important for a full and healthy life. In established communities there is usually a network of neighbourliness and social contacts which ensures contact with other people. Key people within this network are elderly people who contribute to the community by offering advice and support to young people, keeping watch for burglary and vandalism and contributing to community activities. In new towns or in high-rise flats such contact may be sparse. Community resources often include social clubs for elderly people, luncheon clubs, day centres and so on. Industries often provide social clubs for their retired workers. In addition, there may be leisure activities such as exercise groups at the local sports centre, adult education classes and handicraft groups.

The extended family is the centre of all Asian cultures and is responsible for its members at all stages of life. The elderly have a clear and respected role and generally expect to receive loving and respectful care when they need it. Even elderly people still living in Asia continue to have an influence over family members now settled in Britain. It is rare for an Asian family to allow an elderly member to live in an institutional home although there are signs that in Britain the traditional family system is threatened. Immigration poses immense problems of adaptation such as loneliness, climate, language, diet and general lifestyle which may pull the family apart rather than together. Inadequate housing, unemployment, relatively low income, and general ill-health due to changes in climate and diet lessen the family's capacity to care for dependents. Added to this, if the only available work is for unskilled female labour the women may need to leave the home to support the family financially. In some cities with a large ethnic community there is a growing need for support services such as Meals on Wheels and Day Centres.

A study in Birmingham by All Faiths for One Race (1981) found that in the inner city area the incidence of ill-health and poverty was higher amongst elderly black people than their white contemporaries. Black people however tended to be more accepting of this and more fatalistic in their attitude. They suggested that elderly black people, especially those of the first generation in Britain, had difficulty in reconciling their half-forgotten memories of life in the West Indies with present-day life in Britain.

HOUSING

At retirement many people question whether they should remain in their present home or move. There can be many advantages to moving to a dwelling which is suited to limited mobility whilst one is reasonably fit and can cope with the move, although it can be very difficult leaving the home in which one has lived for many years and which one has grown to love. There are often advantages in remaining within reasonable distance of one's family, and to remaining close to friends and the places one is familiar with. Moving miles away to an 'idyllic' retirement town can lead to social isolation.

About 94% of elderly people live in their own homes; only 6% live in residential or hospital accommodation (OPCS, 1976) (see Figure 32). Quality of life depends to a great extent on the comfort and convenience of one's home. If one is old and becoming less mobile the type of housing is even more crucial.

Approximately half of all pensioners live in owner-occupied dwellings; the remainder live in rented accommodation of which more than two-thirds is provided by the local authority. In general terms, the housing of elderly people tends to be older and offer fewer basic amenities such as bath, hot water supply, inside toilet or efficient heating system. They may also be in a relatively poor decorative state because of the cost and upheaval which is involved. 'Do it yourself' is beyond the scope of many elderly people.

Some families manage to care for ageing grandparents by giving them a room in their own house. This may be the only practicable arrangement when the person is no longer able to live alone but may cause friction within the family if it results in teenagers having to share a room, or several people using a kitchen. Some families are able to convert part of their house to a 'granny flat'. This allows close contact between family members whilst

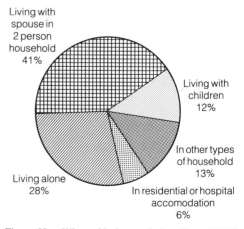

Figure 32. *Where elderly people live. From OPCS (1976).*

at the same time giving freedom and privacy. For those families with the space and the resources, it can prove an ideal arrangement.

In recent years there has been a growth of sheltered housing. These are groups of elderly persons' dwellings grouped together and served by a warden who is either resident or can be contacted by an emergency call linked into the telephone system. These schemes are usually provided by either the local authority or a housing association. They offer specially designed, compact accommodation, usually close to the shops and community resources such as the library. In addition they often develop their own social activities such as coffee mornings and outings. They combine privacy with the security of knowing that someone can easily be contacted in case of need. The call system may be activated by a cord, or a device worn around the wrist or around the neck by those who are very frail and liable to fall. Some schemes, such as the Piper

Network, offer a telephone link to people in their private homes as well as those in sheltered accommodation. A call to the central control unit will put them in contact with a trained operator who can summon assistance if required. Figure 33 illustrates some systems of direct communication for the elderly.

SAFETY

An important aspect of maintaining health is the prevention of accidents. Elderly people are especially vulnerable to accidents in the home. Of all accidents, falls are the most common, especially falls on stairs, and 88% of fatal accidents by falling are to people aged over 65. Table 6 shows the number of fatal home accidents by type of injury and age (Consumer Safety Unit, 1985). Particular dangers are stairs with loose or frayed carpet, inadequate handrails and dim lighting. Very old people depend increas-

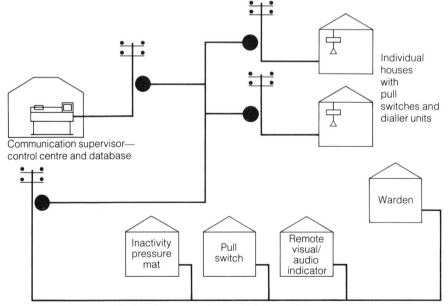

Figure 33.   *Diagram to illustrate systems of direct communication for the elderly.*

Table 6. *Fatal home accidents: type of injury by age.*

Type of injury	0–4	5–14	15–64	65–74	75 and over	Unknown	Total	%
Fracture	18	2	254	302	1823	0	2399	47.5
Poisoning/suspected poisoning	6	8	405	60	58	0	537	10.6
Suffocation	65	42	173	47	114	0	441	8.7
Burn/scald	28	10	109	61	141	0	349	6.9
Foreign body	24	3	125	53	84	0	289	5.7
Concussion	8	1	61	50	137	0	257	5.1
Cut/laceration/open wound	11	3	44	18	57	0	133	2.6
Other internal injury	4	3	49	15	42	0	113	2.2
Dislocation	0	1	4	2	11	0	18	0.4
Bruise/contusion	0	0	1	0	8	0	9	0.2
Ingestion	0	0	3	1	2	0	6	0.1
Sprain/strain	0	0	1	2	2	0	5	0.1
Other	47	25	157	71	144	0	445	8.8
Unknown	3	3	18	13	17	0	54	1.1
Total	214	101	1404	695	2641	0	5055	100.0
%	4.2	2.0	27.8	13.7	52.2	0	100	

Notes

1. Because of the effects of rounding, the percentages do not necessarily add up exactly to 100%.
2. As either one or two injuries can be noted for each patient, the total number of injuries recorded is larger than the total number of accidents.
3. Some of the HASS injury categories are combined in the HADD.

From Consumer Safety Unit (1985) *Home Accident Surveillance System. Report of the 1984 Data*. London: Department of Trade and Industry.

ingly on sight to maintain balance as the labyrinthine function is often faulty, and therefore someone who is quite steady in daytime may be liable to fall in the dark. On the floor, loose mats or mats which are easily 'rucked up' and trailing flexes can cause falls. Older people are particularly likely to lose their balance when their head is hyperextended. An especially dangerous habit is reaching upwards for an object on a high shelf whilst standing on a chair. Some people may feel momentarily giddy when rising from a sitting or lying position and may feel more steady if they pause for a moment before moving.

Slippery floors are a potential danger and non-slip flooring in kitchens and bathrooms is important. In the bathroom, aids are available to prevent slips. A non-slip bath mat and hand rails on the bath and near the toilet can help to prevent accidents and give a reassuring feeling of safety. A bath seat may also be helpful for someone experiencing difficulty getting in and out of the bath.

Medicines are a potential danger. Many elderly people take prescribed medicines and many also take drugs bought at the chemist. Clear labelling is especially important for people whose eyesight is poor. It can be very difficult to remember a regimen involving several drugs and to prevent double dosages (or the forgetting of drugs), but several aids are available such as patient specific drug dispensers (Figure 34). One aid is fitted with a timing device which helps to ensure that

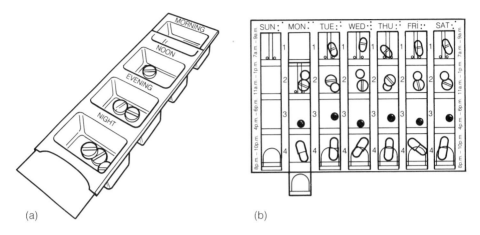

(a)   (b)

Figure 34. *Patient specific dispensing trays for one day (a) and one week (b).*

the correct drugs are taken at the right time.

Other potential hazards include fires, especially for the very elderly. Because of their delayed reaction time, elderly people may be unable to move away from a danger in time and be overcome by smoke or flame. Fireguards are needed for elderly people with fires if they have a history of falling, and smoke detectors have been installed in some sheltered accommodation to reduce the risk of fire.

HYPOTHERMIA

Hypothermia is a condition in which the body temperature drops to below 35°C (95°F). It can occur in people of all ages (babies, mountaineers, skiers and walkers) but it is most common in elderly people and for some may be a serious threat to health during the winter months. Usually when the body temperature falls the temperature regulation centre in the hypothalamus increases the sympathetic tone to the skin and the blood vessels constrict. The direct effect of cold on the skin conserves heat by causing the blood vessels to constrict. In elderly people this mechanism may have become inefficient

so that although the person feels cold heat loss continues. This process is gradual with the body temperature slowly dropping. After some time the person ceases to feel cold and will eventually become drowsy, then comatose. Metabolism is further reduced through the absence of muscle contractions. The body temperature falls even more rapidly and the person may die.

Many factors predispose to hypothermia: being housebound and immobile, lack of hot meals and drinks, depression, some drugs and all alcohol. The most relevant factor however is low income, especially those in receipt of supplementary pensions. Pensioners spend nearly twice as much as the rest of the population on fuel, and it is easy to understand why many try to economize on heating. Some move their bed into the sitting room so that they do not have to sleep in a cold room. Local authority grants may help towards better insulation, and local voluntary groups will sometimes also help with insulation and the installation of more efficient heating systems. Help with heating costs is available to people receiving supplementary pensions. It is slightly higher for those aged 80 and over.

Some elderly people live in considerable risk of accidents and perhaps lie unnoticed for some time. This can create a considerable dilemma for family and health workers who may feel that a move to sheltered accommodation is necessary. This may conflict with the elderly person's desire to stay in their own home and remain independent. In old age, as at any age, the decision can only be made by the person it affects. It is worth considering that a degree of risk taking is reasonable at any age and that quality of life is dependent on many factors. Being safe is important, but so is being happy, and ideally both these criteria should be met.

FINANCIAL ASSISTANCE

Most people can expect to have a considerably reduced income in old age. National Insurance benefits, which include the retirement pension, are paid to claimants who have contributed to the scheme through their work. The non-contributory benefit scheme is means tested and available to those who have not made contributions. In addition to this many also receive an occupational pension. In July 1978 just over a fifth of all retired people were in receipt of supplementary pensions and it was estimated that about 600 000 were not claiming supplementary benefits to which they were entitled. Some elderly people do not claim their benefits because they see it as 'charity', others because they object to the means test and many others because they do not realize that it is available to them. All men over 65 and women over 60 automatically get free NHS prescriptions and those receiving supplementary benefits are entitled to free glasses, dental treatment and hospital travelling expenses. Other benefits which may be available include reduced fares on British Rail and local bus services.

Jordan (1978) in Carver and Liddiard (1983) provides convincing evidence that hardship and need increase with age. He found that 23% of retirement pensioners were living at the officially defined subsistence level and hundreds of thousands below it. The chances of poverty are greater for women. One important factor is the relationship between poverty and sickness and disability which increase with age. Women tend to live longer and so the majority of severely disabled elderly people are women. Moreover, women are also generally worse off financially because of poor or nonexistent occupational pensions. More than twice as many elderly women as men rely on supplementary pensions.

MOBILITY

The second half of the 20th century has witnessed an unprecedented degree of ease of travel. The efficiency of public transport systems and cars have allowed people to move relatively freely locally, nationally and internationally. Loss of mobility usually occurs gradually as one slowly finds that things which one used to be able to do easily and quickly, such as climbing stairs, carrying home the shopping or driving a car, become more difficult and then impossible. Visits to children who have emigrated may become too much even to contemplate. Of all the experiences of ageing this is often described as the most worrying because it brings with it the fear of dependence, the insecurity of wondering who will be available to help and the inevitable loss of one's individual lifestyle and sense of freedom.

Problems relating to mobility are manifold. For instance people of pensionable age in urban and rural areas are much less likely to own a car than younger people, the chief reasons being death of the licence-holder in the partnership and cost. The physical difficulties associated with ageing make it increasingly difficult to cope with public transport and few countries have systematically looked at the adaptation of public transport for the disabled (although they may give fare concessions). In the USA and Sweden experimental schemes have been tried using subsidized taxis but this idea has not been widely adopted. In Britain in recent years buses in rural areas have become restricted if the routes are not economically viable. This has particularly affected elderly people.

Paradoxically the more disabled a person is the more likely he/she is to have to rely on walking, which is fraught with danger. Robson (1978) states that it has been estimated using UK National Travel Survey data that the accident rate of pedestrians was five times that of car travellers. The fatal accident rates for the elderly in the UK are more than two and a half times those of younger pedestrians and for those aged 70 and over it is five times. Problems include uneven pavements, speeding traffic and too short a crossing time at traffic lights. A recent and very serious problem for elderly pedestrians is their vulnerability to mugging. The publicity which often surrounds the mugging of a frail old lady makes the problem appear greater than it actually is. In some urban areas the fear of it keeps otherwise active elderly people indoors even during the day.

SECURITY IN THE HOME

Security in the home is also very important for elderly people. Being frail they are easy victims for thieves. Many elderly people have been robbed by bogus callers and many of these have received serious injuries in the process. General recommendations to elderly people at home are to keep the door bolted, preferably with a chain as well, and not to open the door to strangers no matter how convincing they seem. Special peepholes in doors are useful for identifying bona fide callers. All workmen (and community nurses) should have their identity cards checked before entry. Windows should be fitted with locks so that they can only open a small amount. Doors and windows should always be closed when going out so that nobody has the opportunity to sneak in. Elderly patients who are especially immobile may have an agreement with the district nurse to leave the key in a special place to allow the nurse entry. The key should never be left in the door. If a neighbourhood watch scheme is in operation it can take particular account of elderly people living alone.

After any untoward incident a person is likely to lose confidence and become extra cautious. Following a violent attack or road traffic accident they may need encouragement to venture out again and may well appreciate the company of a friend the first few times. A period of illness or hospital admission may also lead to a period of immobility unless support and encouragement is forthcoming.

SPECIAL NEEDS

There is a saying, much quoted by elderly people, that 'old age doesn't come by itself'. For most people, old age will mean a gradual change in physical or mental health as well as social circumstances. Many problems can be prevented through general health measures; others can be detected at an early stage and adequately managed. Other people must be cared for through sometimes long periods of infirmity. Taylor et al (1983) examined the feasibility of screening elderly people for undetected problems. They identified a potential at-risk group by the following indicators:

- the very old, e.g. 80+,
- recently widowed,
- never married,
- living alone,
- socially isolated,
- no children,
- poor economic circumstances,
- recently discharged from hospital,
- recently changed dwelling.

Williamson et al (1964) found a considerable amount of unmet health needs amongst elderly people in a study carried out in Edinburgh. There is no reason to believe that the situation has improved since then; indeed, the number of very elderly people has increased. There is a strong case to be made for identifying those elderly people who are most at risk to ensure that they receive the health services they require at the earliest possible stage in order to maintain a quality of life and maximum independence. Screening and health surveillance is often provided by the health visitor or district nurse and the general practitioner. Luker (1981) investigated the opinions of elderly women being visited by health visitors and found a high level of appreciation of the service.

Following hospital inpatient care, after-care is very important to ensure that health is being regained, the home situation is satisfactory, and that if relatives are to be responsible for ongoing care they have the support they need. In some hospitals it is usual for a home assessment to be carried out before a frail elderly person is transferred home. This may involve representatives of services such as home care assistants and meals on wheels as well as the district nurse, occupational therapist, medical social worker and GP. They meet with the patient and relatives at home to discuss future plans and to coordinate the relevant services. Joint meetings of everyone involved may be necessary at some stage in the future to review the situation. In some areas voluntary organizations such as WRVS and Age Concern operate settling in schemes whereby elderly people are visited at home following discharge from hospital to ensure that they have basic amenities such as food and heating. Some areas also have voluntary organizations which operate pet fostering schemes for elderly people admitted to hospital.

'Granny battering', abuse of an elderly person by a carer, can occur as a result of stress and an inability on the part of the carer to cope. This stress may take the form of verbal abuse, physical violence, or shutting the person away. The guilt which follows may increase the stress but the shame of admitting the problem to a health professional may be too great and so the problem frequently goes undetected. The emotions involved in caring for someone in one's own family are quite different from caring for a 'patient', and the dynamics of the family may not always be appreciated. In this situation the health needs of all those involved must be recognized and the 'warning signs' noted at an early stage so that additional help, perhaps in the form of respite care or holiday relief, can be offered.

Elderly people who do not have family or friends to care for them, or who cannot be managed by the family at home, must be cared for elsewhere. Those who require nursing care may go to a nursing home. These are usually private although places may be funded by DHSS. There are a small number within the NHS and some are funded by endowments or charities. Some nursing homes provide 'intermittent care' whereby the patient alternates between home and nursing home.

Under Part III of the National Assistance Act, 1948, local authorities are required to provide 'residential accommodation for persons who by reason of age, infirmity or any other circumstances are in need of care and attention which is not otherwise available to them'. Elderly people who cannot manage socially may go to live in a residential home, run either by the local authority or privately. Here they will have all their meals provided and all household chores taken care of. Most people however have their own room and are able to furnish it to their own taste with their own possessions. Most local authorities also provide homes for 'the elderly mentally infirm', usually people with senile dementia who require special care and attention.

Wherever an elderly person lives and whatever their level of dependence and debility, general health needs remain unchanged. Using Maslow's model (see Chapter 8) it involves not only the basic needs but also a sense of belonging and self-esteem. Old age brings for some a daily concern for basic needs such as food, warmth, safety and a little comfort. For others it will offer greater comforts and a sense of fulfilment and the feeling of a life well spent. For many people health in old age is still seen as a lucky bonus. The expectation of health and a sense of wellbeing in old age, and the means by which this can be realized, remains a challenge to us all as individuals, to health care workers, and to society as a whole.

References and further reading

All Faiths for One Race (1981) *Elders of the Minority Ethnic Groups*. Birmingham: AFFOR, Lozells.

Altschul, A. & Sinclair, H. C. (1981) *Psychology for Nurses*, 5th edn. London: Baillière Tindall (especially Chapter 7).

Bilderbeck N. et al (1981) Changing food habits among 100 elderly men and women in the United Kingdom. *Journal of Human Nutrition* **35** (6), 448–455.

Brown, P. (1982) *The Other Side of Growing Old*. London: Macmillan.

Carver, V. & Liddiard, P. (1983) *An Ageing Population*. Sevenoaks: Hodder & Stoughton in association with The Open University.

Consumer Safety Unit (1985) *Home Accident Surveillance System. Report of the 1984 Data*. London: Department of Trade and Industry.

Davies, L. (1981) *Three Score Years and Then. . .? A Study of the Nutrition and Wellbeing of Elderly People at Home*. London: Heinemann.

DHSS (1979) *Nutrition and Health in Old Age*. London: HMSO.

Garrett, G. (1983) *Health Needs of the Elderly*. London: Macmillan.

Gray, M. & McKenzie, H. (1980) *Take Care of Your Elderly Relative*. London: Allen and Unwin.

Hobman, D. (1981) *The Impact of Ageing. Strategies for Care*. London: Croom Helm.

Hunt, A. (1978) *The Elderly at Home. A Study of People Aged 65 and Over Living in the Community of England in 1976*. London: HMSO.

Huskisson, J. M. (1985) *Nutrition and Dietetics in Health and Disease*, 2nd edn. London: Baillière Tindall.

Jerrome, D., ed. (1983) *Ageing in Modern Society. Contemporary Approaches*. London: Croom Helm.

Kastenbaum, R. (1979) *Growing Old. Years of Fulfilment*. London: Harper & Row.

Kinsey, A. C. et al (1948) *Sexual Behavior in the Human Male*. Philadelphia: W. B. Saunders.

Kinsey, A. C. et al (1965) *Sexual Behavior in the Human Female*. Philadelphia: W. B. Saunders.

Longfield, J. (1984) *Ask the Family. Shattering the Myths about Family Life*. London: Bedford Square Press.

Luker, K. (1981) Elderly women's opinions about the benefits of health visitor visits. *Nursing Times* **77** (9), 33–35.

Masters, M. H. & Johnson, V. E. (1966) *Human Sexual Response*. London: Churchill Livingstone.

Office of Population Censuses and Surveys and the Central Office of Information (1984) *Britain's Elderly Population. Census Guide 1*. London: HMSO.

Pincus, L. (1981) *The Challenge of a Long Life*. London: Faber & Faber.

Robson, P. (1978) *Profiles of the Elderly — Their Mobility and Use of Transport*. London: Age Concern.

Stanton, B. R. & Exton-Smith, A. N. (1970) *A Longitudinal Study of the Dietary of Elderly Women*. King Edwards's Hospital Fund for London.

Study Commission on the Family (1982) *Values and the Changing Family: A Final Report from the Working Party on Values*. London: Study Commission on the Family.

Taylor, R. et al (1983) *The Elderly at Risk*. Research Perspectives on Ageing 6. London: Age Concern Research Unit.

Townsend, P. (1963) *The Family Life of Old People*. Harmondsworth: Penguin.

Walker, A., ed. (1982) *Community Care. The Family, the State and Social Policy*. Oxford: Basil Blackwell and Martin Robertson.

Williamson, J. et al (1964) Old people at home: their unreported needs. *Lancet* **i**, 1117–1120.

Young, M. & Willmott, P. (1957) *Family and Kinship in East London*. Harmondsworth: Penguin.

10

Loss and Death

From the moment of our birth we live in a world of constant change and uncertainty. It is a world which gives us things to cherish but which also takes those things away from us. It is a place of birth and death; gains and losses; crises and adaptation. As infants we discover that mother disappears from our world and is not always there when we need her, that pets die, and that our favourite toy can disappear forever down the toilet. We learn early in life that our world is transitory. There are many types of losses, some of which are relatively trivial and pass with just a little sadness, but loss of anything significant in our lives necessitates a period of adjustment and change. This process is called grief.

'RITES DE PASSAGE'

Throughout life there are life events which necessitate 'letting go' of one's current role in order to move onto the next stage. This passage from one role state to another is a crisis point in life and neither the person nor those around them are ever quite the same afterwards. These 'rites de passage' include starting school, puberty, marriage and retirement. Prior to each of these events there is usually a period of anticipatory socialization such as engagement before marriage or pre-retirement courses. Even when the change is expected and desired, there may still be feelings of sadness and loss.

Many parents feel sad when their child starts school because it marks the end of their total dependency on them, and the tears which a parent sheds at the wedding of their son or daughter reflect the sadness at losing 'their child'.

GRIEF

There are times when a significant part of one's life is removed, such as the death of a spouse or the removal of a limb, which is not part of the 'normal' pattern of life and which therefore is not anticipated. At these times people often make comments such as, 'I never thought it could happen to me', or 'I thought it only happened to other people', illustrating the extent to which people refuse to accept the possibility of anything untoward happening in their life. When it does happen the grief response is an attempt to adapt to the trauma. Of all the challenges which we face in life, the loss of something which we hold dear is the greatest.

The notion that someone may die of a broken heart is sometimes taken to be romantic nonsense and yet in the 17th century grief was classified as a cause of death. Today, evidence is building that unresolved or inappropriate grief is a serious threat to health, both physical and mental, and that it may indeed lead to death. A period of grief is essential in order to come to terms with the loss.

Although grief is essentially a personal and private experience, some commonalities in the grief process have been identified. An understanding of these phases of grief is important to enable the sufferer to realize that their feelings are not abnormal, and to help outsiders understand and therefore react appropriately. Grief is ultimately a healing process.

The Phases of Grief

First Phase — Denial

Kubler-Ross (1970) states that most people react to the awareness of a terminal illness with the words, 'No, not me'. Whether it is the prospect of one's own death or the death of someone close, it is a universal initial reaction. This denial may take the form of physical collapse, violent outburst or a dazed withdrawal. Bargaining, such as vowing to change in some way in order to be spared, is also typical. There may be an insistence that the diagnosis is incorrect, or that news of a death is a case of mistaken identity. C. S. Lewis (1961) described his feelings of numbness and shock as, '. . . like being mildly drunk, or concussed. There is a sort of invisible blanket between the world and me. I find it hard to take in what anyone says. Or perhaps, hard to want to take it in'. These feelings may last minutes, hours or days. Denial is a temporary defence or buffer which protects against the shock. The reality of the situation gradually cuts through this defence although to begin with it may seem so terrible that it is quickly blotted out again.

Second Phase — Disorganization

During this phase there is a developing awareness of the true nature of the situation and yet it is essentially a disorganized time when thoughts, feelings and behaviour may seem bizarre and even frightening. Intense periods of pining are experienced along with crying and feelings of physical emptiness. This may alternate with periods of apathy and exhaustion. A common experience is the need to review over and over again the time leading up to the loss as if almost believing that it is possible to alter the course of events. Many people describe a time of restlessness and aimless wandering as if searching. Occasionally they may involuntarily call out or sigh. Following a bereavement, this is sometimes accompanied with a strong sense that the person is there; a widow may repeatedly go to the window feeling her eyes constantly drawn to the bottom of the garden believing that he is there in his favourite spot. She may even believe that she can actually see him sometimes. This strange feeling has been likened to the 'phantom limb' effect when following an amputation the person may continue to feel sensation in that limb. It is as if the mind refuses to accept that this part of itself is missing. For some people this experience can be extremely disturbing; for others it can be strangely comforting and uniquely private.

Rage and anger are typical and take many forms. There may be anger at the health service for not doing something before even though this is unrealistic. The nurse can facilitate the grieving process by allowing anger to be directed towards her and by maintaining closeness and empathy with the people concerned. The anger may be directed towards God for letting them down when they had tried to lead a good life; towards the person who has died for causing them this anguish; and towards themselves. Anger against oneself is often linked to feelings of guilt. Many people faced with a terminal illness try to identify a cause or reason in order to make sense of what is happening. This may be quite unrealistic such as believing oneself to be punished for a past misdemeanour. Bereaved people frequently search for a reason to blame themselves for what has happened and then endure terrible feelings of guilt. Children may actually believe that they caused the death of a parent through once wishing them dead and their guilt can easily go unrecognized and unresolved.

Pincus (1976) describes a period of regression when the bereaved person looks to other people to do things for them and to look after them. They may find decisions and responsibility very difficult and long for someone to come along who will relieve them of the burden; most of all, someone to make everything right again. Life becomes rather chaotic with basic things forgotten and it generally lacks any routine or order. At these times it may be particularly appropriate for the nurse to help with practical arrangements and for the doctor to give even greater support when clinical decisions are necessary. Kubler-Ross states that people faced with terminal illness often use bargaining at this stage. Although there is an acceptance of the inevitability of death there is a belief that that day can be postponed. In some ways this is similar to childlike promises of, 'I will be good if only you will let me do . . . just one last time'.

Often the final stage of this disorganized phase is intense sadness or depression. Memories of how life was may preoccupy thoughts and act as a constant reminder of what has been lost. They may become overwhelmed by feelings of 'If only I had realized how precious those times were, I might have enjoyed them even more'. There may be feelings of regret for the opportunities missed and retribution for the times which were wasted through arguments or the times spent apart. Some people feel that life has become an intolerable burden, that it is not worth living any more, and that it would be better for themselves and the people around them if they were dead. They may become preoccupied with feelings of death and of the futility of life if everything one loves is ultimately taken away. For people with a terminal illness and those bereaved it can help to lead as normal a life as possible and to relearn the lesson, forgotten by most of us, that each day must be lived as it comes.

Third Phase — Resolution

From the turmoil created by grief will eventually emerge resolution and, possibly, acceptance. Kubler-Ross states that given time and help to express the full range of emotions, the dying person will come to contemplate death with 'a certain degree of quiet expectation'. She describes this final acceptance as almost devoid of feelings, not happy and not sad; an emotional resting time. Not all dying people reach this stage of acceptance and some continue to fight in vain hope until the end. For the bereaved, resolution means establishing order into their lives and reorientating themselves into society. This will involve making new social contacts without feeling disloyal. The person who is lost will remain in memories, and most people like to have their photographs around so that they remain part of their lives. To begin with they may be idealized but eventually they will be remembered in a more realistic way and talked about comfortably and with affection.

It must be stressed that the phases described above are not clearcut and not everyone will experience them in the same sequence, at the same pace, or with the same depth of emotions. People often describe grief as a series of waves rather than a steady stream of emotions. Just when they feel they are beginning to come to terms with their grief, something occurs which prompts a surge of anger or depression. The time between these waves gradually lengthens and their intensity lessens. Also, many say that the length of time for this grieving process is generally underestimated, and that grief for the loss of someone very close may last years rather than months. Throughout this whole process one feeling persists: hope.

Anticipatory Grieving

The term anticipatory grief refers to grieving that occurs prior to the actual loss when there is some forewarning. Although it can never match the intensity of feeling following the loss, it seems to have an important function in preparing the emotions in readiness. For many families facing a terminal illness, it is very important for them to be given clear explanations of the condition and its likely outcome as they require it. The withholding of information can prevent the grief response from developing naturally and lead to an even greater outpouring of emotion later on. It is also likely to damage the trust placed in the health care workers. This anticipatory phase is a time when some people like to make practical arrangements. A woman who knows that she is dying may ensure that her husband knows the rudiments of cooking before she dies, and many men like to make sure that their wives know how to deal with mortgages, insurance and so on. Anticipatory grieving is more difficult when the death is relatively unpredictable. Life-threatening conditions which pass through stages of remission may be especially difficult to cope with, as many conditions such as severe brain injury where the person lives for a considerable time but is 'dead' in terms of his former personality.

Types of Loss

It has already been stated that grief occurs when a significant part of one's life is lost. Clearly this includes the death of someone close with whom one has an attachment, and one's own impending death. There are many other situations where grief is apparent but perhaps less well understood. The following examples are not meant to be all inclusive, but rather to give an impression of the presence and extent of grief in everyday life:

1 The loss of any part of one's body, for instance a limb or breast, will lead to grief. The grief is not only for the loss of one's own body image, but also for the anticipated loss of mobility or sexuality.

Grief may be for the nature of the previous relationships which have been lost.

2 The spouse of a disabled person will grieve for the loss of the 'whole' person who was their partner, and for the loss of aspects of their lifestyle.

3 Children of divorced parents will grieve for the loss of the absent partner and perhaps for their lost lifestyle. They may believe that they were the cause of the break-up in the family and experience guilt. Because the absent parent is still alive they may harbour vain hopes of the family coming together again and their grief may remain unresolved.

4 Incest survivors experience intense feelings of anger and depression which are typical of grief. This is for their lost childhood and for the loss of trust in the parent or family member who abused them.

5 Children in hospital experience grief if they are separated from parents. Robertson and Robertson (1952) captured these images on the film *A Two-year-old Goes to Hospital*. These feelings may persist for months afterwards.

6 People who become unemployed experience grief for their lost role in life, status, friendship, paypacket, lifestyle and all those other benefits which work afforded them.

7 The termination of an undesired pregnancy may seem the solution to the immediate problem and yet it is frequently followed by feelings of grief. Horowitz (1978) found that many young women consciously became pregnant afterwards in an attempt to cope with their feelings of loss. Pre- and post-termination counselling are very important.

8 The birth of a handicapped baby may bring feelings of grief. The loss is the 'normal' child who was visualized before the birth. It is not uncommon for parents to alter the baby's name from the one originally planned.

9 Certain disease conditions such as epilepsy and diabetes can lead the sufferer

and family to experience grief because it may make them feel less than whole and it destroys part of their normal lifestyle. People who are HTLV 111 positive suffer grief for similar reasons, and in anticipation of the possibility of developing Acquired Immune Deficiency Syndrome.

Sometimes feelings of grief are expressed which to the outsider seem inappropriate. It is worth considering the possibility that a loss of some kind has been experienced which is not evident to others. The nature of the loss may never become apparent but one's response to that person can still be guided by an understanding of the grief process.

Abnormal Grief Reactions

The normal expression of grief can be hampered by many factors. Fear of the intensity of the emotions by both the sufferer and friends and family can lead to its suppression. Worden (1983) suggests that grief which is not allowed full expression may lead to chronic grief, delayed grief, exaggerated grief and masked grief. Parkes (1972) found that unresolved grief could have a detrimental effect on both physical and mental health especially when the death was 'untimely'. Parkes' study together with other research cited by him, especially that by Maddison and Viola (1968), provides considerable evidence that unresolved grief leads not only to persistent symptoms such as panic feelings, depression, insomnia and other feelings generally associated with grief, but also to less obvious problems such as frequent infections, blurred vision, indigestion and other physical symptoms. Bereavement is also reflected in the Holmes–Rahe inventory which recognizes grief as a major predictive factor in ill-health (see Chapter 8).

Grief is all the more difficult to express when the nature of the loss is not clearly apparent, as in stillbirth. Forrest (1982) describes the problems associated with stillbirth which can lead to prolonged grief reactions of up to 10–20 years. Because the baby never existed to others, a stillbirth (or miscarriage) may not be given the attention it deserves. There is a tendency for it to be swept aside, and well-intentioned people refer to 'the next time' instead of supporting the parents through their present loss. Grief may be more fully expressed if there is a funeral service. Clear information and counselling at this time can help to prevent problems such as marital discord, fear of pregnancy and difficulties relating to a subsequent baby. Self-help support groups can also help parents to acknowledge and express their grief appropriately.

LOSS AND DEATH IN THE FAMILY

In western countries death has become a taboo subject and is no longer recognized as part of living. Improvements in health care in developed countries have led to longer life expectancy so that experience of it within the family is uncommon. Moreover, the trend for people to be admitted to hospital to die means that it is no longer expected as an inevitable part of family life, and for most people direct experience in caring for someone close to them who is dying is limited. More recently it has become accepted that most people would prefer to die at home, amongst their family, rather than in hospital wards. Increasingly therefore families are being expected to cope with death in their midst. Death of any family member will affect the whole family system, and although attention is likely to be fixed on the dying person and the primary carer, every family member must be considered. Families vary in their ability to express and share feelings and part of the nursing care will be to facilitate this. It must include care leading up to the death, and care of the bereaved family afterwards.

It may seem strange to include terminal care in a book about health. And yet recent advances in the care of terminally ill patients and their family, especially the contribution by the hospice movement, have demonstrated that a peaceful death is another dimension of health. More than anything, the hospice movement has been successful in turning a taboo subject into something which can be talked about openly and honestly. Hospice care augments family care by providing short-term care in the hospice, and a home care team of nursing and medical staff who visit the patient and family at home. They are expert in symptom management such as the control of pain and nausea which can greatly improve quality of life. They are also specially trained in counselling skills and so can enable patient and family to recognize and express their feelings and help them to share them openly. They care for the family, alongside the primary health care team, before the death and during the bereavement. What people need most at this time is someone to listen, to share, to provide answers to questions, but most of all someone simply to be there.

CHILDREN FACING LOSS AND DEATH

Bowlby (1953), Spitz (1946), Robertson (1953) and others drew attention to the grief and long-term harm which they claimed could be caused to children through separation from their mother. Bowlby later stated that he had overestimated the adverse effects and that short separations in the context of a loving relationship were not harmful. The crucial factor seems to be the quality of the relationship. Stacey et al (1970) suggest that brief, happy separations from the family, if carefully planned, may help a child to cope with more protracted ones. Indeed, the experience of loss in childhood seems to be helpful in developing the capacity for a grief response and may act as a sensitizing precursor which is adaptive, even creative. The death of a pet may provide an opportunity for grief to be expressed within the security of a loving family. When death of a family member occurs it is important to explain everything clearly and honestly to a child in ways which they can understand so that they too can grieve. The death of a sibling may lead to acute feelings of guilt and blame at still being alive. It may help for them to attend the funeral and see the body. Secrets over what happened only cause children to have even more fantasies and experience more self-blame.

The concept of death develops gradually. Until the age of 5 or 6 years children have little understanding of cause and effect, but engage in 'magical thinking'. Death is likely to be seen as reversible, like sleep. Sometime between the age of 5 and 7 years they begin to understand the concept of cause and effect and the consequences of actions. At about 8 years they begin to see death as irreversible although to make sense of it they tend to fantasize about it being perpetrated by someone or even as punishment. The age at which the death is understood as something which takes place in all life, is final and is not brought about by either oneself or someone else is usually about 10 years although it may not develop until adolescence. Aradine (1976) reviews a number of books about death which are written for preschool and school-aged children to help them understand death. There is little doubt that children of any age are deeply affected by the death of a parent. Van Eerdewegh et al (1982) followed up a group of children aged 2–17 years and found a high level of psychological disturbance 1 month after the bereavement. This had lessened considerably 1 year later. A depressive reaction was especially noted in adolescent boys who had lost their father. Brent (1983) however suggests from a review of other research evidence that bereavement in childhood may lead to longer term behavioural and emotional difficulties.

The care of terminally ill children and their families demands considerable understanding and skill. There is a strong case for children over the age of 3 years to be given their diagnosis at a level appropriate to their understanding. They can also be involved in decision making regarding type of therapy and whether they should be in hospital or at home. Children are particularly adept at picking up non-verbal cues and will quickly realize that something is very wrong. They also seem to have the capacity to amass a considerable amount of knowledge about their condition and the functioning of hospital life. Health workers in the oncology unit at Bristol Royal Hospital for Sick Children have observed children showing an understanding of their illness which greatly exceeds their cognitive capacities in other respects. Moreover, without involvement they may worry unnecessarily about what is likely to happen to them. Given the facts in a way in which they can understand, they can express fears such as fear of abandonment and be reassured that their parents can remain with them. In other ways their behaviour tends to regress and they may need their parent to dress them or put them to bed. Although the approaches used will vary from child to child there seem to be three constant factors: firstly that the child probably knows more than adults expect, secondly that they are more likely to be hurt by concealment of the facts than by frankness, and thirdly the management of their care requires skilled help and time.

Parents of terminally ill children need to be intimately involved with their child's care. Knudson and Natterson (1960) identified three stages of anticipatory grieving: firstly being unprepared and seeking more information, secondly a less intense period with an ostensibly normal life but becoming emotionally distant, and thirdly an overt calm acceptance of the inevitable fatal outcome. Effects on the parents are far-ranging. Schuler et al (1985) noted in families of a child with cancer profound changes in the family life including relationships, work and health. Problems involved parents and their other children. Maquire (1982) found that anxiety and depression reached clinically significant levels in at least one-third of the parents of children with leukaemia. Maquire's study and others have also shown that the rates of deviance amongst siblings is increased at home and at school. However, many parents, following the death of their child, comment on how much they gained from the experience. It is difficult for the outsider to understand how such a loss can lead to gain but then an outsider does not experience the love and depth of feelings which such a situation generates.

CULTURAL INFLUENCES

All societies develop ritualized ways of coping with death. The mourning process conforms to a clearly set pattern designed to facilitate the grieving process. Foremost are the funeral rites which take place after a specified period of time and which allow everyone concerned formally to say goodbye to the deceased and to share their grief. Speck (1978) states that for this ritual to be relevant it must meet needs at three levels: the psychological, by giving a framework for the expression of grief; the theological or philosophical, by making sense or giving meaning to what has happened; and sociological, through sharing the experience with others and being reaccepted into society.

The way in which different cultures ritualize death varies considerably (see Chapter 12). It seems however that some facilitate the grief process better than others. In Britain, restraint over emotions is considered 'proper' and those who break down and cry at funerals are pitied and gently frowned on. Many bereaved people comment on the way in which they are avoided by others. They notice people crossing the street or staying away from them. The reason for this is usually attributed to them not knowing what to say, and finding 'it difficult'. Even in hospitals dying patients and grieving relatives are sometimes avoided because everyone feels uncomfortable in their presence. Bereaved people usually find this avoidance especially hurtful.

Some cultures use the rituals surrounding death to encourage freer expression of emotion than would normally be expected in Britain. The period of mourning may be more clearly defined enabling a person to do their 'grief work' free from other social pressures. Below is an outline of the ways in which some other cultures deal with death and mourning:

1   *Islam*. Special prayers are said for the dying and are always recited in arabic. When a Muslim dies members of the family wash the body according to the Islamic faith and prepare it for burial. There are specific burial rites, for instance the body should be placed in the grave so that it faces Mecca.

2   *Hindus*. It is customary for the family and friends (of the same sex) to wash the body in a ritualized way and dress it for cremation. Bereavement is both a family and a community experience and there is a defined period of mourning when everyone expresses their emotions openly. Throughout this period the bereaved family is not left alone. Traditionally the eldest male lights the funeral pyre. On return from the funeral the mourner is symbolically cleansed and the obligations within the family are determined. The ashes are collected the following day so that they can be strewn in the Holy Rivers with the appropriate services. In Britain the ashes can be collected from the crematorium. The 'uthalia' marks the formal end of the first stage of mourning.

3   *Buddhist and Shinto*. In these religions mourning rituals are prescribed which encourage a continuing relationship with the person who has died. An altar is built which may be visited when advice is needed on a problem or when a feeling needs to be shared.

4   *Judaism*. At death emphasis is placed on what the person has done in their life and in particular the good they have achieved which remains as a testament to their life. Orthodox Jews insist on a Rabbi or member of the family being present at the patient's bedside prior to death to recite prayers. The last offices are carried out by officials from the local Jewish burial society who are specially trained in the Tahara rite. The body must not be left unattended.

These practices may seem very strange in some respects but it is worth considering the function of mourning which is to heal both the bereaved and the community. Rites surrounding death which bring the bereaved into intimate contact with deceased, and mourning which encourages expression of grief within the context of family and community support may ultimately be more healing for all concerned.

References and further reading

Aradine, C. R. (1976) Books for children about death. *Pediatrics* **57** (3), 372.

Benians, R. (1984) The bereaved child. *Maternal and Child Health* **9** (1), 4–8.

Bowlby, J. (1953) *Childcare and the Growth of Love*. Harmondsworth: Pelican.

Bowlby, J. (1981) *Attachment and Loss*: Vol. 3, *Loss. Sadness and Depression*. Harmondsworth: Penguin Education.

Brent, D. A. (1983) A death in the family: the pediatrician's role. *Pediatrics* **72** (5), 645–651.

Chapman, C. M. (1977) *Sociology for Nurses*. London: Baillière Tindall.

Forrest, G. C. (1982) Coping after stillbirth. *Maternal and Child Health* **7** (10), 394–398.

Horowitz, M. H. (1978) Adolescent mourning reactions to infant and fetal loss. *Social Casework* **59**, 551–559.

Knudson, A. G. & Natterson, J. M. (1960) Participation of parents in the hospital care of fatally ill children. *Pediatrics* **26**, 482–490.

Kubler-Ross, E. (1970) *On Death and Dying*. London: Tavistock.

Lewis, C. S. (1961) *A Grief Observed*. London: Faber & Faber.

Madison, D. C. & Viola, A. (1968) The health of widows in the year following bereavement. *Journal of Psychosomatic Research* **12**, 297.

Maquire, P. (1982) Psychological and social consequences of cancer. In: Williams, C. J. & Whitehouse, J. M. A., eds. *Recent Advances in Clinical Oncology*, pp. 375–384. Edinburgh: Churchill Livingstone.

Parkes, C. M. (1972) *Bereavement. Studies of Grief in Adult Life*. London: Tavistock Publications.

Pincus, L. (1976) *Death and the Family. The Importance of Mourning*. London: Faber & Faber.

Robertson, J. (1953) *A Guide to the Film A Two-year-old Goes to Hospital*. London: Tavistock Child Development Research Unit.

Sampson, C. (1982) *The Neglected Ethic. Religious and Cultural Factors in the Care of Patients*. London: McGraw-Hill.

Saunders, C. (1959) *Care of the Dying*. London: Macmillan.

Schuler, M. B. et al (1985) Psychosocial problems in families of a child with cancer. *Medical and Pediatric Oncology* **13**, 173–179.

Speck, P. (1978) *Loss and Grief in Medicine*. London: Baillière Tindall

Spitz, R. A. (1946) *Grief, a Peril in Infancy* (film). New York: New York University Film Library.

Stacey, M. et al (1970) *Hospitals, Children and their Families: The Report of a Pilot Study*. London: Routledge & Kegan Paul.

Van Eerdewegh, M. M. (1982) The bereaved child. *British Journal of Psychiatry* **140**, 23–29.

Wolkind, S. & Rutter, M. (1985) Separation, loss and family relationships. In: Rutter, M. & Hersov, L. eds. *Child and Adolescent Psychiatry: Modern Approaches*, 2nd edn. Oxford: Blackwell Scientific.

Worden, J. W. (1983) *Grief Counselling and Grief Therapy*. London: Tavistock Publications.

11

The Family

At the heart of our experiences at every stage of life is the family. We will influence, and in turn be influenced by, the family from, arguably, our pre-conceptual stage to beyond death. The family exists in some form in all cultures, and from archaeological evidence appears to have existed since earliest times. Some definitions of 'a family' state that it must involve a marriage bond and span at least two generations. Other definitions suggest that the only essential ingredient is at least two people who share a 'significant' relationship. The essential features of the family lie not so much in the rules and regulations determining its structure but rather the functions which it performs. At the root of these functions lies the quality of the relationships, and their capacity to care, to share, to love and to provide comfort and security, but perhaps above all to express genuine concern for each other's welfare. The family has therefore a significant part to play in health and consequently ill-health.

One of the great strengths of the family is its flexibility to adapt and adjust to changing times and situations. Attitudes to it have however changed dramatically. Farmer (1970) suggests that 40 years ago it was viewed as 'a decaying, outworn institution, denuded of almost all its functions, visibly in the terminal stages of a protracted senility'. However in 1968 Fletcher indicated that the family was stronger than ever when he stated 'the family is now concerned with a more

detailed and refined satisfaction of needs than hitherto. . .'. There are few people today who would seriously question that the family is the agency through which attitudes and behaviour are largely learned and where most care is given and received. The family is once again being viewed as the focus of a health care system which is being increasingly based on community care. The family is not only expected to be the principal caregiver to the old, the dying and the handicapped amongst its own members but in some instances to extend this care to provide fostering and respite care for others.

SOCIALIZATION

The family is capable of transmitting through generations such attributes as skills, knowledge, attitudes and behaviour. It does this through the process of socialization. From our first days of life we are influenced by those who care for us. We learn that crying brings food and comfort and that smiles are returned with coos. Later as toddlers we attract unreserved pleasure and pride when we are charming and cute, but scowls when our sticky fingers probe inside the video. We come to find that fine dividing line between what is, and what is not, socially acceptable through trial and error, pain and pleasure. The sounds we hear through infancy eventually become our own language, and the clothes we are given to wear become the clothes of our choice when we are old enough to dress ourselves.

But the child is not an inert object to be moulded like playdough. Each has a unique personality which will itself influence the family. We must all know mothers who tell us that their first child was 'easy' but that their second was 'always difficult'. The child's reaction to situations influences the rest of the family, and Stern (1977) observed that it was frequently the child who instigated interaction with the carer. The process of socialization is always reciprocal; parent teaches child but child also teaches parent. Moreover, although its strongest influence is in the early years the process continues throughout life. The influence of the family may be superseded to some extent by influences from outside such as education or work but there will be no time when we are completely devoid of this influence. Cohler and Grunebaum (1981) argue that throughout our lives we are constantly in touch with family members to share problems, ask advice or request material support. There are those who argue that even after the death of a parent the child remains influenced by what their mother or father would have thought or done in a given situation. The process of socialization therefore manages to combine the innate drives of the infant with the expectations of society and distils out a unique personality who can respond appropriately to the demands made by self and others.

CHILD CARE IN THE FAMILY

A 'mother figure' particularly during the early years is seen as an essential factor for future emotional and mental health. However, Bowlby (1979) stated that 'almost from the first many children have more than one figure towards whom they direct attachment behaviour; . . . the role of the child's principal attachment figure can be filled by others than the natural

mother'. The most important factor seems to be the quality of these relationships. The concept of shared care is not new, as generations of people cared for by nannies, childminders and, of course, grandparents can testify to. The idea that childcare should be the exclusive province of the mother and be contained within the nuclear family is relatively recent. Roles and attitudes to childcare are however constantly changing. Longfield (1984) cites evidence that in Britain in 1979 more than 50% of women with dependent children were in paid employment, although in 1984 a survey found that a large number of people were opposed to working mothers. In fact there is no conclusive research evidence that mothers' employment has consistent, direct effects, either positive or negative, on children's development or educational outcome. It is, however, important to consider what happens to children whose mothers work.

Some parents choose to share a full-time post. This is occasionally possible in professions such as teaching, social work and banking. For some couples it may be the case that the mother is capable of earning a higher wage than the father or in a time of high unemployment may be the only one able to find a job. There are some couples where the father chooses child care and the mother prefers to go out to work. Men who adopt the role of primary caregiver are a small but growing group and need information and support both in preparation before the baby is born and afterwards.

Absence of the wage-earning parent from the home can in certain instances have adverse effects on the family. Long periods away through work, or the effect of unsocial hours associated with shift-work, nightwork, etc., will inevitably influence family life and such situations have been associated with a high incidence of marital breakdown. The absent parent may assume either an unwarranted importance or conversely insignificance until the period of adjustment is over.

The effects may be reduced if there are relatives living nearby who can support and so unite the extended family.

The extended family appears to be providing greater contact and support than is generally supposed, and preschool children are still mainly cared for within the family. Apart from the father, relatives, especially the grandmother, help out. Recent studies suggest that about 25% of children under five whose mothers work outside the home are cared for by their granny. Where the mother is a lone parent and employed 57% of the children involved may be cared for by other family members. These figures do not take into account all the other practical help and support which is given by the family such as babysitting in the evening or at weekends, shared holidays, financial support, help with housework, gardening and so on.

THE GENERATION GAP?

Some years ago the phrase 'generation gap' was coined to describe the seemingly irreconcilable differences which may exist between parents and their children as a consequence of the rapid changes in society. Although the world of young people is in many ways very different from that of their parents, fundamental issues remain relatively unchanged; the difficulties of establishing relationships outside the home, the prospect of unemployment, fear of war and so on are always with us, and these are what concern people most. A survey by Rutter et al (1976) of all 14-year-olds on the Isle of Wight found that in only 4% did parents feel an increase in alienation at this age, and only 5% of the adolescents reported actual rejection of their parents. A further 25% reported some degree of criticism. In some ways there may be an even greater understanding between grandparents and children. In general there appears to be continuity between the generations with a tendency for grand-

parents to be more in tune with their grandchildren than the middle generation on political issues, liberal and permissive behaviour, ageing and death.

In their book, *Mothers, Grandmothers and Daughters*, Cohler and Grunebaum (1981) followed the lives of four families each with three generations of women. They found that even though many problems (marriage difficulties, separation, return to work), they maintained continued and frequent personal contact even when they were living some distance apart. Although the relationships were often ambivalent the women stayed mutually supportive. Relationships within the family as people get older are only an extension of how those relationships have unfolded over their years together. If a daughter and mother have disagreed throughout their lives it is unrealistic to expect them suddenly to get on well together as they become older. However if the individual members have been sensitive and adaptable to each others needs and lifestyles the pattern is generally maintained.

THE ROLE OF GRANDPARENTS

For many people one of the joys of having children is the prospect of grandchildren. This relationship is often very close and quite unlike the parent–child relationship. Grandparents are often rather more indulgent towards grandchildren in a way that they may not have been with their own children and their inclination to give sweets and treats and allow them to 'get away with things' may conflict with parental wishes and lead to family disputes.

When grandparents are distanced from their grandchildren, for instance through emigration, it becomes more difficult to maintain this role and develop the closeness normally expected. Letters and gifts at Christmas and on birthdays help to redress this, and in recent years cheaper air travel, direct dial telephones and homemade videos have enabled families to maintain closer contact than before. In any industrialized country it is likely that families will move around to gain education, employment and promotion. Many grandparents therefore see their grandchildren only infrequently although they usually manage to keep in contact. Indeed many people prefer not to be overly involved in family situations and choose to live at a 'safe' distance, just close enough for visiting and mutual assistance. This allows grandparents to pursue those interests which they have not had time for before unfettered by the demands of work or dependent children. It is sometimes claimed that in western countries elderly people are not valued and that their wisdom goes unrecognized. This may be true although it is often the grandparent or great grandparent who recalls those stories which offer an historical perspective and give a sense of their roots and a concept of continuity through the generations.

The accusation is often made that families no longer care for their elders as they used to. Vague reference is made to a 'golden age' when elderly people were loved and cherished and looked after at home. It is interesting that as long ago as 1832 a Royal commission claimed that the care of elderly family members was neglected in England. It should always be remembered that elderly people are not a helpless group who need to be looked after. About three-quarters of the over-65s are in reasonably good health and take an active part in family and community activities. However the proportion of very elderly people is increasing in Britain and most western countries and there is an increasing number of frail elderly people who are no longer able to manage on their own. In these situations it is the family which is in the front line with statutory and voluntary services supporting when and where they are available.

WOMEN AS CARERS

Wilson (1982) states that community care means family care and family care means care by women. The Equal Opportunities Commission in 1980 found that over three-quarters of those caring for the elderly were women and other studies have shown that these are usually daughters or daughters-in-law. It is also the case that, because women tend to live longer than men, about three-quarters of these frail elderly people are women. Most of us probably have a mental picture of these 'daughters' as fit, healthy young women. In practice it may be the case that a 90-year-old woman is being cared for by her daughter who is herself 70 years old and may have health problems. The role of carer can be physically and emotionally stressful. In addition it may necessitate the woman giving up her work or career with few prospects of becoming employed again when her role as carer is over. For many women this leads to a considerable reduction in income as well as lost contact with colleagues. Voluntary organizations such as the Carers Association are very supportive and informative on rights and benefits. Invalid care allowance is payable to people caring for a dependent person at home.

FAMILY ATTITUDES TO HEALTH

The family is the place where most of our early attitudes and behaviour is established. What we learn through childhood, particularly from our parents, will form the foundation of the way in which we view health and ultimately the way in which we choose to live our lives. For instance, if our parents attend the dentist six monthly for routine checks and they start to take us with them from an early age we may be likely to continue this practice through our adult life. Families who belong to sports clubs and swim or play tennis together at the weekend will probably anticipate that their children will adopt a lifetime of healthy sporting activity.

Of course, it is not always as simple as this. Children as they grow older begin to question the dictates of the family and during adolescence may rebel against them. This may have either positive or negative effects on the health of the child and family. They may reject the values of their parents and begin to smoke or abuse drugs even though their parents have tried desperately hard to prevent this. Or they may choose a different lifestyle for themselves by, for instance, insisting on a vegetarian diet on animal rights grounds when the rest of the family are meat eaters.

Children can themselves be educators and can do a great deal to influence attitudes and behaviour within the family. In immigrant families it is usually the children who are the first to learn the host language and the new ways and pass them on to their parents and elders. Children, even juniors, can be very influential in introducing new ideas which they have learned, sometimes in health promotion programmes in school. How many parents will have given up smoking because their child has lucidly and accurately described the health risks and the pathological processes involved?

Although attitudes to health are largely formed within the family, other influences, particularly school, are also important. This can lead to conflict if parents do not agree with what is being taught. The subject of sex education has always been controversial and there are some parents who believe that it can undermine the integrity of the family. They state that such matters should only be discussed within the family. They further believe that such teaching can lead young people to adopt attitudes and forms of behaviour which run contrary to their own. The problem for teachers and nurses working in schools is that they are aware of the confusion and ignorance which still exists among young people and the health problems, such as unplanned

pregnancies, which can result. Families do not always discuss intimate matters with their children as Farrell (1978) found. This may be because they are too embarrassed or do not know how to because their parents were unable to talk to them. Many parents are very grateful that schools are prepared to tackle these issues and would like extra help on problems such as drug taking. It is important that parents are made aware of the content of health promotion programmes and are given the opportunity to discuss them fully with the school nurse or teachers concerned and that they can withdraw their child from it if they wish.

FAMILY MEALS

There are many factors which influence family foods, one of which is what the person doing the shopping and preparing the meals considers to be healthy and 'good'. Other factors include cultural influences, personal taste, storage space, availability of certain foods, ease of preparation, effects of advertising and, not least, the amount of money to spend. Health Education reports such as the NACNE Report (1983) (see Chapter 2) and the HEC booklet, *Guide to Healthy Eating*, suggest ways in which a healthy balanced diet can be achieved. The main message is to reduce fats, sugar and salt and increase fibre. The use of the terms 'healthy' and 'junk' foods is somewhat misleading. Highly refined and processed foods have relatively low nutritive content but some convenience foods form an important part of the diet. For instance, frozen peas have a higher vitamin content than so-called 'fresh' peas which have been sitting around for a few days. Tins of sardines, baked beans, tomatoes, unsweetened fruits, unsalted nuts, dried fruits, frozen fish and vegetables are all good buys for the family table.

The family mealtime has traditionally been a time when the family sits down and spends time together. It may be the opportunity to share plans for the day, discuss issues, or simply to spend a short time quietly all together. Special foods or dishes can help to enhance the unity of the group and so favourite family foods tend to develop. Cultural foods are very important to preserve national, religious and group solidarity. For Jewish people the meal table is the centre of family unity and the kosher foods and special dishes reinforce their sense of racial distinctiveness. Ethnic peoples usually preserve their foods habits long after they have become integrated into the new land and foods will be available locally which reflect the ethnicity of the area. It is arguable that in western countries many families have less opportunity for shared meals. One influence is television and the temptation to take meals whilst sitting watching programmes.

EMPLOYMENT AND UNEMPLOYMENT

When families were self-sufficient, work was divided between the available family members and all contributed to the welfare of the family. Today most families rely on an income from outside employment so that one, or perhaps more, become the 'breadwinners'. Outside employment does not only offer monetary rewards it also affords status. As a consequence therefore unpaid work within the home becomes relatively low status. In Britain, housework and even home-based jobs which bring in money (such as childminding) are seen as low status. In Africa, although between 60 and 80% of the food is produced by women, it is the men who produce cash crops such as coffee who reap the rewards of money and recognition. In western countries during the 1960s and 1970s women began to demand equal opportunities in employment. The effect of this has been far reaching. More women today delay having babies until their late twenties or early thirties and return to their job or

career after maternity leave. Although housework may be shared, a large amount is still done by women who therefore have to carry responsibility for family, home and work.

Employment can provide money, status, development of skills and talents, relationships with workmates and colleagues and a sense of identity and purpose. Entry into the labour market and retirement from it are major landmarks in most people's lives. There are two major factors which influence a young person looking for a job; firstly their qualities and qualifications and secondly the availability of jobs. In some communities based on mining or farming there is a tendency for generations to follow in the same line of work. This is also the case in some professional groups such as nurses, doctors, teachers and in publishing. People tend to move around the country because of their work, especially as a consequence of redundancy or promotion. In some areas when factories close down large numbers of people from the community may move away to find work. Apart from the disruption to the wage earner concerned and the immediate family, parents and grandparents may be left behind, thus fragmenting families and making it much more difficult to provide practical support at times of illness or crisis.

In recent years there has been a considerable rise in the number of people unemployed. In Britain the rate of unemployment has accelerated from 1.3% in 1961 to nearly 14% in 1985. In some areas it is particularly high, for instance in Northern Ireland 20.6% and in Northern England 17.7%. Among those aged 18–24 years 35% report some unemployment in the past year. The employment figure for women has changed little during this time although the proportion of married women with children working dropped between 1980 and 1984. Loss of any part of oneself will evoke an emotional response of grief and mourning. Loss of a job is likely to be met with a sense of numbness and shock, 'this can't be happening to me'. Quickly, feelings of depression arise as the reality of the situation becomes apparent and with it a sense of rejection and worthlessness. The person may yearn for things to be as they were and realize how much they depended on it; life may seem meaningless without it. Gradually these feelings give way to emotional acceptance and finally adjustment. This process may be delayed, suppressed, postponed or extended depending on the importance which that person (and their family) placed on work, whether there are others 'in the same boat', and the way in which the job was lost.

Fagin and Little (1984) noted the effects of unemployment not only on the person concerned, but also on the whole family. Unemployed men tended to visit their GPs more often with symptoms of sleeplessness, anxiety, palpitations and gastrointestinal disorders leading them to conclude that there is an association between ill-health and unemployment although this link is far from straightforward. There was also an increase in cigarette smoking (for the men and their wives), although a reduction in alcohol probably because of the expense and the reluctance to participate in social activities due to feelings of shame. Occasionally the wives of unemployed men grew in emotional strength as they supported their husbands and families and some even noticed a reduction in their own ill-health. However, others sank into depression and despair with their husbands. Effects on their children's health included disturbances in feeding habits and sleep, minor gastrointestinal complaints, increased accidents and behavioural disorders. In the words of Jeremy Seabrook (1982), 'Love is stretched thin . . . People turn on those who love them best because there is nobody else you can take the pain and humiliation to'.

MAKING AND BREAKING RELATIONSHIPS

'Evidence is accumulating that human beings of all ages are happiest and able to deploy their talents to best advantage when they are confident that, standing behind them, there are one or more trusted persons who will come to their aid should difficulties arise' (Bowlby, 1979). One of the primary functions of the family is to establish relationships which warrant this trust. The 'bond' which forms between mother and child is well documented, but other relationships are also fundamental such as those between father and child, between siblings, and between grandparents and grandchildren. These may become closer as the years pass. The ability to form relationships within the family seems to have an influence on relationships with others. Young people who grow up in a closely knit family where they are encouraged and supported seem to readily build new relationships with peers and create a social network which draws together family and friends.

The search for a partner, whether of the same or opposite sex, often begins in adolescence and there may be several before one becomes permanent. In most families in the western world it is expected that young people will find their own partner although families usually have strong views on whether they approve or not and encourage or discourage the budding romance accordingly. Each person will bring to a marriage their own ideas which they want to express, and their own needs which they want met. Inevitably they will be influenced by their own family background. Initially there is likely to be some conflict as they establish their relationship and either work things out together or agree to differ. If their backgrounds are dissimilar, for instance if they come from different ethnic groups, this process may be more difficult and take longer. The making of a marital relationship may be adversely affected by events over which the couple have little control such as unemployment, financial hardship, poor housing and an unplanned pregnancy. If the couple manages to cope with such difficulties the relationship may ultimately be strengthened but it may also lead to stress and irreconcilable differences.

Within the family some relationships must also eventually be broken. The death of grandparents and older members is a feature of family life. However the unexpected death of younger members, death of children, stillbirths, miscarriage and so on can lead to grief which is difficult to express even within the family. Separation and divorce, emigration, severe injuries leading to personality changes will all cause the breaking of a previous relationship. The pain of grief can be borne more easily because of the strength which exists between the family members who remain. Families usually gather at such times of crisis to offer each other support (see also Chapter 10).

As divorce rates rise so 'reconstituted' families become more commonplace. Many families comprise a step-parent and other children from a previous marriage. For the child this involves establishing relationships with others whom they have not grown up with, and can lead to conflict and misunderstanding. The role of step-parent is known to be fraught with difficulties; less well documented is the relationship between step-siblings and half-siblings. It might be reasonably assumed that there will initially be some resentment, perhaps hostility, and that only careful nurturing of these relationships, open discussion, and perhaps some compromise, will lead to trust in each other and the feelings of security which in time will draw the family together.

FAMILY CARE IN ASIAN FAMILIES

Asian cultures are as varied as European cultures and it is therefore difficult to draw generalizations. However, the extended family is a common feature of all Asian cultures. For Asians who have settled in Britain it remains the most important influence in their life. Each family usually includes three generations (see Figure 35). Sons remain at home and bring their wives to live with them when they marry. When a young woman leaves home to marry she therefore marries not only the man but the whole family. She becomes an essential part of the family, responsible for the day-to-day care of children, both her own and others. She has an important role in religious and moral upbringing. She will also be expected to care for the elders in the family and any frail or handicapped members. They may keep such people very much in the background but the care they give is loving and respectful. It is unusual

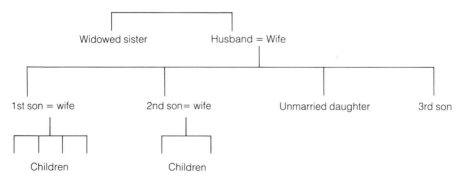

Figure 35.   *An extended family household. From Stanford, J. Testicular Self-examination,* The Professional Nurse, *February 1986.*

for Asian families to allow a member to live in an institutional home. Women have traditionally remained in the background although they are now entitled by Indian law to inherit property and attitudes are changing towards equal rights. Men are chiefly responsible for dealing with public authorities and the outside world in general. There exists within an Asian family therefore a system of mutual responsibility and obligation and a considerable capacity to care.

Throughout his or her life an Asian remains dependent on the family. The happiness and reputation of a family will always take precedence over an individual's needs or ambitions. Brothers vow to care for their sisters throughout their lives and this creates a strong bond. Important decisions will be taken jointly by the family, and it is not uncommon for the whole family to consult a doctor when one member has a serious health problem. The dependence on the family back home in the Indian subcontinent also remains strong. Money will be sent home on a regular basis even if the family is second or third generation in Britain. Families endeavour to make visits to them and will be influenced in their way of life in Britain by what they think the family would approve or disapprove of.

Arranged marriages are found in the Far East, Middle East and Indian subcontinent. Because the marriage is so vital to the whole family it is considered too important a decision to be left to two young and immature people. Where the couple are older, and perhaps less emotional and a little wiser, they may be allowed more freedom to make their own choice. In some cultures a dowry may be expected from the young woman's family. Marriages which break up affect everyone. Often the woman is blamed whatever the circumstances because she is regarded as the one whose duty it was to fit in. Pressure is therefore put on her to make the marriage work. Her position in society will be greatly affected, although it is likely that her own family will have

her back. In some cultures it is unlikely that she would remarry. Problems within the family may arise if the couple have been brought up and educated in the west. The conflict is usually between the desire to marry the person of their choice, which will result in a break with the family, or comply with their parents' culture and marry someone they may not know or love. For some young people this conflict leads to considerable distress and even physical or mental illness.

THE ONE-PARENT FAMILY

Lone parents no longer elicit the raised eyebrows or whispers behind curtains which they might have even 10 years ago. Social attitudes to children born outside marriage and to divorce and separation have become much more accepting. And yet this liberal outlook in some ways masks the social innuendos and harsh problems which lone parents still face.

There are several routes to lone parenthood. Marital breakdown accounts for about two-thirds and unmarried mothers and death of one parent each make up about half of the rest. Cultural attitudes are also relevant. For instance in Britain nearly half of births to mothers who had themselves been born in the West Indies take place outside marriage although there is considerable support from the extended family. The roots of this style of family life can be traced back to the days of slavery when marriage was prohibited and partners separated as soon as a child was born. In contrast only about 1% of births to mothers born in the Indian subcontinent take place outside marriage. In 1983 it was estimated that there were about one million one-parent families involving one child in eight. Of these 90% were headed by women. However the difficulties experienced by lone fathers should not be underestimated. Many such fathers are able to cope reasonably well with the early years and with the traditional female tasks of cooking and sewing but tend to find the adolescent years the hardest, particularly if they have a daughter. It is difficult to know how many people will at some stage of their lives be part of a one-parent family because of the tendency to move into the situation through temporary separation and out of it through remarriage.

Lone parents are still a disadvantaged group compared to the general population and their experiences may range from social embarrassment at one end of the scale to poverty at the other. Although attitudes are changing they remain ambivalent and lone parents may still find themselves or their children excluded from social functions primarily centred on two-parent families. Non-married non-working mothers may be at risk of mental distress because of their isolation, lack of friends and severely restricted social life. Lone parents are constantly concerned with the burden of sole responsibility for the care and development of their children. This strain can be lessened if they have others around with whom they can share their feelings and fears.

They may meet with prejudice from prospective employers who choose not to employ them because they wrongly anticipate less commitment or more workdays lost through problems relating to their children. For those working there is the problem for women of jobs being concentrated in low-status, low-paid occupations with limited opportunity for further training or advancement. For any lone parent there is the problem of finding suitable day care for their child, and this may limit opportunities for promotion if a move is necessary. Lone parents are more likely to have to rely on state benefits.

Adequate housing is yet another problem. Popay et al (1983) cite several studies which consistently show that one-parent families are less likely to be owner occupiers; more likely to share accommodation; more frequently live in overcrowded conditions; lack basic amenities; move house more frequently; own fewer consumer durables such as washing machines and telephones; and spend a greater proportion of their income on housing and heating than two-parent families. There is also evidence to suggest that lone parents are more likely to be allocated flats rather than houses and to be concentrated in the 'poor' neighbourhoods in inner city areas.

DISADVANTAGED FAMILIES

Lahiff (1981) describes poverty as a condition of want, of insufficiency, or of deficiency and it can apply to material objects or to emotional or social concepts. It is a matter of comparison; as material wealth becomes more available to more people those unable to benefit from it stand out. Emotional 'poverty' can result from the effects of unemployment or from having children one can neither understand nor control. People who are faced with repeated failures in life soon lose their self-esteem and develop a self-image of worthlessness. They become acutely sensitive to outside criticism and may get caught up in a self-fulfilling prophecy in which because of their repeated failures society does not value them thereby confirming their own poor opinion of themselves. Social 'poverty' may come from living in an area surrounded by others with a sense of hopelessness. Poor housing in an inner city area or damp housing in an outer suburb with an infrequent, costly bus service can compound the sense of isolation and despair.

Such families come to feel that they have no control over their lives and that there is no way out. They may come to mistrust statutory services because they feel that their values are different from their own and that they will at best offer unhelpful advice and at worst criticize. They may not open their door to the health visitor or social worker, defer seeing the GP, or only go to the school when they feel a need to complain. Workers in disadvantaged areas are now changing their approach so instead of simply doing things for people they aim to enable them to find ways of making choices which affect their lives so enhancing self-esteem. For instance it may involve finding a successful way of getting their houses treated for dampness.

The term 'cycle of deprivation' was coined to describe the transmission of disadvantage through the generations. Rutter and Madge (1976) collected research evidence on many aspects of disadvantage such as delinquency, child abuse, ineffective parenting behaviour and psychiatric disorder to investigate whether problems literally continue to reproduce themselves. Their findings were generally optimistic. They did find continuities of disadvantage across the generations but they also found discontinuities. They concluded that 'at least half of the children born into a disadvantaged home do not repeat the pattern of disadvantage in the next generation. On the other hand, even where continuity is strongest many individuals break out of the cycle and on the other, many people become disadvantaged without having been reared by disadvantaged parents'. Moreover, they found the problems to be much weaker over three generations than two. The cycle of disadvantage does not seem to be as all-encompassing as has been suggested. Other causal processes are also highly significant; these include regional and cultural differences, poor housing and inequality of income.

INHERITED HEALTH DISORDERS

Some families know that they carry a risk of transferring on to the next generation genetic disorders. Some conditions may be so distressing, for instance Huntington's chorea, that they choose not to have children. If the condition is transmitted

by a recessive gene, for instance cystic fibrosis, there is a one in four chance that the child will be affected. If the disorder is transmitted by a dominant gene, for instance neurofibromatosis, there is a one in two chance that the disorder will be transmitted. Affected families are usually offered genetic counselling so that the risks of an affected child can be explained to them and they can make an informed decision on whether to plan a pregnancy. Some disorders which are sex linked, such as muscular dystrophy, can be detected *in utero* and termination offered if the child is of the sex likely to be affected. This raises many ethical issues (see Chapter 7 for details of abortion legislation). Many maternity hospitals are now offering preconception care so that any prospective parent concerned about familial disorders can gain access to expert advice and counselling.

There are some families where there is a tendency for certain disorders to affect many members through generations. Diabetes, familial hypercholesterolaemia, schizophrenia, and even some cancers seem to occur with regularity in some families. This can have a considerable effect on the outlook of the family members and their expectations for their own health. For instance, a person in a family with a history of hypercholesterolaemia may be prompted to positively promote their own health in order to prevent a heart attack. They may decide to attend their GP for regular blood tests, pay particular attention to a diet with relatively low fat, take regular exercise and learn relaxation techniques. On the other hand the stresses involved in living closely with others who have developed a particular form of health problem may lead to denial of the problem and a refusal to believe that it could possibly happen to oneself, or even to reckless behaviour as if deliberately challenging fate. In some families it may lead to hidden stresses if feelings and fears are not allowed to be expressed. Open discussion of the relevant health problems within the family usually helps and a counsellor may be necessary to facilitate this.

INTERVENTION AND SUPPORT

There are many stages of the family life cycle when it turns to the outside for help and support. In the past most diseases and health related problems were seen as pertaining to one particular member and health care was focused accordingly. Nowadays it is recognized that most health conditions are influenced by attitudes and behaviour within the family and that the healing and caring process will affect the whole family. Health care is therefore becoming increasingly family focused. The family is a unit and if one part falters, the whole system is weakened or thrown into disarray. Careplans, whether in hospital or in the community, should always involve everyone concerned so that the aims are mutually agreed and understood. For instance, there is little point in making care plans on the basis that the patient's daughter will assume the role of carer when her elderly mother is discharged from hospital if she has little idea of what will be expected of her.

Family support from voluntary organizations is especially important and often complements the work of the statutory agencies. Voluntary organizations may be national bodies or locally based. They may exist specifically for a particular care group, such as HEADWAY (The National Head Injuries Association), and Alzheimer's Disease Society, or be more general such as The Association of Carers which was established in 1981 to offer support, information and opportunities for self-help to anyone leading a restricted life because of their responsibilities to a person of any age who is mentally or physically handicapped or ill or impaired by infirmity. The work of voluntary organizations usually revolves around three main aims; the establishment of self-help groups, information, and respite or relief care for the carers.

OTHER 'FAMILIES'

The benefits of family life are so convincing that they are being increasingly viewed as preferable to institutional care and this has greatly influenced service provision. A pregnant, unsupported young woman may stay with a foster mother to help her through the early months; some local authorities such as Avon have introduced sponsored childminding schemes so that preschool children can be cared for within a family; handicapped children go to foster families for respite care instead of being admitted to hospitals; children 'in care' are placed with foster parents instead of children's homes; elderly people who are no longer able to live alone can, in some areas, spend their last years as boarders with a surrogate (or foster) family. There are many families who are prepared to 'adopt' another member and to take them to their hearth and their heart.

'Families' are even being created in some situations. For instance children who cannot be fostered now live in Family Group Homes with houseparents. These are provided by social services and aim to create a homely atmosphere by having a small group of children of varying ages together. Mentally handicapped people are being moved out of long-stay hospitals into ordinary homes where they can live together in small groups, lead their own lives and enjoy the comforts, security and support (and the squabbles and tears) that we might all reasonably expect from our family.

References and further reading

Bowlby, J. (1979) *The Making and Breaking of Affectional Bonds*. London: Tavistock Publications.

Cohler, B. J. & Grunebaum, H. U. (1981) *Mothers, Grandmothers and Daughters.* Sussex: Wiley-Interscience.

Craven, E. et al (1982) *Family Issues and Public Policy.* London: Study Commission on the Family.

Dominian, J. (1980) *Marriage in Britain 1845–1980.* London: Study Commission on the Family.

Fagin, L. & Little, M. (1984) *The Forsaken Families. The Effects of Unemployment on Family Life.* Harmondsworth: Penguin.

Farmer, M. (1979) *The Family,* 2nd edn. Harlow: Longman.

Farrell, C. (1978) *My Mother Said . . .* London: Routledge & Kegan Paul.

Firth, R. (1956) *Two Studies of Kinship in East London.* London: University of London Press.

Fletcher, R. (1968) *The Family and Marriage in Britain.* Harmondsworth: Penguin.

Garrett, G. (1985) Family care and the elderly. *Nursing* **2** (36), 1061–1063.

Great Britain Central Policy Review Staff and Central Statistical Office (1980) *People and their Families.* London: HMSO.

Harbert, W. & Rogers, P. (1983) *Community-based Social Care. The Avon Experience.* London: Bedford Square Press/NCVO.

Lahiff, M. E. (1981) *Hard to Help Families.* Topics in Community Health. Aylesbury: HM & M Publishers.

Longfield, J. (1984) *Ask the Family. Shattering the Myths About Family Life.* London: Bedford Square Press/NCVO.

National Advisory Committee on Nutrition Education (1983) *Proposals for Nutritional Guidelines for Health Education in Britain.* London: Health Education Council.

Pincus, L. & Dare, C. (1978) *Secrets in the Family.* London: Faber & Faber.

Popay, J. et al (1983) *One Parent Families. Parents, Children and Public Policy.* London: Study Commission on the Family.

Rose, V. (1984) A family matter. Familial hypercholesterolaemia. *Nursing Times* **80** (12), 21.

Rutter, M. & Madge, N. (1976) *Cycles of Disadvantage.* London: Heinemann.

Rutter, M. et al (1976) Adolescent turmoil: fact or fiction? *Journal of Child Psychology and Psychiatry* **17**, 35–56.

Seabrode, J. (1982) *Unemployment.* London: Quartet.

Skynner, R. & Cleese, J. (1983) *Families and How to Survive Them.* London: Methuen.

Stern, C. (1977) *The First Relationship: Infant and Mother.* London: Fontana/Open Books.

Study Commission on the Family (1982) *Values and the Changing Family.* London: Study Commission on the Family.

Willans, A. (1983) *Divorce and Separation. Everywoman's Guide to a New Life.* London: Sheldon Press.

Wilson, E. (1982) Women, the community and the family. In: Walker, A., ed. *Community Care.* Oxford: Basil Blackwell and Martin Robertson.

12

The Community

The term 'community' is widely used but rather difficult to define. Although it usually conjures up images of nestling houses, it is the people who are the essential ingredient. A 'community' implies a 'community spirit' where a sense of belonging and a common identity draws people together. It also suggests a sense of caring; that those people who live in close proximity to each other will experience a sense of duty, moral obligation or desire to help each other. Mitford (1982) described it as 'a little world . . . where we know everyone and are known to everyone, and authorized to hope that everyone feels an interest in us'. The nature and structure of communities varies greatly but certain functions are virtually universally present irrespective of culture, climate or country. The nature of the community in which one lives, works or socializes has a profound effect on health and wellbeing. Alongside the family it provides the framework which determines one's way of life. It may also be a safe haven where, whatever one's circumstances, one can rely on the support of others, or at the very least not to be forgotten.

Industrialization has altered the shape of communities and throughout the world pre- and post-industrial types can be found. The classical comparison between these two types of community was made by Tonnies, the German sociologist. He delineated two ideal types which he termed Gemeinschaft (community) and Gesellschaft (association). He suggested that in the 'community type' people were usually rural and lived off the land. This led to them living in extended families and having long-lasting patterns of interaction with their neighbours. Their concerns centred on themselves, their families and immediate friends. Attitudes and beliefs were largely traditional folkways and new ideas were either rejected or slow to be accepted. Conversely, in 'association type' the families were more likely to be nuclear with social interaction superficial and transitory. Life was urban and influenced by industry leading to people becoming concerned with business, travel and the wider issues of the world. They tended to be receptive to new ideas and change. These ideal types are useful when considering the effects communities have on health and general wellbeing although it is clear that most communities are, in effect, a blend of both.

TYPES OF COMMUNITY

Rural Communities

Rural communities are traditionally based on agriculture or fishing. They take the form of scattered villages which work the neighbouring land or sea. To support the people living there they contain places to worship, to buy provisions, to go for health advice, and to meet on a daily basis and for special occasions. The people often have several different roles and more than one occupation. For instance, the storekeeper may double as the publican and church warden. During the year there are usually a few events which unite all the people and confirm the cohesiveness of the community. This may be the village fête, a money-raising event for a new lifeboat, or the harvest festival. These communities combine in one place the three social areas which in cities are usually split; the locality in which the person lives, their occupation, and their social affiliations. In Britain there are still communities which function in this way although with increasing mobility people often look to the nearby towns for work and social life. Mobility has also enabled people to move to villages from the cities and commute to work daily. Some have been dubbed 'dormitory villages' suggesting that people use them only to sleep in. In reality these families have often contributed a great deal to village life and have helped to invigorate communities which were beginning to suffer from depopulation. Traditional rural communities are more usual and typical of third world countries.

In rural communities health care is largely contained within the family and the local community. For instance, a young mother is likely to have her own mother nearby and will also know other mothers in the village with young children. Likewise, old people are known within the community and their ability to cope and their state of health is quietly, often unconsciously, monitored. Help with the gardening, lifts to local events and an occasional meal are offered almost as a matter of course (indeed some people may find the perpetual scrutiny somewhat intrusive). When an old person begins to find it difficult coping on their own it is usual for the family to offer increased help with the household chores or for them to go and live with their family. Although such a community is by nature self-supporting, the closeness of family members and the intensity of the relation-

ships can lead to conflict. Internal conflicts may be much greater in a small community because the members are closer to each other. It is not uncommon for extended families to be split by disagreements or bitter feuds and for contact between close family members to be severely restricted or even lost.

Urban Communities

In Britain the movement of people from the countryside to the city took place during and after the industrial revolution. Within towns and cities communities developed where people were largely self-supporting in terms of work, shops, places of worship and social amenities such as pubs and clubs (rather like clusters of villages). During the Victorian era a trend began for people to move out of the towns into the suburbs. The cities beloved of the Georgians were considered unfashionable and unhealthy. The concept of the 'garden city' developed which combined the benefits of the countryside with closeness to the facilities of towns and cities.

The trend continued throughout the 20th century and most cities have suburbs which extend outwards from the city centre becoming progressively more modern. In the post-war years many more urban communities, such as Bethnal Green in East London, were split up by the slum clearance programme when people were moved to new housing estates on the outskirts of cities. However, the improvements in terms of physical conditions were often outweighed by the loss of community spirit and neighbourliness. In reality, instead of combining the best of two worlds some combined the worst. Amongst a mass of housing families found themselves relatively isolated from the city and from each other. In recent years there has been a revival in urban living and these areas with their period properties have become fashionable again with many young professional people choosing to buy houses there. There have also been some sensitive urban renewal schemes whereby the community has been preserved. Families have been moved out of houses which have become unfit for occupation, new houses have been built on a similar plan and the people moved back to resume life very much as before.

Inner-city Areas

In the 1980s inner city areas have become synonymous with multiple deprivation, high crime rates and poor health. In recent years there have been several serious inner city riots notably in London, Liverpool and Bristol. Inner city problems exist in cities throughout the United Kingdom; in Scotland, notably in Glasgow; in South Wales; in Northern Ireland, especially West Belfast and West Londonderry; and in England in cities such as Bristol where the relatively poor quality of health in inner city areas has been highlighted by Townsend (1984).

However, a report on Primary Health Care in Inner London (DHSS, 1981a) commented that, although many deprivation factors are to be found to a greater or lesser extent in other urban environments, the scale and combination of problems in different boroughs and neighbourhoods in London is unique. The programme of slum clearance undermined family unity and support and led indirectly to high mobility of the population and social isolation. Housing stock is poor and many do not have sole use of basic amenities. Also, the proportion of the population living in rented property is high, and those living in high-rise accommodation is vastly in excess of the national figure. The lack of social stability is reflected in the incidence of illegitimate births, abortions and children in care. The proportion of elderly people living alone is above the national average and because of the break-up of the extended family many have nobody to rely on when illness or crises occur. As the economically successful have moved out,

those who have gravitated towards inner London have tended to be vagrants, drug addicts, alcoholics and the young single homeless. The latter group are especially vulnerable to drug abuse, mental illness and suicide.

During the 1950s and 1960s immigrants tended to move into inner city areas because the discriminatory housing policies made it difficult for them to get mortgages or local authority tenancies in any other area. In 1981 about 40% of births in inner London were to mothers born outside the UK. These communities have developed their own culture which is reflected in the community activities and carnivals. Many people of ethnic minority groups prefer to stay in these areas amongst a community where they feel they belong and where they feel relatively safe. Home Office statistics state than an Asian is about 55 times more likely to be physically attacked than a white person. It is one of the reasons why Asian families continue to live in close proximity to each other with only the more affluent moving out. In some cities urban renewal projects have sought the views of local people and have managed to sensitively improve living conditions to include facilities relevant to the ethnic mix and so enhance the community spirit.

New Towns

The New Towns Act of 1946 paved the way for the development of what were to be the ultimate in 'garden cities'. These towns would provide high-standard housing in a clean environment. Development corporations were established to plan the town, attract industry and most importantly attract the people from cities with run-down housing and old redundant industries. They were largely successful although some suffered during the 1970s from the failure of industry and subsequent rise in unemployment. Also, many people had failed to realize the extent to which they would miss the community they had left and suffered from loneliness as a result. Most new towns attracted predominantly young people leading to an imbalanced age structure in the population which lacked middle-aged and elderly people. In addition, leisure and shopping facilities were sometimes lacking in the formative years of the new town. All of these factors contributed to new towns acquiring a reputation for promoting poor mental health; an image which perhaps became rather exaggerated. However, it is probably fair to say that it was a considerable time before new towns developed true communities amongst the people living there.

HOUSING

In England and Wales nearly 90% of people live in suburban or urban areas. Between 1971 and 1981 there was an increase in the number of people living in suburban areas whilst at the same time the number of people living in dense urban areas more than halved. Another significant trend during this period has been the increase in owner occupancy which in 1983 accounted for around 60% of all stock (38% in Scotland which has the highest proportion of local authority rentings). This has been brought about by two main factors; the sale of local authority houses and the relative increase in private sector building over local authorities and new towns. There has been a sharp fall in private rentings and between 1979 and 1983 a fall also in local authority rentings. The last decade has seen a gradual improvement in amenities in houses such as baths, showers and central heating which has been supported by the increase in home improvement grants and housing benefits.

INDUSTRY AND THE COMMUNITY

Any community is intrinsically linked with the work it provides. This link is most stark in areas which have suddenly experienced high unemployment such as Corby New Town. Corby was founded on a single industry, steel. When the steelworks closed in 1980 unemployment peaked to 37%. A consequence of this was the initial rise in crime rates and the depression, anxiety and disharmony in family life which is associated with unemployment. A sudden change in the type of employment can also adversely affect a community. One of the most dramatic changes in Britain was the advent of the oil industry in Scotland. At Sullom Voe in the Shetlands a deal was agreed in the mid-1970s whereby an oil terminal was established on condition that the islanders maintain planning control. Even with the involvement of local people within a few years there were increases in drunken driving, petty crime and vandalism, illegitimacy, wife battering and marital breakdown. At the same time the traditional industries of fishing and knitting suffered through not being able to compete with the high wages. Even greater problems may begin when the oil runs out after the end of the century and there is no longer any viable industry to sustain the community.

HEALTH PROMOTION IN THE COMMUNITY

Health and wellbeing can be influenced either favourably or adversely by the community within which one lives. Although the community to some extent dictates the state of wellbeing experienced by people living there, it is also in turn influenced by them. For instance, the type of food available in local shops and 'take aways' will greatly influence one's diet. However, repeated requests for certain foods such as wholegrain bread (if only white bread is normally sold) will inform shopkeepers that there is a market and encourage them to reconsider the products they stock.

Provision for sport varies between different communities although in general there has been a proliferation of sports centres in towns and cities. These include sport and leisure provision for disabled people. In most areas there is opportunity for some form of leisure activity such as football, cricket or tennis clubs, and in most towns there is a swimming pool. Local action groups and pressure on councillors can influence the provision of local facilities. Many churches have opened their halls for drop-in centres, youth clubs and sports clubs because of the need expressed by the community.

Campaigns to promote health within a local community can be a very successful means of responding to an expressed need of the community or of raising awareness of a health issue. The community targeted for the campaign may be the working place, school, college or a neighbourhood, and it may be entirely local or part of something on a wider national level. The crucial factor is that it is relevant to the lives of the people involved. For instance, in inner city areas where the incidence of muggings and assaults is relatively high it may be relevant to launch a campaign on how to avoid potentially dangerous situations and where to go to learn self-defence. General precautions could be based on those advocated by Lowe et al (1984) in their book, *Streetwise*. The following are examples of campaigns at local and national level:

1 The Tyne Tees Alcohol Education Campaign began in 1974 in the north-east of England and aimed to help people to recognize their drinking problems and to seek help; also, to promote sensible drinking. It made extensive use of the local media backed up by local talks and workshops. The campaign was evaluated and found to be an effective means of promoting health in relation to alcohol.
2 In London a helpline is available for people concerned about Acquired Immune Deficiency Syndrome. Information on where to go for help is given on posters displayed on underground trains.

3 Action on Smoking and Health (ASH) is a national body which has detailed and made available information on the damaging effects of smoking on health. Its recommendations have been extensively adopted by health authorities as part of their health promotion policy for staff and patients. In Bristol, GASP, the Group Against Smoking in Public successfully lobbied cinemas and restaurants to provide non-smoking areas or to ban smoking completely.

NEIGHBOURLINESS

A 'good neighbour' is considered by many to be someone who arrives on the scene to listen to troubles and offer advice or a little practical help just when it is needed. At all other times they are quietly in the background. Ball and Ball (1982) defined neighbourhood care as an 'informal social support at neighbourhood level, generally of a routine kind but extending to some crises, given by households whose occupants regard each other as neighbours'. In their study of neighbours they found evidence of local networks in several different types of community from villages to large towns. Certain features were consistent such as the reciprocal nature of the involvement. This is typified by the neighbourhood watch schemes whereby people take turns to watch each other's houses for signs of break-ins. They found that some types of housing could enhance contact between people and that empty houses could disrupt the rhythmic pattern of the neighbourhood. Another feature was the emergence of a natural leader who could act as spokesperson on local issues or inform professional health workers of the support needed. Newcomers frequently enhanced neighbourliness by making a positive effort to meet people and offer help. They also tended to acknowledge skills in local people which had not previously been recognized. Ball and Ball comment that where such neighbourliness exists it is crucial that professionals do not damage it, but listen to the natural spokespeople and enhance what is happening through their interest, encouragement and admiration.

Neighbourhood schemes have been developed in many areas in an attempt to harness some of this local goodwill. The success of such schemes is obviously partly determined by the nature of the community. However, it has frequently provided a catalyst for many more people to offer support, especially to those who are elderly, frail or disabled. Kent's Good Neighbour Scheme attempted to combine altruism with payment by paying volunteers to be good neighbours and visit elderly people who were waiting for residential care. The volunteers were recruited by a project leader and came from varied backgrounds although they were often mothers with a young family. The fee paid was a recognition rather than a reflection of the work involved and volunteers tended to visit far more frequently than agreed. The scheme seemed to foster goodwill, and fears that the payment would damage the nature of the relationships seemed to be unfounded.

COMMUNITY CARE

The main argument for community care is the quality of life which it can afford and which is generally regarded as superior to long-term institutional care. The DHSS report *Care in the Community* (DHSS, 1981b) outlined the philosophy for extending community care with particular reference to mentally handicapped and mentally ill people. It acknowledged the belief that these people should be moved out of long-stay institutions into homes of their own where they could experience a more 'normal' lifestyle. For many mentally handicapped people this has meant the loss of the familiar, secure but inevitably authoritarian hospital community

for the alien and sometimes dangerous 'normal' world. This transition will take a very long time for some people although early reports suggest that they are integrating into the community and are indeed experiencing a quality of life which was not possible for them before. In order to achieve this the report suggests that resources concentrated on hospitals should be released to support the more informal, community-based care which is necessary. It is sometimes argued that community care is cheaper than hospital or residential care. This is debatable as the costs involved vary considerably from person to person and for some people requiring extensive support involving many services it may actually prove more expensive. However, in order to promote health and general wellbeing it is important that everyone has a choice in where they live and in who cares for them.

For community care to be successful it involves care by the community as well as care in the community. This means acknowledging and supporting the private informal care which is carried out by family, friends and neighbours. The role of informal carers is being increasingly seen as central to community care and statutory agencies are turning their attentions to finding ways of harnessing and developing it. The reasons for this are two-fold; firstly, the realization that continuous care for someone who is dependent on others is not possible without it; and secondly that the whole community becomes stronger as a result of being involved (and conversely weaker as a result of professionals usurping the caring role of the community). Informal care may be unorganized such as a neighbour who 'pops' in occasionally, or it may take the form of a highly organized voluntary group such as the WRVS with Meals on Wheels.

The care offered by volunteers and neighbours is usually of a reciprocal nature whereby each gains from the relationship. The volunteers may gain in self-confidence through the acknowledgement and development of their skills. Simply having contact with other people may be helpful to those who might otherwise feel isolated, such as women whose children have recently started school. Ideally within a community a 'caring network' will develop within which formal and informal care will interlace and complement each other with everyone being valued for the part they play. From the earlier description of types of communities it is clear that some lend themselves to care by the community more than others. For instance, in inner city areas it will be necessary for the statutory services to take much more of a leading role and to assume responsibilities for the care of people in the absence of supporting families than would be acceptable or necessary in rural communities.

Community Care Schemes

Listed below are a few examples of the many community-based schemes which have developed in an attempt to provide support for the different care groups within the local community. All of them acknowledge the role of the family as the primary carer and aim to incorporate the support of the local community and the statutory services into a caring network which can be not only sensitive to the needs of the individual family but also flexible in the support offered. Effective community care schemes, even those organized at a national level, have as their hallmark a considerable sensitivity to what local people both need and want.

Children

Home-start. This began in Leicester in 1970 but has since been extended to a national consultancy network. It aims to promote the parenting abilities of young parents who are finding difficulty in coping with the needs of their young children. In this way it promotes the overall development of the child phys-

ically, socially, emotionally and intellectually. The volunteers, who are unpaid, are mothers who have shown that they are able to cope with the needs of young children. They have support from their organizer and colleagues in the field, and the back-up of local resources such as playgroups and toy libraries. The volunteer befriends the mother and visits her over a period of time, sometimes years, encouraging and nurturing her parenting skills. Typically the mothers being visited have very low self-esteem and one of the aims of the scheme is to develop confidence in their parenting abilities. An essential feature is the trust and friendship which develops between the two women. The scheme has been carefully evaluated and has been found to be successful in achieving its aims and is well liked by parents, volunteers and statutory services.

Under-fives Infophone. In some areas, particularly urban areas, a major difficulty is simply obtaining information about available provision. Families with children under five may be confused about the difference in the types of provision such as a day nursery or a nursery school. Statutory agencies may be able to assist but may be relatively uninformed themselves on voluntary provision. One way of overcoming this problem is to provide a book such as *Titch Hiker's Guide to Bristol* (1983). However such guidebooks are almost always out of date by the time they are published. Another way is to use a constantly updated automated system. In June 1978, the Islington preschool infophone service began which maintained updated information on a wide range of provision including crèches, toy libraries, childminding, volunteer schemes and statutory services. It made this freely available to anyone by telephone and was widely advertised in the media. Such a system can facilitate neighbourliness by putting people in touch with what is happening locally. In communities which lack cohesiveness it can go some way towards overcoming isolation. It can also help to identify communities where there is a demand for certain types of service but no provision.

Handicapped and Disabled People

Contact-a-Family. This arose from a pilot project in two London boroughs which aimed to meet the needs of families with disabled children. It aimed to bring together families with similar experiences within a neighbourhood so that they could offer support and guidance on a self-help basis. From the start the project aimed to facilitate maximum integration with local people and local facilities using volunteers whenever appropriate. A community worker is seconded from the national office to the local area whose primary function is to develop a caring network within the local community. This is achieved by initiating contact between the group, facilitating self-help, support and problem-solving, and recruiting, training and deploying volunteers. Practical initiatives include playschemes, babysitting, transport, family clubs (which take into account the needs of siblings) and a whole range of respite, recreational and educational activities.

Association of Crossroads Care Attendant Schemes Ltd. This scheme was piloted in 1974 in Rugby, Warwickshire, and aimed to support the carers of disabled people living at home. It had been observed that admission to hospital or residential care became necessary when a breakdown occurred in the family due to continual stress and strain, rather than through choice. Crossroads provides a care attendant who is trained to give both nursing assistance and domestic help similar to that normally provided by a caring relative. Their philosophy is to give a little help at the right time, help that is continuous (which means it does not stop over Bank Holidays, at weekends or at night), is reliable and given regularly. In particular the care attend-

ants can relieve the family when the primary carer is ill or in need of a holiday. The scheme also complements care given by the District Nurse when skilled nursing care is needed or when the disabled person needs two people to assist him/her. There are now many schemes throughout the UK and The Netherlands. It is organized nationally and has been funded by the DHSS since 1977. In 1981 it extended its care to include mentally handicapped people.

Elderly People

The Pathfinder Scheme. This began in 1981 in Leicestershire and uses volunteers to offer a domiciliary service to elderly mentally infirm people and their caring relatives. Volunteers are recruited from the local area and are provided with training for their work which is very varied but which includes check calls, getting people ready for day centres and hospital appointments, sitting in, escort duties, shopping, emptying commodes, preparation and supervision of meals and the support of caring relatives. These volunteers form part of a caring network which usually also includes day hospitals and day centres, community psychiatric nurses and social workers. The volunteer can do a great deal to enable the person to remain in the community and to relieve strain on the family.

Support for the Elderly Mentally Infirm (SEMI). In Bristol the voluntary organization SEMI was formed to give recognition to the elderly mentally infirm as a group. It is a relatives support group which includes a neighbourhood day care project. Staple Hill Day Centre began as a joint venture between health and social services and the local church where the centre was eventually based. Volunteers were recruited largely through the Methodist minister who, through his inspiring sermons, tapped the goodwill of the local community. Volunteers were offered some training before helping in the day centre and organizing transport and meals. Positive benefits in terms of the mental health of the members and the general health of the carers was a clear sign of the success of the scheme.

INFORMATION NETWORKS

Within a community, information about statutory agencies, the national organizations that are active locally and neighbourhood groups tend to be disseminated in a number of different ways. Local agencies such as health visitors and social workers can often put people in touch with organizations which may be helpful for them. In close-knit communities information is usually spread by word of mouth. However, there is an inherent problem in ensuring that people within the local community can have ready access to useful and accurate information even on problems concerned with day-to-day living such as welfare rights and support services.

One of the most obvious and accessible places to look for information is the local library. Libraries are usually conveniently sited with easy access for disabled and elderly people, and in rural areas there is often a mobile service. Librarians are professionally trained to provide information in the most effective way. They can coordinate and assist in the provision of information from a variety of different bodies and organizations. Most libraries have notice-boards and information racks but some are beginning to use computerized databases to ensure that information is easily accessible and up to date. For instance, the Wiltshire Information Network has an information directory for the county of Wiltshire which lists the name, address and telephone number of organizations together with details of their objectives. For someone who needs advice or help on a problem, this is a good place to start looking.

References and further reading

Abrams, P. et al (1982) *Action for Care: A Review of Good Neighbour Schemes in England*. Berkhamsted: The Volunteer Centre.

Ball, C. & Ball, M. (1982) *What the Neighbours Say. A Report on a Study of Neighbours*. Berkhamsted: The Volunteer Centre.

Beresford, P. & Croft, S. (1986) *Whose Welfare*. Brighton: The Lewis Cohen Urban Studies Centre.

Chapman, C. M. (1977) *Sociology for Nurses*. London: Baillière Tindall.

Davies, G. (1985) Mental handicap care in the community. *Nursing* 2 (36), 1065–1067.

DHSS (1981a) *Primary Health Care in Inner London*. Chairman Professor D. Acheson. London: HMSO.

DHSS (1981b) *Care in the Community. A Consultative Document on Moving Resources for Care in England*. London: HMSO.

Ewles, L. & Simnett, I. (1985) *Promoting Health. A Practical Guide to Health Education*. Chichester: John Wiley.

Frankenberg, R. (1969) *Communities in Britain. Social Life in Town and Country*. Harmondsworth: Penguin.

Harbert, W. & Rogers, P. (1983) *Community-Based Care. The Avon Experience*. London: Bedford Square Press/NCVO.

Lowe, T. et al (1984) *Streetwise. A Basic Guide to Self-defence*. London: Ariel Books/BBC.

Mitford, M. R. (1982) *Our Village*. Oxford: Oxford University Press (first published by Harrap, London 1947).

Osbourne, P. (1984) The Crossroads Care Attendance Scheme. *Nursing Times* **80** 40–41.

Peach, C., Robinson, V. & Smith, S. (1981) *Ethnic Segregation in Cities*. London: Croom Helm.

Phoenix, T. et al (editorial committee) (1985) *The Titch Hiker's Guide to Bristol. A Handbook for Parents with Babies and Young Children*. Bristol: National Childbirth Trust, Bristol Branch and Avon Under-5's Liaison Group.

Richardson, A. (1984) *Working with Self-help Groups: A Guide for the Local Professional*. London: Bedford Square Press/ NCVO.

Smith, C. (1982) *Community Based Health Initiatives. A Hardbook for Voluntary Groups.* London: NCVO.

Susser, M. W. & Watson, W. (1971) *Sociology in Medicine.* London: Oxford University Press.

Townsend, P. et al (1984) *Inequalities of Health in the City of Bristol.* Bristol: Department of Social Administration, University of Bristol.

Van Der Eyken, W. (1982) *Home-Start. A Four-Year Evaluation.* Leicester: Home-Start Consultancy.

Van Der Eyken, W. (1980) Under Fives Info-Phone. The implementation and initial evaluation of a telephone based service to parents of young children. *Early Child Development and Care* **6**, 155–178.

Walker, A., ed. (1982) *Community Care. The Family, the State and Social Policy.* Oxford: Basil Blackwell and Martin Robertson.

Whitehouse, A. (1978) Kent's Good Neighbours. *Community Care* No. 205, 15–16.

Young, M. & Willmott, P. (1957) *Family and Kinship in East London.* Harmondsworth: Penguin.

13

The Environment

In the past some of the most dramatic improvements in health have been brought about through environmental health measures. A classic example is the control of cholera which occurred in a series of outbreaks in London in the first half of the 19th century. Dr John Snow observed that the people affected had all drunk water from the Broad Street pump. Without any understanding of the link between water and the disease he proceeded to remove the handle from the pump thereby preventing the consumption of water and hence the spread of the disease. The disappearance of enteric fever, a major killer of the 19th century, was brought about by improved sanitation, and mortality from tuberculosis began to decline through reduction of overcrowding, improved nutrition, and a general raising of personal hygiene. In the latter part of the 20th century some of the major concerns which people have regarding their health are the effects of pollution and the possibility of radiation from industrial accident or war. The influence of the environment on health ranges from the home to global issues.

THE HOME

In his hierarchy of needs Maslow states that the basic needs are food, shelter and warmth. The home is therefore the basis of our health and wellbeing. To provide shelter and warmth houses must be suit-able for the climate in which they are built. In cold countries warmth is retained through insulation and snow is shed from the roof, while in hot climates the houses must be cool and shady with wide eaves or verandas to keep out the direct heat of the sun. It is difficult to generalize about other attributes which houses should have as styles and functions vary especially between cultures. However, there are certain general conditions which need to be met. The house needs to be in a state of good repair in order to afford protection. It must be dry and have adequate lighting, heating, water supply, drainage, and storage for food and fuel. At the most basic level it needs to include space for cooking, washing, sleeping and general living. Most people in developed countries expect considerably more from their home in the way of comfort and amenities in order for them to experience a sense of wellbeing. In Britain there are however many homes without sole use of basic amenities although the number is reducing, and there are many houses which are persistently damp. Such conditions can lead to physical and mental ill-health.

In a new housing development consideration is given to the immediate environment. In some new towns the roads sweep round the outskirts of the residential areas so the space between the houses can be landscaped with walkways making it quiet, safe and attractive. Some housing estates are designed so that even in an area of high-density housing residents have a sense of privacy. Many new developments include a small number of houses or flats specially designed for elderly and disabled people. Most new developments include facilities that will be needed locally such as shops, health centres, churches, parks, libraries, community centres, places of entertainment and ideally work opportunities. Car parking space and public transport is also important. Adequate local facilities are essential if the people living there are to develop into a community.

The standard of housing has a marked effect on the health of the residents. The Black Report (Townsend and Davidson, 1984) found that people living in disadvantaged areas had significantly higher mortality rates although this was largely related to socioeconomic class. A study by Brennan and Lancashire (1978) showed that death rates for children (especially younger children) were related to extent of overcrowding, lack of basic amenities, extent of unemployment among the male working population and extent of council house occupancy. The Acheson report on primary health care in inner London (DHSS, 1981) notes high mortality rates from conditions such as pneumonia, bronchitis, emphysema, accidents and suicide, and high admission rates from tuberculosis and mental illness.

Poor housing conditions can have a devastating effect on the whole family. Apart from ill-health due to physical disease it can also lead to depression and anxiety as well as financial problems. Children are affected because they cannot study or pursue hobbies in rooms which are overcrowded, poorly lit, badly ventilated, cold and damp. Dampness is often cited as the major problem. This can be caused by defective roofs and gutters, rising damp percolating up from the ground due to lack of a damp-proof course, condensation due to inadequate ventilation and often poor insulation. Families living in damp houses are often instructed to keep the heating on and the windows open and so are forced to spend excessive amounts on heating bills to make up for the structural flaws. They may also have to replace bedding and clothes ruined by mould growth. Any attempts to brighten the home with redecoration is ruined by dampness and the growth of mould on walls.

In the post-war years tower blocks of flats were built as a solution to the housing problem. They illustrate how the needs of people living in a home go beyond physical amenities. 'High-rise' living can create loneliness and social isolation, especially in certain groups of people, and have also been associated with a high incidence of ill-health. The problems are also acute in young children who are confined in a relatively small space without the opportunities for outdoor or 'messy' play. Old people may also feel imprisoned and cut off from street activity and 'callers by'. The daily routine of people moving around helps to structure time for elderly people confined to their homes and without this contact they may become lonely, disorientated and neglected.

Multiple Occupation

Many problems are created by squalid living conditions produced by one house being occupied by many families. Each family may have only one room with the basic amenities being shared. This is a particular problem in inner city areas, especially amongst immigrants who may be unable to find other accommodation and in addition may be charged high rents by unscrupulous landlords. The Housing Act of 1961 gave powers to local authorities to control this problem by insisting on additional facilities being made available and by limiting the number of people who may live in a house. The work is usually carried out by environmental health officers.

Infestation (see also Chapter 2)

One consequence of poor housing can be infestation. Old houses may be infested with *Cimex lectularis* (bed bugs) which do not carry disease but which can cause considerable irritation and discomfort from their bites, and in addition have an unpleasant smell. They live in walls, furniture, crevices, books and mattresses from which they migrate at night to bite anyone sleeping in the house. Eggs are laid in the hiding places and full development takes 6–7 weeks. The adults then exist for 6–8 weeks and are most active in hot weather. The bugs can exist for months without a meal so uninhabited property is still a risk. Infested property needs to be fumigated by the environmental health department or other pest control specialist. The most effective preventive measures are still cleanliness, sunlight and fresh air. (The traditional 'spring-clean' still has its place.) Although fitted carpets cannot be taken outside to be beaten most modern vacuum cleaners do an adequate job.

Musca domestica (house flies) do not act as vectors of infectious disease but may spread faecal-borne disease. Their legs become contaminated with faecal material which is then transferred to any human food on which they subsequently alight. The danger is greatest in areas where sewage systems are primitive and where they have the opportunity to alight on human faeces. However in any country there is the risk of flies spreading pathogenic bacteria from animal faeces to man via food. Diseases which can be spread in this way include typhoid, cholera, dysentery, poliomyelitis and infantile gastroenteritis. Flies breed in rotting vegetable matter therefore it is important to keep compost heaps, dustbins and manure as far from the house as possible. Food must be kept covered or in the refrigerator to prevent contamination. Control of flies in shops which have foods on open display is important.

Culex pipiens (mosquitoes) spread malaria and yellow fever in tropical countries but not usually in temperate climates although there have been a small number of isolated incidences of malaria in areas close to airports. The bites can be very irritating. In the home control can be effected by mosquito nets around beds. (See also Chapter 16.)

Cockroaches are mainly found in old houses, bakehouses, hospitals and institutional kitchens. There are two common species: black beetle and German cockroach. They are nocturnal in habit and usually live behind cupboards and stoves and in crevices. They are a sign of dirty and therefore unhygienic conditions and have been known to carry pathogenic organisms such as *Salmonella*, dysentery, tubercle bacilli, the cholera vibrio, streptococci and staphylococci, and are implicated in the spread of disease.

Vermin such as rats and mice are a constant menace and are implicated in the spread of disease. In some countries rats carry diseases such as plague, foot and mouth disease, rat-bite fever, *Salmonella* infections, and possibly also typhus and trench fever. Routine destruction of rats is carried out in sewers and drains and any building where food is stored. Refuse that might provide feeding materials and places that encourage the breeding of vermin must be disposed of. Dustbins should be covered whilst awaiting refuse collection.

Ventilation

Efficient ventilation means a regular interchange of air and is important for health and comfort in any building where people gather. The balance between heat lost and heat gained by the body is influenced by three main factors in the air; temperature, movement and moisture content. Heat is lost from the body in the following circumstances:

- if the air is cold;
- if the air is moving, as this increases evaporation from the body surface (hence the use of fans in hot climates);
- if the air is dry, because it can then absorb more water vapour so evaporation is more effective and cooling power is increased.

The discomfort felt in stuffy rooms, especially when a large number of people gather in a small enclosed space, is due to heat stagnation which is brought about by increased air temperature, excess moisture and lack of air movement all resulting in inadequate heat loss.

Heat can be lost from the body in three main ways; evaporation, convection and radiation. The relative importance of these factors depends on the temperature of the surrounding air. In the temperature range 13–24°C radiation is responsible for about 45% of heat loss. When the atmospheric temperature rises above 24°C heat loss by evaporation becomes important while at temperatures above 37°C it is the only method of losing heat. This is why perspiration becomes more profuse as the temperature rises. It also explains why humidity is so important a factor. Low humidity will assist evaporation and cooling but a high humidity will diminish heat loss; an atmospheric temperature of 29°C in a high humidity is more uncomfortable than 43°C in a low humidity.

Natural ventilation is aided by the provision of adequate air inlets and outlets. The inlet should be large enough to allow air to diffuse slowly but steadily throughout the room so that it does not cause a noticeable current of air; a draught. Doors and windows usually act as inlets even when they are closed although double glazing may greatly reduce this. Air also enters a room through walls especially on the windward side as most building materials are porous. Air is drawn out of a room through chimneys or ventilators placed in outside walls near the ceiling. Ventilation is also aided by movement of masses of air of unequal temperature. Convection is the movement of air due to heating. Hot air being lighter rises and is replaced by a current of colder heavier air. In this way there is a constant circular movement of air around a room (see Figure 36).

Artificial ventilation is usually used in public buildings, including modern hospitals, houses in hot humid climates and in some forms of modern transport. Air conditioning can ensure that the temperature and moisture content of the air are maintained at comfortable levels. The system depends on fresh air being forced into a building and foul air extracted. The air entering the building

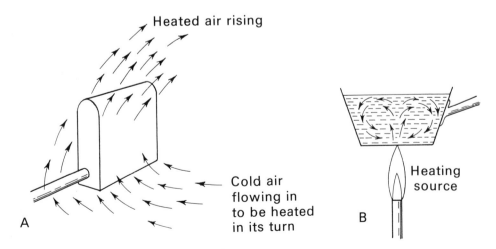

Figure 36. *Room ventilation.*

is regulated for temperature and moisture content before being driven by fans along ducts into the rooms.

In recent years a number of outbreaks of Legionnaire's disease have occurred in hotels and hospitals with air conditioning. The mode of spread is airborne where the water used to cool the air has become contaminated with the causative organism, a gram-negative bacillus. It is a serious respiratory disease and is often fatal, especially amongst elderly people who develop the disease. It is important that in any air conditioning system only water sterilized by chlorination treatment is used and that the system is cleaned out and checked regularly. Drip trays should not be allowed to collect stale water. Any pool of water used in the system should be maintained either well below or well in excess of 35°C, the temperature at which the *Legionella* bacillus thrives.

Heating

The room temperature of any building is dependent on two main factors; the heating system and insulation. The type of heating used will depend on many factors such as the size of the rooms, whether heating is continuous or intermittent, and constraints on the types of fuel that can be used. Most heating depends on radiation (the direct passage of heat from a warm object through the air to a cooler object or person), convection, and to a limited extent conduction. Methods which rely principally on convection are the most efficient. A central heating system in which 'radiators' heat the air coming into contact with them and warm the room by convection is probably the most efficient and constant type of heating. It also warms the fabric of the house, reduces condensation and enables all the accommodation to be fully used in comfort. Ideally the temperature of the main living rooms should be maintained at about 18°C. The minimum temperature for all offices and shops under the Offices, Shops and Railway Premises Act, 1963 is 16°C.

Many different types of heating apparatus and fuels are used. Smoke control areas in cities and the trend towards labour-saving methods have led to the reduction of open coal fires especially in the south of England although solid fuels such as coal are still favoured in some areas and wood and peat are still used widely in rural areas. Full central heating fired by oil, gas or electricity is becoming more popular. Solar heating is gradually becoming more efficient although its use is always likely to be limited in temperate climates.

Insulation to prevent heat loss from the building is becoming increasingly important as the cost of fuels increases. Double glazing can reduce heat loss through windows by providing an air space between the two panes of glass which cuts down loss by conduction; cavity wall insulation reduces heat loss through the walls; and lagging of roof spaces is probably the mose useful because it prevents the rising hot air from escaping through the roof. It is also important to ensure adequate draught-proofing of windows and doors to avoid excessive entry of cold air. Because of the energy savings many local authorities give grants for home insulation.

With elderly or disabled people and young children, careful planning can help to improve the heating arrangements. The room where they spend most of their time should ideally be south-facing, have three inner walls and a heating system which gives a constant, uniform warmth.

Lighting

Lighting is an essential consideration in the home and workplace. It can promote a restful environment and reduce accidents yet its contribution to a sense of wellbeing is often unacknowledged. Natural light is ideal and many new homes and office blocks are built with large windows to use this light to its full extent. Electric light is the usual form of artificial lighting. Fluorescent electric lighting is often used in kitchens and offices because it produces a steady stream of light with a minimum of shadow. The type of artificial lighting which people tend to find most restful is that which illuminates the subject matter adequately, is reasonably even with no sharp contrasts between light and shadow, and has no flickering or glare. Poor lighting is an important contributory factor in the falls which elderly people have on stairs.

Water Supplies

A constant supply of safe clean water is essential for health and it is one of the aims of the World Health Organization that there should be clean water for all. It is generally estimated that 5 litres of water per day is required for each person for domestic purposes although a more realistic figure is probably 15 litres. A person living in the developed world consumes on average in excess of 100 litres per day. Apart from domestic usage it is also required for industrial and agricultural purposes and increasingly for leisure use. In countries with temperate climates such as the UK the heavy rainfall produces water in abundance. The main sources of water are as follows:

1   *Underground water.* This is water which is created by rain water sinking into the soil until it meets an impermeable stratum of rock and forms an underground lake. Most of the earth's fresh water is locked up in underground reservoirs. By sinking a shallow well it is possible to tap this source and this is the usual method of supplying isolated rural dwellings which are not connected to the mains. The water needs to be tested at regular intervals to ensure that it has not been contaminated with sewage as this is always a possibility. The other main drawback to this system is that shallow wells tend to run dry after a prolonged drought. More permanent supplies can be tapped by sinking a deep well which draws water from below the first impermeable stratum (see Figure 37). Purification of water in wells occurs by a biological process in the passage of water through the soil. The deeper the well, the greater the purification so that artesian wells (deep wells where the water is under pressure) provide very pure water.

2   *River water.* Rivers provide water for many cities and large towns including London. River water is usually polluted by sewage and waste from the towns it has passed through. In the 19th century Britain had some of the most polluted rivers in the world. Since then there has been greater control of the discharge of trade and sewage effluents. The Control of Pollution Act, 1974 extended control

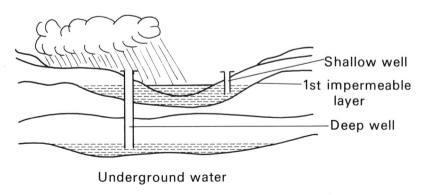

Underground water

Figure 3.7.   *Distribution of underground water and wells. By permission of OPCS.*

on the entry of polluting matter into rivers, coastal waters and sewers. The water may also be very hard owing to dissolved minerals. Rivers have the capacity for self-purification providing the pollution is not too great. Further purification is necessary to turn it into a satisfactory pure water supply.

3 *Upland surface water*. The majority of artificial water supplies are provided by the construction of a dam which collects a large volume of water from moorland districts where the water is usually pure and soft. In the UK most of the reservoirs are in the mountainous regions of Scotland and Wales. Water is carried by aqueducts to cities such as Glasgow and Birmingham.

In arid parts of the world other methods of obtaining fresh water have been attempted with limited success. These include desalination of sea water and the transportation by sea of ice flows from polar regions.

Water Purification

Before any water supply is safe for consumption it must be completely purified. This entails three stages:

1 *Storage*. Apart from providing the necessary reserve for a constant supply storage helps purification in three ways; by sedimentation of impurities and suspended matter, by the sterilizing effect of wind and sunshine, and by bacteria in the water outgrowing their food supply.

2 *Filtration*. This is the next stage in the process and consists of one of the following:

    a Slow sand filters—the sand acts as a filtering agent but its efficiency is due to the accumulation on its surface of a jelly-like mass of organic matter which holds up the impurities. In time this impedes the flow of water and must be removed and the sand cleansed.

    b Rapid chemical filters—powerful coagulants such as aluminium silicate form the jelly-like layer which acts as a filter. When the deposited impurities become too thick, compressed air is passed in the reverse direction through the filter and by agitation washes it clean.

3 *Sterilization*. This is the final stage in the process and is carried out using chlorine which oxidizes the organic matter and kills micro-organisms. To ensure that sterilization is complete the cholorination process should be introduced into the water supply at least 1 hour before the water is withdrawn. Other methods of sterilization are the use of ozone or ultraviolet rays. Water reaches the consumer in water mains which are sealed so that there is no contamination from sewage. The most likely contamination at this stage is from lead in old water pipes in houses.

Regular bacterial and chemical sampling of water is undertaken at various stages in the process to check on the efficiency of the purification process and to ensure that the water which reaches the consumer is safe.

Travellers to countries where purification of water supplies is not carried out to such exacting standards need to take extra precautions. One method of ensuring that water is safe to drink is to boil it for 5 minutes. A quicker method is to use proprietary chlorine tablets in all water to be drunk, used for brushing teeth or washing fruit. Bottled mineral water if it is available is also safe. Potassium permanganate can be used for washing fruit and vegetables and in some areas is added to wells. In regions where typhoid and cholera are rife inoculations are essential and scrupulous attention to clean water is still essential.

Fluoridation

The incidence of dental caries is partially related to the content of natural fluoride in the water drunk by the people in that area. The DHSS therefore advises all water authorities to introduce artificial fluoride in areas where the content is low and to bring it to the level of one part per million. Where this has been carried out a substantial reduction in the amount of dental caries has been observed. However some people object to this on the grounds that it is enforced medication and therefore an infringement of individual liberty.

Sewage

The system for disposing of sewage is dependent on many factors but the main aims are always to prevent possible contamination of water supplies and food, and to provide as convenient and inoffensive a system as possible.

1 *Latrines*. In camps or temporary dwellings simple latrines can be constructed. A deep hole 6–8 feet deep is dug at a distance from water supplies and cooking facilities. Earth is provided to cover the excreta so protecting it from flies. Organisms in the soil quickly render it harmless. Most latrines have some sort of seat, and a cubicle for privacy. Deep-bore latrines are used in the tropics where the risk of contamination and ill-health is greater. The hole is much deeper and the excreta is disposed of by bacterial action and subsoil water.

2 *Chemical closets*. These are the most satisfactory method for isolated houses, caravans, coaches, etc. They consist of a closet containing a powerful disinfectant. After a short period of time sterilization of the excreta is complete and the contents can be buried in a trench.

3 *Water closets*. Where water is freely available the water carriage system is the most effective way of transferring sewage from domestic premises. The water closet (WC) should not open directly into rooms where food is prepared, and should be adequately ventilated. Provision should

be made for hand washing. Sodden soap, wet nail brushes and damp hand towels are all suitable breeding grounds for bacteria. In one's own home they do not usually cause a problem although in public lavatories or in institutions they are a potential source of infection.

In a combined system waste from sinks, lavatories and baths mixes with rainwater from roofs and streets and is carried in the main sewer to the treatment works. The pipes carrying waste water from all parts of the house pour into the house drain which in turn empties into the main sewer. There are inspection chambers where these pipes meet to allow the drains to be cleaned. The sewers are laid to follow the downward slope of the land so that gravity flow aided by pumping conveys the water to the treatment plant. There are manholes approximately every 100 metres to allow for inspection and cleaning. About 140–230 litres of waste water and sewage per person per day passes through this system.

Sewage Treatment

The raw sewage is first passed through a screening process to remove coarse particles and larger solids. These are sometimes shredded and returned to the flow. The sewage then flows into tanks where the solid matter (sludge) is separated from the liquid matter (effluent). The effluent is purified by filtration through stones and chippings in graduated sizes during which time the natural cleansing processes of bacterial action and oxidation render the liquid safe to be discharged into rivers or streams. In some coastal areas treated sewage is discharged into the sea. This is done well below the water line and only at ebb tide but even so there is some danger of pollution of the beaches. Constant chemical and bacterial sampling is carried out to ensure that the sewage is safe for disposal.

Septic Tanks and Cess Pools

In rural areas where there is no main drainage system the sewage must be processed differently. Septic tanks are watertight structures with impervious linings into which sewage is retained long enough for the partial disintegration, digestion or liquefaction of the solids. This is a biological process which is carried out by anaerobic bacteria and their enzymes. The liquefied effluent is then discharged into subsoil drains or biological filters where it is purified by aerobic bacteria. The resulting effluent is discharged into a river, soakage pit or land drain and the tank is desludged approximately yearly. Cess pools are similar but they must be emptied regularly by pumping the contents into a tanker which then takes the sewage to treatment works for disposal.

Refuse Disposal

Refuse has become an increasing problem in recent years with the greater use of disposables and packaging materials and the decrease in the number of homes with facilities for burning rubbish. Plastic is a particular problem because it is not biodegradable. Refuse disposal is carried out in a number of different ways. Whilst awaiting collection it is important that refuse is stored in sound containers to keep out flies, vermin, cats and dogs. The refuse is collected in specially designed vehicles which reduce dust and scattering of rubbish. Many vehicles contain a mechanism for crushing the contents so that more can be carried in one van.

Disposal works usually deal with refuse either by incineration or by controlled tipping. With the latter method the refuse is deposited in layers not more than 6 feet thick and then sealed on all sides and covered with earth. It is important that it is not left uncovered for longer than 72 hours in order to prevent fire and infestation. Tipping can help to fill in uneven land or quarries but this must be carefully monitored by the local authority to ensure that consideration is given to the landscape so that it is not allowed to become unsightly. Some refuse is carried considerable distances by rail to refuse disposal sites. In some areas refuse is disposed of at sea but this must take place far enough out to prevent pollution of the coastline.

Recycling

Over recent years it has become increasingly clear that the earth's resources are finite. 'Waste' is no longer viewed as disposable and worthless but rather as a collection of materials to be recycled. The materials now routinely recycled are glass, paper, metal and organic waste. The key to material recovery and recycling is separation. Many towns organize special collections for papers and provide 'bottle banks' for glass. Organic waste can be used for compost. The recovery of metals is more complex and involves an industrial process. Some metal is removed from municipal waste by magnets but much comes from scrap. The world steel industry uses scrap for about 45% of its iron requirements and some countries reach 75%. Aluminium can be recycled from drink cans and some towns now provide collection points for these. Apart from the savings on raw materials, recycling also helps to stop land being used up for waste disposal. There are two main ways in which recycling can be encouraged; firstly by making people more aware of conservation issues and the benefits to the environment, and secondly by offering financial inducements such as deposit payments on bottles and cans.

TRANSPORT

A powerful influence on the shape of the environment is the infrastructure of transport. During the 1960s the first phase motorways were built in Britain. This facilitated economic development by linking industrial areas and speeding up the transportation of goods, nationally and internationally. The building of the motorways also coincided with a massive increase in the number of car owners. Motorways made the more remote parts of the country accessible and increased the mobility of people for work and leisure purposes. The volume of traffic has created problems in some towns and villages from the noise, dirt and danger. This has been reduced in some by diverting long-distance traffic, particularly heavy goods vehicles, onto by-passes or orbital roads. The second phase of motorways built in the 1970s linked every major city with a population of more than 250 000 and all major ports and airports.

Public transport systems include road, rail, sea and air and they may be locally or nationally organized. Public transport is especially important in rural and remote areas although it may be uneconomic to run and therefore very limited as a service. Country bus services linking villages with neighbouring market towns, and air and sea services to outer islands, sometimes come under threat of closure for this reason. The maintenance of roads is the responsibility of the highways department of the local authority.

LEISURE

The infrastructure of roads and public transport has helped the leisure industry to develop. Areas of outstanding natural beauty such as the Lake district, the Highlands, the Gower peninsula and the Cornish coast are all relatively accessible for holidays and weekends. The pressure on some of these areas especially during the summer months has led to the need for conservancy measures to protect the environment from erosion. There is always the risk that communities will be adversely affected by the leisure industry.

In the 19th century huge areas of the highlands of Scotland were turned into grouse shooting and deer hunting playgrounds for the wealthy, thereby destroying some of the crofting communities. Today some communities in remote beautiful villages are effectively being depopulated by the buying of holiday and weekend cottages. However some places such as historic towns, areas of natural beauty and specially designed leisure parks are dependent on tourism for their economy. With careful attention to problems such as traffic, car parking and the protection of the natural environment, and with the provision of necessary amenities, these areas can successfully serve the needs of those who live there as well as those who visit.

THE ATMOSPHERE

Fresh air has long been regarded as one of the fundamental requirements for health. Yet it remains unclear what constitutes clean air or, conversely, the level of pollution that constitutes a health hazard. There are several forms of air pollution including dust, gases, fogs, vapours, smoke and chemicals. A major pollutant which is often overlooked is cigarette smoke in the home. Chen et al (1986) found that exposure of children to household smoke in early life increased the risk of severe respiratory disease. This frequently necessitates hospital admission. Other associated health problems include asthma, angina attacks and bronchitis.

Smoke

A major cause of pollution in Britain is the domestic coal-burning fire which is responsibile for about 85% of the smoke in the atmosphere. It produces more smoke and grit per kilogram burned than factory chimneys. In the more prosperous South many families burn smokeless fuels or have central heating. In the North and

Midlands the preference for open coal fires remains strong and in some cities leads to serious air pollution. The Clean Air Act, 1956 enables local authorities to declare smoke control areas by which the emission of smoke from any chimney is an offence. Over 90% of the Greater London area is covered by smoke control areas demonstrating the success of clean air policies.

Traffic

Pollution from motor vehicles is a sizeable problem in many urban areas and includes a mixture of noise, gases, grit and dust, and lead. Diesel engines if properly maintained are relatively inoffensive. Petrol engines on the other hand emit a complex mixture of pollutants, particularly carbon monoxide.

Lead

Each year an estimated 450 000 tonnes of lead are released into the air, compared with 3500 tonnes from natural sources. Half of this comes from vehicle exhaust as it is added to petrol to improve its combustion properties; other sources include paint, surma, and lead shot used by anglers. Lead does not decay and therefore once it has accumulated in the soil or the body it is permanent. In Britain about 280 000 homes still have lead pipes which are responsible for tap water which is in excess of the European Commission directive and it may be the 1990s before this situation is rectified. Lead particles are taken into the body in food, water, inhalation and on fingers and lead accumulates in the bones where it replaces calcium. It is a neurotoxin and has been associated with a number of health problems in children, including behaviour problems, low achievement, IQ loss and even brain damage. Children who live near busy traffic are particularly at risk. Some countries are now changing to lead-free petrol to reduce this health risk. Low-lead petrol has been sold in

the UK since December 1985 and from 1991 all new cars will be built to run on lead-free petrol. Since July 1987 lead has not been added to paint.

Carbon Dioxide

Carbon dioxide is steadily rising in the atmosphere due to the combustion of fossil fuels and the removal of forests which produce oxygen. Carbon dioxide has a role in maintaining warmth and therefore it is theorized that there will be a gradual rise in temperature. This is known as the 'greenhouse effect'.

Sulphur Dioxide

This is produced wherever sulphur is burned and as sulphur is present in nearly all fossil fuels it is emitted freely in industrialized countries. The effects on health are not fully understood but it is a toxic component of smog. Smog is formed when fog traps impurities and causes a build-up in their concentration. In 1952 4000 people in London died in a smog which lasted 5 days. Sulphur dioxide with associated sulphates and acids combines with water vapour in the atmosphere to form droplets of sulphuric acid, 'acid rain', which is causing serious ecological damage in parts of Europe and North America.

Chlorofluorocarbons

There is a theory that chlorofluorocarbons which are released from aerosol cans, refrigerators and air conditioners break down and permanently damage the ozone level in the atmosphere. It is believed that this may take decades and therefore the damage has not yet been felt. Ozone is responsible for filtering radiation from the sun and if damaged could lead to an increase in skin cancers as well as having adverse effects on crops. In view of this the United States has banned the use of these substances.

Asbestos

There are three forms of asbestos: white (chrysotile), brown (amosite) and blue (crocidolite). They form a group of impure magnesium silicate minerals which occur in fibrous form and have been used extensively for fire protection and insulation. Asbestos dust is now recognized to be harmful to health under certain conditions. People at risk are those who work with the material and anyone in prolonged contact with the dust, for instance workers in buildings where it has been allowed to deteriorate unchecked. Conditions associated with asbestos are asbestosis, pleural plaques and diffuse pleural thickening, cancer of the lung and mesothelioma.

Chemicals

There are two main groups of chemicals that are in common use as pesticides. Organochlorines (or chlorinated hydrocarbons) are persistent and non-biodegradable in the environment. It has been found that 50% of DDT is still in the soil after 10 years. It is toxic and selectively soluble in fat and has even been found in the fat of penguins of the Antartic. When ingested in food or water it is stored in the bodies of animals and man where it accumulates. In the USA high levels in body fat led to a ban on its use there in 1972. Another group of pollutive chlorophenol compounds widely used in industry are polychlorinated biphenyls (PCBs) which are similar to DDT and which are also toxic and persistent and accumulative in body tissue. The second group, organophosphorus compounds, are synthetic organic insecticides; an example is carbaryl which kills insects and is used to treat head lice. These are unstable, do not persist and are biodegradable. They kill pests by attacking the nervous system. Because they do not accumulate in the body they are less harmful although they are highly toxic to

anyone in direct contact and need careful storage and use.

Aside from the accumulative effect in the environment, chemicals may cause considerable damage to health from industrial accidents. An accident in Seveso, north Italy, in 1976 led to a wide area becoming contaminated with dioxin. Dioxin, or TCDD, is a by-product of the production of the herbicide '245T'. The long-term effects of dioxin toxicity are totally unknown and no effective tolerance for humans has been established. It is however known to be highly persistent in the ecosystem. Health problems which followed the incident included skin damage, liver complaints, spontaneous abortions and significantly higher levels of congenital deformities. A similar industrial incident in Bophal, India, was responsible for over 2000 deaths as well as blindness and severe lung damage.

Townsend's work on inequalities of health in the city of Bristol (Townsend et al, 1984) found areas of unexpectedly high mortality and noted that these tended to be near the sites of heavy industry. A causative link has not been established but only by continually monitoring the health of people in industrial areas will problems be highlighted.

Radiation

Atmospheric radiation emanates from both natural and man-made sources. Background natural sources include cosmic rays, rocks, soil, natural building materials and the human body. The three main sources of man-made radiation are:

1 X-rays used in medicine and dentistry. This is the major source and should be used sparingly in diagnostic work. The effect is cumulative in the body and the total amount over a lifetime needs to be monitored. Radiation affects cells most when they are reproducing and larger doses cause the cells to lose their reproductive powers entirely. Reproductive

organs must therefore be shielded to prevent possible sterility or congenital malformations in children. Pregnant women should not be X-rayed unless absolutely necessary because of the potential damaging effect on the unborn child. Radiography departments are shielded and workers wear protective clothing. The level of radiation is continuously monitored. Radiation is also increasing from the use of radioisotopes in industry, research and medicine.

2 Fallout from nuclear weapons and their testing. The survivors of the nuclear attacks on Hiroshima and Nagasaki serve to remind us of the lasting damage from radiation. They have a higher incidence of chronic myeloid leukaemia and congenital abnormalities. Fallout from nuclear weaponry testing still occurs although it has diminished since 1963. It may still affect the health of the people involved in the work before that time.

3 Industrial emissions, especially from nuclear reactors and processing installations. High-level waste is sealed in containers and dumped at sea and there are stringent regulations controlling this. There is some concern however that in the long term these might leak and radiation enter the marine ecosystem. Low and medium activity wastes are either stored on land or disposed of at sea. In the UK 75% of total waste is produced at Sellafield in Cumbria and liquid effluent is discharged into the Irish Sea where it is adsorbed onto rocks on the sea floor. Study continues into the environmental pathways of radioactive waste and the chemical changes which occur in polluted sediments to check that it does not reach the coast where it could be absorbed by plants, animals and people.

The levels of radioactivity along the Cumbrian coast and the health of people who live in that region are monitored. Alleged 'clusters' of cancer cases in the area around Sellafield particularly amongst young people with leukaemia led to an independent investigation into this issue in 1983. Because the numbers involved were so small the findings were inconclusive. The studies demonstrated that in West Cumbria as a whole mortality from childhood cancer was near the national average, particularly for cancers other than leukaemia. But it did not exclude local pockets of high incidence and noted a higher incidence of leukaemia in young people resident in the area although there was no proof that this was caused by nuclear discharges from the plant. The report made a number of recommendations including further study of young people with cancers and closer monitoring of the health implications of radioactive discharges around Sellafield.

Nuclear energy has some advantages over fossil fuels. Health risks to the workers are far below those in the coal-mining industry, and nuclear power produces no sulphur and therefore is not associated with the formation of acid rain. Safety standards are particularly stringent although there is always the risk of accidents, and radioactive leaks are known to occur from time to time. In April 1986, a devastating incident occurred at Chernobyl in the USSR. It led to a large number of people becoming contaminated with radioactivity, an area with a radius of about 100 miles was evacuated, and the cloud of radioactive dust affected several neighbouring countries. This together with the incident at Three Mile Island at Harrisburg, Pennsylvania, in 1979 reminds us that the use of nuclear power whether for energy or weaponry is potentially the most serious threat to the environment which man has created.

References and further reading

Arvill, R. (1983) *Man and Environment. Crisis and the Strategy of Choice*, 5th edn. Harmondsworth: Penguin.

Brennan, M. & Lancashire, R. (1978) Association of infant mortality with housing status and unemployment. *Journal of Epidemiology and Community Health* **32**, 28–33.

Carson, R. (1965) *Silent Spring*. Harmondsworth: Penguin.

Chen, Y. et al (1986) Influence of passive smoking on admissions for respiratory illness in early childhood. *British Medical Journal* **293**, 303.

Dix, H. M. (1981) *Environmental Pollution*. Chichester: John Wiley.

DHSS (1980) *Lead and Health. The Report of a DHSS Working Party on Lead in the Environment*. London: HMSO.

DHSS (1981) *Primary Health Care in Inner London* (chairman Professor D. Acheson). London: HMSO.

Lenihan, J. & Fletcher, W. W. (1976) *Environment and Man*. Vol. 3, *Health and the Environment*. Glasgow: Blackie.

Meredith Davies, J. B. (1983) *Community Health, Prevention Medicine and Social Services*, 5th edn. London: Baillière Tindall.

Myers, N. (1985) *The Gaia Atlas of Planet Management*. London: Pan Books.

Price, B. C. (1983) *Friends of the Earth Guide to Pollution*. London: Maurice Temple Smith.

Report of the Independent Advisory Group (chairman Sir Douglas Black) (1984) *Investigation into the Possible Increased Incidence of Cancer in West Cumbria*. London: HMSO.

Rogers, R. (1981) *Lead Poison*. London: New Statesman.

Smith, M. et al (1983) *The Effects of Lead Exposure on Urban Children*. Institute of Child Health, University of Southampton.

Townsend, P & Davidson, N. (1984) *Inequalities in Health. The Black Report*. Harmondsworth: Penguin.

Townsend, P. et al (1984) *Inequalities of Health in the City of Bristol*. Department of Social Administration, School of Applied Social Studies, University of Bristol.

14

Food Hygiene and Health

The worldwide distribution of food provides the most dramatic illustration of the difference between the world's poor and rich nations. During the 1980s pictures of starving people in the north-eastern countries of Africa pricked the consciences of those in the affluent west where mountains of unused food were collecting. The production and distribution of food therefore has to be viewed in global terms. However, the problems of the third world countries should not completely detract from the tremendous advances that have been made in developed countries to make available food that is wholesome, convenient, enjoyable, varied, relatively cheap and in plentiful supply. Methods of food production and marketing have led to an ever-increasing variety of foods, and for certain seasonal foods to be available throughout the year. This has given us an unprecedented choice in what we eat and contributes greatly to our standard of living and sense of wellbeing.

NUTRITION

Nutrition is a major factor in health maintenance and the prevention of certain diseases. Substances which serve as food for the body are those which it can use as fuel for providing warmth and energy and those which provide body-building materials for the growth and repair of tissues. Nutritional needs vary

depending on health status and physical characteristics, for instance children require additional body building material because of their growth. However, the general principles of nutrition apply to everyone.

Proteins

Proteins are essential for building cell protoplasm and are therefore necessary for growth and repair of tissues. Proteins are formed from amino acids which contain nitrogen, a vital element which is present in all known forms of life. Plants and vegetables are rich sources of protein, especially peas, beans and cereals. The protein in animal foods is similar to human protein in composition and is found in meat, fish, eggs, cheese and milk. The body requires about 22 amino acids and all but eight of these can be produced in the body. Those which cannot be produced are called 'essential amino acids' and must be supplied in the diet simultaneously and in the correct proportions. Foods which contain all the essential amino acids are called complete proteins; most meat and dairy products are in this category. If one of the essential amino acids is missing, all amino acids are reduced in the same proportion as the one that is low, e.g. a food containing 100% of lysine requirement but only 20% of methionine requirement results in only 20% of the protein in that food being used as protein by the body. Most cereals, fruits and vegetables are incomplete protein foods and therefore a vegan diet, which contains no animal products, requires careful planning.

Carbohydrates

These are the chief sources of body fuel and include starch and sugar. The substance is made in nature by the action of sunlight on the chlorophyll in the leaves of growing plants. Most carbohydrate foods are obtained from plants in the form of cereals, vegetables and fruit and most contain sugar. Simple sugars, or monosaccharides, dissolve quickly and are easily absorbed. There are three main types: glucose which is found in fruits such as grapes, vegetables, especially sugar cane, sweet potatoes, new potatoes, sweet corn and onions, and honey; fructose which is also found in fruits, vegetables and honey; and galactose which is principally found in milk.

Fat

This also serves as body fuel. It is obtained from both animal and vegetable sources. Glycerol molecules are constant in all fats but the structure and length of the three fatty acids with which they combine varies considerably. Their chains consist of carbon atoms linked together with hydrogen atoms attached along their length. Carbon atoms have the capacity to join with four other atoms and the link between adjacent carbon atoms accounts for two of these bonds. The remaining two are free to combine with hydrogen. In 'unsaturated' fats the free links on the carbon chain have not all combined with hydrogen. 'Polyunsaturated' fats are those in which there are many unfilled spaces. When all the spaces have been filled the fat is described as 'saturated'. In general, vegetable fats are largely unsaturated and are liquid at room temperature, although there are exceptions, e.g. coconut. Animal fats are saturated and are hard at room temperature. Mar-

garine is made hard by saturating it with hydrogen atoms. There are now several soft margarines which are 'high in polyunsaturates'. There is some evidence that saturated fats contribute to an increase in the level in cholesterol in the blood which is believed to be a contributory factor in coronary heart disease.

Vitamins

These are essential for normal health. Without them deficiency diseases occur. Vitamins A, D, E and K are fat-soluble and are therefore found in fat-containing foods. Vitamin A is present in animal fats and, in a slightly different form, in green and yellow vegetables and fruit. It is necessary for growth in children and vision. It aids the growth and repair of body tissues and helps maintain the condition of the skin; it also protects mucous membranes against the effects of air pollution and infection. Vitamin D is present in animal fats and fish oils and is also manufactured in the body when the skin is exposed to sunlight. It is necessary for the development of bones and teeth in children and because it aids the absorption of calcium and phosphorus it is important in maintaining normal heart action and the blood clotting mechanism. The vitamin is utilized more effectively when taken with vitamin A. Vitamin E is recognized as being essential though no deficiency syndrome has been identified. It has been linked to infertility in animal studies and is thought to protect certain sex hormones. Together with B group vitamins it is sometimes recommended for women at the time of the menopause. It is found in corn, whole grains, peanuts and eggs. Vitamin K is necessary for the formation of prothrombin, a substance which is essential for the normal clotting of blood. It can be manufactured in the intestine in the presence of certain bacteria. The vitamin occurs naturally in leafy green vegetables, milk, eggs and polyunsaturated fats but, as with all fat-soluble vitamins, it can only be absorbed in the presence of bile. All fat-soluble vitamins can be stored in the body and therefore excessive intake can result in poisoning.

Vitamin C and the B group vitamins are water-soluble. They are not stored in the body but are excreted in the urine. B group vitamins are found in a similar group of foods and have a functional relationship. They help to provide the body with energy by converting carbohydrate to glucose and are vital in the metabolism of fats and proteins. They are also necessary for the normal functioning of the nervous system. Almost all the B vitamins are found naturally in brewer's yeast, liver and whole-grain cereals; they are also produced by the intestinal bacteria. It is possible that the action of antibiotic drugs may reduce this source. Vitamin C is present in most fresh fruit and vegetables, but is destroyed by long cooking or by keeping foods hot for long periods. It plays an important part in the healing process because it facilitates connective tissue formation; it is necessary for the manufacture of red blood cells, and is effective against certain infections.

Mineral Salts

These are required by the body for a variety of functions including the regulation of tissue activity. They are inter-related in human physiology and cannot be considered in isolation from each other. This makes their supplementation for deficiencies more complicated than vitamin supplementation. Most are present in adequate amounts in a mixed diet. Calcium, iron and iodine are the three minerals whose supply is particularly critical. Calcium is found in milk and most dairy produce and in green vegetables such as broccoli and kale. It is absorbed more efficiently in the presence of vitamin D and is necessary for normal clotting of the blood and functioning of the nerve tissue. Iron is obtained from lean meat, egg yolk and green vegetables and plays an essential role in oxygen transport and cellular respiration. It is necessary in the diet to prevent certain types of anaemia, particularly in women during the child-bearing years when iron is lost during menstruation and pregnancy. Iodine is necessary for the manufacture of thyroid hormone and is found in seafoods and vegetables grown on iodine-rich soils. The use of iodized salt is a successful way of ensuring adequate iodine uptake in iodine-poor regions although people who eat low-salt diets may need supplements.

Water

This accounts for approximately two-thirds of the body weight and is not only the most abundant but also the most important nutrient. It is involved in nearly every body process, is the primary mode of transport for nutrients and is necessary for all building functions. In addition it helps in the maintenance of normal body temperature and is essential for carrying waste materials out of the body. Virtually all food contains water, particularly fruit and vegetables. The average adult requires up to 3 litres of water daily, of which about 1.5 litres are taken as drinks and just over 1 litre in food. A similar quantity is passed out of the body as perspiration and excretion.

Fibre

This is not a nutrient because it cannot be digested. It is however essential for normal functioning of the bowel as it increases the bulk of the stool and stimulates peristalsis. It prevents constipation and has an important role in the prevention of other bowel disorders such as haemorrhoids and cancer of the bowel. It is found in whole grains, wholemeal bread, bran cereals, vegetables and fruit.

FOOD PRODUCTION IN THIRD WORLD COUNTRIES

Detailed consideration of the complex problems regarding the production and distribution of food in third world countries is beyond the scope of this book. However, it is impossible to discuss food and health without reference to hunger and hunger-related diseases. Whilst it is certainly true that the earth can provide enough food for everyone, an estimated 500 million people (more than one in ten on the planet) consume less than the 'minimum critical diet' to stay healthy and maintain body weight, and about 40 million people die each year from the effects of hunger. Nutritional deficiency syndromes have been categorized as follows:

1 protein–energy malnutrition (PEM), kwashiorkor, marasmus,
2 vitamin A deficiency, xerophthalmia,
3 vitamin B1 deficiency, beri-beri,
4 vitamin B2 deficiencies, pellagra, ariboflavinosis,
5 nutritional neuropathies.

For further information see Manson-Bahr and Apted (1982), Chapter 35.

The areas worst affected are Africa, Asia and Latin America. There are many factors which contribute to inadequate food supplies. These include:

1 demineralization of the soils in tropical areas through tropical storms,
2 ravaging of crops by pests (in temperate climates winter is a natural pesticide),
3 overgrazing of grasslands, leading to soil erosion,
4 deforestation leading to soil erosion,
5 overworking of soil leading to soil exhaustion and erosion,
6 desertification—the advance of the desert as a result of overgrazing and devegetation,
7 excessive use of land for cash crops for export which reduces available land for subsistence farming,
8 population pressures,
9 inadequate farming methods,
10 lack of money for investment in new technology (the foreign exchange for cash crops, such as coffee and peanuts, is relatively small and prices fluctuate wildly on the world market).

These problems however are not insurmountable and in some parts of the world, notably China, tremendous strides have been made to improve the situation. The main aim is for people to be able to produce enough food to feed themselves. This involves making better use of the existing farmlands and restricting advancement into marginal lands. Relief aid to famine-stricken countries has been directed towards long-term changes as well as immediate relief. Measures include:

1 Protecting the borderlands of the natural desert by maintaining or planting shrubs and bushes which serve as barriers to hold back dunes.
2 Planting shelter belts of trees along roads and tracks to act as aerodynamic windbreaks.
3 Prevention of devegetation of lands through rotational grazing which gives overworked pastures time to recover.
4 Improving devegetated lands by planting legume grasses, such as clover and alfalfa, which help to restore soil fertility.
5 Intensified use of good lands which involves growing crops in rapid rotation and interplanting several crops at a time. Crop residues and other mulch can be used as 'green manure'.
6 Careful use of medium-value land for crops that withstand long rainless spells, e.g. millet, sorghum, certain beans and fast-maturing maize. Rotation with other crops and fallow periods are needed to restore the soil's fertility.
7 Genetically engineered crops which can thrive in harsh environments.
8 Establishing a careful balance between the use of land for cash crops to bring in money for investment and its use for subsistence crops.

FOOD AND HEALTH IN THE UNITED KINGDOM

In the UK a national nutritional policy ensures that basic requirements regarding the availability of food and the nutritional status of certain vulnerable groups are met. They are:

1 All essential foodstuffs should be available to the whole population at reasonable cost.

2 Certain priority foods should be provided for specific sections of the community. These include: (a) vitamins and subsidized dried milks for mothers and young children; (b) free school meals for children whose families are on low income; (c) meals on wheels and lunch clubs for elderly people (both services are subsidized).

3 Standards of milk production are controlled nationally. This also includes other dairy products such as ice-cream.

4 Minimum standards are maintained for many foodstuffs and constant sampling ensures that these are reached.

5 Some foods are fortified to guarantee adequate supplies of vitamins, e.g. vitamins A and D in margarine.

6 Adulteration of foodstuffs is prevented by extensive legislation controlling the use of preservatives and additives.

7 Foodstuffs must be free from disease. This is achieved by meat and food inspection at ports, abattoirs and markets.

8 Food handlers must observe hygiene measures to avoid contamination of the food (see below).

9 Continuous health education is carried out to promote healthy eating. Recent reports on food, notably the NACNE Report (National Advisory Committee on Nutrition Education, 1983) and the COMA Report (Committee on Medical Aspects of Food, 1984), have provided guidelines which aim to reduce the incidence of heart disease and other food-related disorders (see Chapter 2).

Food Hygiene

Food hygiene is usually taken to mean those aspects of food production and handling which deal with the prevention of food-borne infections and diseases caused by chemical poisons. To ensure that the food which reaches the consumer is clean and safe it is necessary to prevent contamination and to ensure that microorganisms which exist in food in spite of all precautions are not allowed to increase to a level which will cause ill effects. This involves everyone in contact with the food; the producer, manufacturer, distributor, retailer and consumer. Legislation is necessary to safeguard food hygiene and the Food Hygiene (general) Regulations, 1970, Act aims to eliminate food contamination in shops, restaurants and factories. Environmental Health Officers make periodic checks to ensure that the standards are maintained. Clearly, those people who work in restaurants, institutions or factories must be especially vigilant. However, for prevention to be effective everyone involved needs to understand the basic principles. The main requirements of food hygiene are:

1 *Personal hygiene.* Contamination can easily occur during the handling of food. Clean hands and fingernails are therefore essential and food should be handled as little as possible. Hands must be washed before handling food, after going to the toilet and after blowing one's nose. Cuts or abrasions need to be covered with a waterproof dressing. Working clothes should be clean and the hair covered. There should be no smoking over food. Anyone with an illness such as a sore throat, cold or gastroenteritis should refrain from handling food. In the home, when this is not feasible, extra attention to hygiene can help to prevent the rest of the family being affected.

2 The water supply must be safe.

3 Sewage, liquid waste and garbage must be carefully disposed of to prevent the spread of disease.

4   Food must be protected from contamination at all times. This includes regular cleaning of refrigerators and any place where food is stored. Raw foods, especially meats must be stored away from cooked foods. In shops adequate shelving and other storage space, preferably enclosed and dustproof, must be available as it is against the regulations for food to be placed lower than 18 inches from the floor.

5   Utensils and equipment must be washed and kept clean when stored. Electric dishwashers clean more thoroughly than washing up by hand. Dishcloths and tea towels need to be changed frequently.

6   The premises must be kept clean and maintained in a way to deter vermin, insects and rodents. The walls and floors of food rooms therefore need to be in good repair and constructed of easily washable, impermeable material. Toilets also need to be in good repair with hot running water and clean towels and soap. There needs to be adequate light and ventilation.

food production

Milk

milk is a valuable food because it contains protein, carbohydrate and fat and is rich in calcium and phosphorus. It is however a particularly good medium for the growth of bacteria. Cow's milk is most widely available although the production of goat's milk is increasing. By law milk must contain not less than 3% fat or 8.5% of milk solids other than fat. No colouring matter, water, dried or condensed milk, skimmed or separated milk or preservative may be added. Dairy farmers must be registered by the Ministry of Agriculture, Fisheries and Food who ensure, by regular veterinary inspection and testing, that the herd is free from disease and that the milk is being produced in hygienic conditions. The milk is immediately cooled and kept cool until

collection. A dairy worker must notify the 'Proper Officer' of the local authority if he/she contracts food poisoning, gastroenteritis or other specified diseases, and any employee may be medically examined if suspected of suffering from a disease likely to cause infection in milk. Tuberculosis has virtually disappeared from the herds in Britain, and brucellosis can be prevented from infecting humans by pasteurization.

At present there are four special designations for milk; untreated, pasteurized, sterilized and ultra-heat-treated:

1   Untreated milk (green top) receives no heat treatment but strict regulations control its production and retail. It is placed directly into retail containers.

2   Pasteurized milk is the most commonly available. The object is to destroy all pathogenic bacteria including tuberculosis bacilli, *Brucella abortus*, streptococci, staphylococci, typhoid and paratyphoid bacilli and diphtheria bacilli. Pasteurization involves heat treatment in one of the following ways: (a) the milk is raised to a temperature of $62.8 - 65.5°C$ and maintained there for at least 30 minutes and then rapidly cooled to a temperature of not more than $10°C$ ('Holder' process); or (b) the milk is kept at a temperature of not less than $71°C$ for at least 5 seconds and immediately cooled to not more than $10°C$ (High Temperature Short Time—HTST—process).

3   Sterilized milk is filtered and homogenized, heated to $108.9°C$ for 10–12 minutes then cooled. The bottles are sealed so that if they remain unopened the milk will keep for a long period. The disadvantage of this method is that the flavour and colour of the milk are affected.

4   Ultra-heat-treated (UHT) milk has been retained at a temperature of not less than $132°C$ for a period of not less than 1 second, and then immediately placed in sterile containers in which it is supplied to the consumer. It can be safely stored for several months if unopened.

Milk is available in several different forms apart from the traditional 'doorstep' fresh milk. Dried milk produced by spray drying will keep for many months although once reconstituted must be treated as fresh milk. It is useful where fresh milk is unobtainable. Evaporated and condensed milk is fresh milk from which the water content has been reduced. It is then sealed in tins and can be kept for a long time provided the tin is not damaged. Condensed milk usually has some sugar added. Once opened they must be stored and treated as fresh milk. Skimmed and semi-skimmed milk is readily available. It is cheaper than full cream milk and is also low in fat and calories.

Other Dairy Produce

Ice-cream must contain not less than 5% fat and not less than 7% milk solids other than fat. It must be heat treated at either 65.5°C for 30 minutes or not less than 71°C for 10 minutes. After heat treatment the mixture must be reduced to a temperature of 7.3°C or less within 1 hour and kept at this temperature until freezing is carried out.

Butter is prepared by churning cream until the globules of fat adhere together. Not more than 16% moisture is allowed in butter and no preservatives or colouring matter may be added.

Margarine is made from either vegetable oils or a mixture of vegetable and animal fats. It must not contain more than 16% water or 10% of butter fat. It is usually fortified with vitamins A and D. Some margarines are made from polyunsaturated fats which it is believed produce less cholesterol in the bloodstream.

Cheese is prepared by coagulating the caseinogen of milk with rennet. There are no legal standards and the composition varies with the locality. Cheese is usually prepared from pasteurized milk because tubercle and typhoid bacilli are not destroyed in the cheese-making process.

However some varieties are made from untreated milk. The fat content of cheeses is subject to considerable variation depending on the type of cheese, its age and the composition of the initial milk. Ripe, hard pressed cheeses usually have the highest fat content, at about 35%; semi-hard cheeses have about 33% fat content; and soft cheeses about 29% fat.

Eggs must be sold whilst they are fresh and under EEC regulations must be date stamped.

Meat

All meat is examined prior to sale and slaughter houses must be registered and inspected regularly. All imported meat must bear a certificate from the country of origin which must show that the meat was inspected before and after slaughter and that precautions were taken in its preparation to prevent endangering public health. If there is any sign of the disease the whole or part of the carcase may be condemned. Meat which is fit for human consumption is stored in refrigerated rooms, and in refrigerated lorries if transported over long distances. Some meat is prepared in a highly specific way for religious purposes; kosher meat for Jews and halal meat for Muslims.

Apart from inspection for disease there are regulations concerning the use of hormones to promote growth, tenderizers and antibiotics in animals and poultry. Antibiotics, by means not fully understood, have been found to promote more efficient use of nutrients and so accelerate growth, as well as preventing infection. However, given prophylactically in feeds they perpetuate resistant strains of pathogens and are therefore recommended for treatment only. However, *Salmonella* in animals from infected feedstuffs makes the widespread use of antibiotics inevitable. This is especially the case when animals are placed in conditions of great stress such as transportation over long distances.

Shellfish

Shellfish may be infected with typhoid, hepatitis A, paratyphoid or *Salmonella* if collected from areas contaminated with sewage. Collection is therefore prohibited in such areas. However, over 500 cases of hepatitis A and acute gastroenteritis, in which cockle consumption was frequently implicated, were reported to the Disease Surveillance Centre in England and Wales in the first half of 1985. It is even more important to avoid raw or partially cooked shellfish in countries where cholera is common. Oysters are usually cleansed by placing them for two days in sea water which has been purified by ultraviolet light. Some stations may be ineffective if the water is taken from a polluted source or if the output of ultraviolet light is low. Mussels and other shellfish are usually cleansed by covering them with freshly chlorinated seawater for two days.

Bread

Most bread in the UK is made from wheat flour although some is available made from rye and other grains. Wholemeal bread is made from flour in which 90% of the original wheat grain is used. It is brown, has a 'nutty flavour' and contains higher proportions of proteins, vitamin B1 and nicotinic acid than whiter flours of 70% extraction. Its higher fibre content also has a valuable role in digestion providing bulk to the stool and thereby regulating bowel motions and preventing constipation. In recent years wholemeal bread has increased in popularity as a 'health food' and because of its superior flavour. Bread is rarely a vehicle for food poisoning because its low moisture content does not encourage bacterial growth. However, bacteria causing typhoid and dysentery may be transported from the hands of a carrier to the consumer and all bread should therefore be wrapped. Also there is growing concern about mould on bread which has

been found to be associated with liver disease in animals.

FOOD PRESERVATION

Food may be preserved by the following methods:

1 *Freezing or chilling.* This principle relies on the inability of bacteria to multiply at low temperatures. Freezing occurs at temperatures below $-4.4°C$; chilling at temperatures between $-3°C$ and $-1°C$. Quick freezing in individual retail packs has become increasingly popular and this involves passing the food through the critical temperature range within 1–2 hours. Apart from the convenience of this food it also preserves taste and nutrients. However, once frozen food is thawed bacterial multiplication begins again and so the food must be cooked and eaten without too much delay. Thawed food should never be refrozen.

2 *High temperatures.* This principle is used in canning and bottling. The food is put into the container, covered with liquid and then cooked, sterilized and sealed. The food will remain sound if the container is properly sealed so that air cannot enter. Cans are often cooled under water and it is important that the water is pure. The 1964 Aberdeen typhoid outbreak was caused by unclean water entering a tin of corned beef through a tiny pinhole. Some canned foods can remain safe for consumption for many years. However, in some, slow chemical changes may occur and it is therefore advisable to consume all canned foods within 1 year.

3 *Curing or smoking.* This method is traditionally used for bacon, ham and fish to enhance the flavour. Phenolic compounds in the wood smoke enter the flesh and inhibit the growth of organisms. Excessive consumption of smoked foods has been associated with a significantly high incidence of cancer of the stomach.

4 *Drying.* This is an effective way of preserving substances such as egg, milk, fish, fruit, vegetables and pulses. Bacterial growth is inhibited by the lack of moisture whilst the vitamin content is not appreciably affected.

5 *Air-conditioning.* By careful regulation of the temperature, humidity, carbon dioxide and oxygen content of the air, fruit such as apples and tomatoes can be kept in near-perfect condition. This allows fruit and vegetables to be preserved commercially on a large scale.

6 *Irradiation.* This method involves subjecting foods to small doses of gamma rays and is not yet sanctioned in the UK. It is being recommended for several different types of foods including packs of frozen boneless meats and egg products when the usual hygienic methods fail to prevent contamination, especially with *Salmonella.* It may also be used to extend the 'shelf-life' of fruit and vegetables by destroying micro-organisms. Test have found that radiation is not detectable in the food afterwards. However, this method remains controversial mainly because it could be used to conceal the early stages of deterioration in foods.

FOOD ADDITIVES

The use of preservatives, emulsifiers, antioxidants, flavourings and colourings in foods represents a growing controversy in the food industry. All additives are controlled and by law they must be included in the list of ingredients. This gives the consumer the opportunity to become more aware of the hidden substances which include sugar, artificial sweeteners, salt and other additives.

Millstone (1986) distinguishes five main functional groups of additives:

1 *Consumer protectors.* Preservatives are food additives which are used to inhibit the growth of bacteria and prevent contamination and spoilage. Food which is highly processed, such as mechanically recovered meat, is particularly vulnerable to bacterial contamination and can therefore be used only in combination with preservatives. The aim is to prevent acute food poisoning but the incidence in Britain continues to rise. Moreover there is controversy over the chronic long-term effects which certain preservatives may have on health. The safety and toxicity of the synthetic antioxidants E320 and E321 which are used to preserve fats and oils continue to be investigated.

2 *Shelf-life extenders.* Antioxidants prevent the unpleasant flavour and odour of rancid oils and fats caused by decay; humectants prevent food from drying out; others include anti-browning agents such as E300, vitamin C. Approximately 35 different chemicals are permitted for use in the UK and they can be identified by their E numbers, E200–E320s.

3 *Cosmetics.* These include organoleptic modifiers which affect the colour, flavour and aroma of foods; and textural modifiers such as jelling agents, gums and thickeners which affect how the products feel to our hands and mouths. Flavouring additives constitute the largest single group. They are not allocated specific E numbers and so although their presence is indicated on the label it does not state which ones. Flavour enhancers, notably monosodium glutamate, are chemicals which give the impression that the food has more flavour than it really has. They are indicated on labels by the numbers 620–635. Colourings are added to foods to make them appear enticing. As a group they are the most thoroughly tested and a number have been found to be toxic and have consequently been banned. E123 amaranth, E102 tartrazine and E142 acid brilliant green have been banned in the USA and USSR. Acute problems associated with colourings include rashes, asthma and hyperactivity in children. Tests on their safety continue and doubts remain as to their potential chronic effects on health.

4 *Processing aids.* Anti-caking agents and lubricants are used to aid the processing of foods. One group, polyphosphates, are used in meat and fish products as water-retaining agents.

5 *Nutritional additives.* These are mainly vitamin and mineral supplements. Legislation requires the fortification of bread and margarine with some nutrients and this has been found to be beneficial to impoverished families and elderly people. However, the essential problem is not so much replacing nutrients but rather preventing their removal in the first place during food processing.

It is certainly the case that without these additives the shelf-life of many foods would be shorter and their quality, arguably, poorer. They give the choice of 'convenience' foods which many people find are suited to the modern lifestyle. However, there is now clear research evidence implicating food additives with health problems. Eggar et al (1985) report a double-blind study which links additives, especially artificial colorants and preservatives, with overactivity in children. At best there remains some doubt over both short- and long-term health implications of food additives in general. This seems to have caused an increasing number of people to feel uneasy about them. As a consequence consumers have begun to demand more information on them which in turn has helped to reduce the amount of additives to foods. Market research has found that there is a growing market for foods which can carry the label 'additive and preservative free'. (For a list of additives implicated in hyperactivity and intolerance see the appendix in Millstone (1986).)

FOOD ALLERGIES

Food allergies remain a medical controversy. Whilst some clinicians claim that virtually any food can cause a variety of allergic reactions in sensitive people, others reject it completely. Diagnosis is difficult and depends on either the demonstration of a skin-sensitizing antibody or the presence of specific IgE antibodies in the serum. Cow's milk allergy in early childhood appears to be the most common form of food allergy affecting an estimated 0.3–10% of children but, again, there is controversy over its incidence and importance. Another food allergy which is claimed is migraine in response to cheese, chocolate and red wine. This is believed to be due to an idiosyncratic reaction to tyramine which is contained in these particular foods. Treatment is the elimination of the offending food(s) from the diet.

ORGANICALLY GROWN FOOD

The term 'organically grown foods' is relatively new although the concept and the methods used are very old indeed. Black's *Agricultural Dictionary* defines organic farming as 'systems of farming which avoid the use of artificial fertilizers, pesticides or herbicides and concentrate on methods of crop rotation and the use of home-grown feed, organic fertilizers and manures, and ley farming'. The main reasons for growing organically are related to personal and environmental health.

Environmental Health

The widespread use of pesticides and herbicides has had a considerable effect on plant, insect and animal life. There are several major problems in the use of these poisons; firstly although they kill off most of the pests some will escape to produce offspring which are immune; poisons are not selective and so the useful insect life is killed off along with the destructive insects; the pest's natural enemies such as birds, hedgehogs and other insects are poisoned when they eat contaminated insects; some poisons such as DDT and 245T have persistent effects which build up, not only in the soil but also in the fat of the animals and humans eating the contaminated foodstuffs. In any ecological system damage to one part will ultimately have a deleterious effect on everything else. The damage which is being done to the balance in nature is described by Rachel Carson (1965) in her book *Silent Spring*.

Personal Health

The arguments for organically grown food are mainly two-fold; firstly it is claimed that the use of poisons and the excessive use of nitrogenous fertilizers on food may be linked to serious health problems including cancer of the stomach; secondly that plants grown using chemical fertilizers may be deficient in essential vitamins and trace elements such as zinc and iron. Organic fertilizers such as manures, seaweed and compost create a well balanced soil which will produce healthy plants and therefore nutritious and uncontaminated foods. Interest in organically grown foods is growing and such foods are becoming increasingly available in shops to meet this demand. Organically raised meat is also available at certain butchers. Families with even very small gardens are finding that they are able to produce quite a few organic crops for themselves.

FOOD POISONING

Bacterial food poisonings can be divided into:

1 toxin food poisoning caused by staphylococci, *Clostridium perfringens* (*Cl. welchii*), and botulism;
2 infective food poisoning, e.g. salmonellosis.

Toxin Food Poisonings

Toxin food poisonings are those in which the poisonous substance ingested is a bacterial enterotoxin produced by prior bacterial multiplication in the food. The toxin is heat stable and therefore contaminated food cannot be rendered safe by cooking or pasteurization.

Staphylococcal toxin food poisoning can occur if the strain is *Staphylococcus aureus*, if the food provides a suitable culture medium (e.g. cold meats, fish, vegetables, unpasteurized milk), and if food is stored at a temperature of between 10 and 49°C for a period of 8 hours or longer. In most instances, human staphylococcal lesions such as abscesses, paronychia, nasal infections or infected nails are the source of contamination. Over 10% of persons carry staphylococci in their noses and so food contamination is a constant possibility. Prevention involves the consumption of foodstuffs within 2 hours of preparation whenever possible, storage of foods in cool conditions, and ensuring scrupulously clean conditions whilst handling or preparing food.

Clostridium perfringens (*Cl. welchii*) spores are widely disseminated in earth and faeces and it is almost inevitable that they will gain access to kitchens and raw meat. In commercial kitchens raw meat is given separate shelf-space or refrigerators from uncooked foods. In any kitchen it is important to prevent blood from meat contaminating fresh foods by dripping onto it or mixing with it on chopping boards. Heating tends to activate these spores and therefore the heating up of precooked foods, especially meat dishes, carries this risk. Prevention includes avoiding the precooking of meat, or, if it has to be precooked, it should be cooled rapidly and stored below 10°C. Food should not be stored between 10 and 49°C for more than 3 hours. These measures are especially important for services such as Meals on Wheels where food has to be prepared some time in advance then delivered hot. Careful gutting of fish and game is also important to prevent contamination of the flesh with faeces from the intestine.

Bacillus cereus is an organism which has been responsible for food poisoning in people eating rice in Chinese restaurants and from 'take-away' shops. The organism is often present in uncooked rice grains and survives cooking by means of spores which can withstand near boiling temperatures. The bacilli which arise from the germinated spores produce toxins in the food as they grow and multiply. The problem arises if large quantities of boiled rice are prepared in advance to be heated up or fried at short notice. Only changes in food preparation methods to cut out the hours of storage after cooking will prevent this type of food poisoning.

Botulism is a very rare disease caused by the anaerobic *Clostridium botulinum*. It is a serious disease with a high mortality. It is very rare in the UK but cases are still reported in Europe and America. Sources of infection are usually traced to tinned meat or fish, or home-bottled vegetables in which there has been inadequate sterilization with anaerobic conditions being produced. Prevention includes avoidance of bottling of vegetables and proper control of commercial canning.

Infective Food Poisoning

Infective food poisoning is a true bacterial infection in which the small intestine is attacked by various salmonella bacteria producing a gastroenteritis. The size of the infecting dose bears a close relationship to the speed of the onset of symptoms and to the severity of the illness.

Salmonellosis is the most common form of food poisoning in the UK, accounting for about 70% of all outbreaks. Many types of salmonella are responsible, the commonest being *Salmonella typhimurium*. Symptoms occur about 12–24 hours after eating the food and include vomiting, diarrhoea, fever and malaise and last on average 2–3 days. It can prove fatal in young children and elderly people. There are five main sources of infection; human cases and carriers, domestic animals and rodents, duck eggs (and

occasionally hen eggs), pigs and poultry (it is present in most commercially reared poultry). It may also be present in animal feeding stuffs, sun-dried fish meal, spices such as peppercorns and imported bone products. Prevention involves careful handling of raw meats, especially poultry and pork. Chopping boards, plates, knives, etc., should be thoroughly cleaned afterwards so that they do not contaminate other foods. Meats should be thoroughly thawed before cooking so that any bacteria close to the bones will be destroyed during the cooking process. Turkeys need a carefully estimated cooking time. Outbreaks in elderly persons' homes and hospitals have led to many fatalities in the past.

INTERNAL PARASITES

Oxyuris vermicularis (threadworms) appears in the stools as small white threads, the eggs having been swallowed with infected food or from unwashed hands. The worms migrate out of the anus at night causing intense irritation and scratching. The hands may become a vector for the parasite and the wearing of gloves at night may help to prevent reinfestation. Treatment consists of administering a drug such as piperazine. All affected family members should be treated. Ointment containing a local anaesthetic may reduce irritation.

Taenia saginata (tapeworm) is found in beef and *Taenia solium* is found in pork. These are uncommon in the UK because of the strict regulations controlling meat production. An infested person will have gastrointestinal upset and weight loss, and will see segments of the worm passed in the stools. Treatment consists of the administration of oral dichlorophen and careful inspection of the stools to check for the excretion of the worm.

Ascaris lumbricoides (roundworms) is also uncommon in Britain. Eggs are taken in with contaminated water or food, and treatment is with a drug such as piperazine.

References and further reading

Carson, R. (1965) *Silent Spring*. Harmondsworth: Penguin.

Committee on Medical Aspects of Food (1984) *Report of the Policy Panel on Diet in Relation to Cardiovascular Disease (The COMA Report)*. London: DHSS.

Eggar, J. et al (1985) Controlled trial of oligoantigenic treatment in the hyperkinetic syndrome. *Lancet* **i**, 540–545.

Hay, J. (1986) *Vegetables Naturally. Organic Growing for Small Gardens*. London: Century Arrow.

Hobbs, B. C. & Gilbert, R. J. (1978) *Food Poisoning and Food Hygiene*, 4th edn. London: Edward Arnold.

Lessof, M. H., ed. (1984) *Allergy, Immunological and Clinical Aspects*. Chichester: John Wiley.

Meredith Davies, J. B. (1983) *Community Health, Preventive Medicine and Social Services*, 5th edn. London: Baillière Tindall.

Manson-Bahr, P. E. C. & Apted, F. I. C. (1982) *Manson's Tropical Diseases*, 18th edn. London: Baillière Tindall.

McLaren, D. S. (1981) *A Colour Atlas of Nutritional Disorders*. London: Wolfe Medical Publishers.

Millstone, E. (1986) *Food Additives. Taking the Lid Off What We Really Eat*. Harmondsworth: Penguin.

Myers, N., ed. (1985) *The Gaia Atlas of Planet Management*. London: Pan Books.

National Advisory Committee on Nutrition Education (1983) *Proposals for Nutritional Guidelines for Health Education in Britain (NACNE Report)*. London: Health Education Council.

Pulling, J. (1985) *Additives. A Shopper's Guide*. London: Century.

15

Health Problems

Wherever one lives and whatever one's style of life, there are always threats to health to contend with. Some are a result of outside influences over which one has relatively little control, such as pollutants in the environment. Others may be through personal choice such as participation in a high-risk sport. Life expectancy in western countries is far higher than that in developing countries but health problems are still significant in terms of the disablement caused as well as mortality. The nature of health problems changes over time. In Britain, the main health problem of the 19th century was infectious disease. Today the major issues relating to health are accidents and violence, circulatory disease, cancer and respiratory disease (see Figure 38). The general health measures outlined in Chapter 2 suggest ways of protecting health against many of the problems described here.

Certain terms are used in the study of communicable disease. *Epidemiology* is the study of all factors connected with the incidence and spread of disease. A disease is *endemic* if it occurs constantly in any area, such as measles in Britain. A sudden increase in a particular disease is described as an *epidemic* and a series of similar epidemics throughout the world is a *pandemic*. Scattered cases of communicable disease with no connection between them are said to be *sporadic*. The *incubation period* of any disease is the period of time between infection and

the first signs or symptoms of illness. The *prevalence* of a disease refers to the amount of a certain disease which is present in a community at a point in time; *incidence* refers to the number of new cases which emerge within a community over a period of time (see Figure 39).

COMMUNICABLE DISEASE

Communicable or infectious diseases are those which can be spread either from person to person or from animal or insect to a human. The cause (aetiology) of such diseases is by infection of the body with bacteria or viruses or their products. There are five main methods of spread:

1 *Airborne or droplet infections*: bacterial diseases include whooping cough, streptococcal tonsillitis, tuberculosis; virus diseases include measles, influenza, rubella, the common cold, Legionnaire's disease.
2 *Faeces-borne or gastrointestinal infections*: bacterial diseases include typhoid, botulism and food poisoning; virus diseases include infective hepatitis and poliomyelitis.
3 *From animals*: diseases include anthrax, brucellosis, toxoplasmosis, bovine tuberculosis from infected milk, rabies and Lassa fever.
4 *By contact*: man — diseases include sexually transmitted diseases, e.g. syphilis

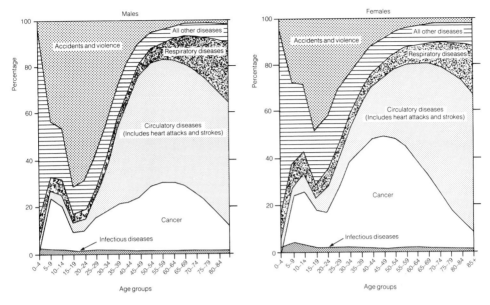

Figure 38. *Selected causes of death by age and sex, 1979. Source: OPCS, General Register Office (Scotland and Northern Ireland).*

and gonorrhoea; injury — diseases include tetanus, especially by puncture wounds with items such as rusty nails and gardening implements.

5 *From insects*: diseases include malaria and typhus.

There are three main factors which determine the development of communicable disease:

1 environment, e.g. seasonal variations, overcrowding, inadequate ventilation;

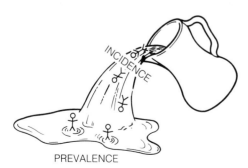

Figure 39. *Incidence and prevalence of disease: diagram to illustrate the difference.*

2 properties of the infecting bacteria or viruses, especially their virulence and the size of the infecting dose;

3 characteristics of the person, especially natural or artificial resistance.

The prevention of communicable disease demands that the spread of the disease be interrupted in some way. This may be achieved in four main ways:

1 By altering the environment in some way such as ensuring a clean water supply to prevent cholera and provision of uncontaminated food to prevent food poisoning.

2 By increasing resistance through immunization against diseases such as whooping cough, influenza, tetanus and typhoid.

3 By contact follow-up for diseases such as tuberculosis and sexually transmitted disease. This method was largely responsible for the eradication of smallpox.

4 Health education is important to prevent the spread of all diseases.

Tuberculosis is an example of a disease in which all these methods of control are relevant. It is more common in areas where there is high unemployment, poverty and overcrowding. Heaf or tine testing can detect those people who have a natural immunity, those who have the disease in some form, and those who are not immune. BCG (bacille Calmette–Guérin) can protect against infection and is given routinely to certain vulnerable groups such as newly born babies where a member of the family has had the disease. In some areas it is given routinely to all non-immune schoolchildren at the age of about 13 years. Some Health Authorities have discontinued this because of the low incidence of the disease in Britain and offer Heaf testing to establish levels of the disease and natural immunity in the community. Contacts of those found to have the disease are followed up and screened for the disease. In the past, mobile radiography units screened large sections of the population. The consequence of these measures is that the incidence of tuberculosis has been greatly reduced in developed countries.

Sexually Transmitted Diseases

The incidence of sexually transmitted diseases is increasing worldwide. The number of people attending departments of genitourinary medicine in the UK has risen three-fold in the past 15 years. The steepest rise is amongst young women. This increase is probably attributable to many factors such as changes in sexual behaviour, a lowering of the age of sexual activity and an increase in the number of sexual partners, and the trend away from barrier methods of contraception which afford some protection against disease. The apparent increase may however be attributable to the facts that more people seek medical help due to greater awareness of the risks of infection and that clinics are more easily accessible.

The diseases most commonly seen in Britain are non-specific genital infection, gonorrhoea, genital warts, trichomoniasis, genital herpes (increasing more than any other STD), pediculosis pubis and syphilis (increasing amongst gay men). Diseases such as chancroid, granuloma inguinale, lymphogranuloma venereum, yaws and pita are rare in Britain but are significant in some tropical areas.

The aims of the health service are firstly to inform people of the risks involved so that, through modification of sexual behaviour, infection can be prevented (see Chapter 2 and the Health Education free booklets, *Guide to a Healthy Sex Life* and *Herpes, What it Is and How to Cope*). It is important also that people are aware of the signs and symptoms so that they can seek help at an early stage and that clinics are well advertised and accessible. Treatment for bacterial, parasitic, protozoan and fungal infections is relatively simple and straightforward. Management of viral infections such as herpes simplex is more difficult as the disease tends to recur. Counselling of patients is important to enable them to come to terms with the disease and its effect on their sexuality. Contact tracing has been largely discontinued. Instead the patient is encouraged to make contact with past sexual partners and take the responsibility of informing them.

Acquired Immune Deficiency Syndrome

AIDS was first recognized in young homosexual men in the USA in 1981. The first case in Britain was reported later in that year and by 1984 a clear pattern of reported cases had emerged initially in the larger cities of the world, notably New York, San Francisco, London and Sydney. The disease also exists in Central Africa where it appears to be spread mainly through heterosexual contact. The Centers for Disease Control (CDC), Atlanta, which is a branch of the US Government responsible for monitoring epidemic infectious diseases established the following definition: 'AIDS is caused by a chronic infection of the T lymphocytes (especially helper subtype) by a novel retrovirus. AIDS can be diagnosed when this infection has caused damage sufficient to increase the risk of malignancies and opportunistic infections.' The retrovirus is known as human immunodeficiency virus (HIV). The long-term effects of the viral infection are unknown although it is generally recognized that of the people who become infected, some may remain symptom free, but some will develop AIDS which is invariably fatal. Estimates of the number of HIV-positive people who will develop AIDS range from 30 to 70%.

HIV is a fragile virus which is readily destroyed outside the body and does not pass easily from person to person. It is not transmitted through casual or social contact. DHSS and RCN guidelines are available for nursing and other personnel in contact with AIDS patients and people of high-risk groups. The recommendations are similar to those necessary to prevent the spread of hepatitis B and reinforce the importance of good technique in procedures such as withdrawing blood and sound basic hygiene. Only three methods of transmission have been identified:

1 Sexual contact. Homosexual and heterosexual. In Australia there are reports of women being affected from artificial insemination by donor when the semen was infected.
2 Injection or transfusion of blood or blood products including sharing injection needles with an infected person.
3 From mother to baby. This may be *in utero*, at birth or through breast milk.

Groups of people most at risk are:

1 *Gay and bisexual men*. Over 90% of cases of AIDS in the UK are in this group and about one-third of the gay and bisexual men tested in central London clinics were antibody positive to the HIV virus in early 1985. A study by the San Francisco Health Department and the Centers for Disease Control found a zero level of antibody in a group of gay men in San Francisco in 1978. However, by the middle of 1984 59% of a selected group of very sexually active gay men had developed antibodies to the virus and by October 1985 73% of this group had become infected.
2 *Haemophiliacs*. This is due to transfusions of infected blood products, especially factor VIII. In 1985 of the estimated 4000 haemophiliacs in the UK, about 1000 were HIV-positive, making this the second largest group at risk. People in high-risk groups are asked not to donate blood. All blood donated to the blood transfusion service since October 1985 is screened and all factor VIII is heat treated to destroy the virus. This has dramatically reduced, and possibly abolished, the risk.
3 *Drug users who inject*. This group is becoming increasingly vulnerable in the UK and HIV-positive rates of up to 30% have been found amongst this group in some cities.
4 *Recipients of blood transfusions or organ transplants*. People in high-risk groups are asked not to offer their organs for transplant.
5 *Central Africa contacts*. AIDS is found in several Central African countries, especially Zaire and Uganda, and seems to be spread primarily through heterosexual contact. Some estimates suggest that as many as one in five of the population may have come into contact with the virus and be HIV-positive. Anyone living there in the past 6 years who had sexual partners is at risk.
6 *Sexual partners of other risk groups*. This includes wives of bisexual men and homosexual and heterosexual partners.
7 *Babies born to HIV-positive parents*. This may occur before or after birth. Around 50% of these babies will be antibody-positive at birth and an estimated 50% of them will die of AIDS in the first 2 years of life.

A test to detect HIV antibodies is available but is generally not recommended because there is no treatment to offer and because of the adverse effects which a positive result can have on a person's life. It cannot detect whether the active virus is still present although everyone with antibodies is considered infectious. Another problem with the test is that it may take up to 3 months after the virus has entered the body for seroconversion to take place and for the test to become positive. During this time the person will be infectious. The test is indicated for women in a high-risk group who are planning to become pregnant because of the risk to their own health and the child's. If the test is used, pre- and post-test counselling is essential. A positive result, apart from the practical difficulties such as possibly not being able to obtain life insurance or a mortgage, will certainly affect one's sex life and relationships.

The Terence Higgins Trust is available to help anyone who has AIDS, or is just concerned about AIDS. It has produced a number of information leaflets such as *AIDS — The Facts* and *AIDS — More Facts for Gay Men* which is an explicit leaflet about sex. They also offer a telephone counselling line and a range of support services for people who are known to be HIV-positive. A support group called Body Positive is a social group with a fortnightly disco which offers support and counselling. This is to prevent the social isolation which may result if friends and colleagues know, to give each other emotional support especially to those whose friends have died from AIDS, and to deal with practical issues such as employment, housing, insurance and mortgage problems. They have developed a positive approach to health advocating good diet and exercise as well as guidance on sexual practices which are risk free or low risk. A support group for women who are HIV positive began in 1986. There is also a 'buddy service' to support and give informed advice to people with AIDS.

In 1986 the government launched a national health education campaign to alert people to the risks of AIDS, and to dispel some of the myths surrounding the transmission of HIV. The message reiterated the ways in which HIV can be spread and stated clearly that it can not be caught through social contact, or by coughs or colds. It also emphasized that AIDS is everyone's business and that in the absence of a vaccine or cure protection can be maintained through avoiding practices that are known to carry a risk, i.e. drug addicts sharing needles and syringes, sexual intercourse (heterosexual or homosexual) with multiple partners. The use of the sheath and spermicide is recommended where there is any possibility that a sexual partner may have become infected with HIV (specially strengthened sheaths are available for anal intercourse). Newspaper, radio and television advertising space as well as leaflets through the letter boxes of every home in the UK was used to inform people of the risks.

Hepatitis

There are two types of viral hepatitis: hepatitis A (infective hepatitis) and hepatitis B (serum hepatitis). They both cause liver disease and almost identical symptoms. They differ in their incubation periods; that of hepatitis A is 10–40 days, and of hepatitis B is 60–160 days. Their modes of transmission are also dissimilar. Hepatitis A is mainly spread by food, milk and contaminated water. It is therefore especially important that food handlers pay particular attention to hygiene. It may also be transmitted by blood and blood products by the parenteral route and there is some evidence that urine and nasopharyngeal secretions may be a source of infection. In countries where the disease is endemic there is a theory that insect bites may also transmit the disease. The virus may continue to be excreted in the faeces of people for some time after their recovery from the disease and in the faeces of the carriers.

Worldwide, hepatitis B infection is the main cause of chronic liver disease. The source is the blood of persons who have the disease or who are carriers. It is transmitted parenterally through blood, serum or plasma and by equipment which is in contact with blood. The disease may be transmitted through needle prick injuries of contaminated blood, through infected blood coming into contact with cuts and mucous membranes and through tattooing. It may also be spread by the oral route. The organism is found in faeces, urine and all body secretions. It is especially important that scrupulous attention to hygiene is carried out when nursing patients and that hands are washed with soap and water as soon as possible after exposure. All personnel working in hospital units such as renal wards where blood is being handled should be screened for the antigen in order to protect the patients. The disease is most likely to prove fatal in patients who are already weak through illness. It is estimated that 1–2% of the population is positive for the hepatitis B antigen. The high-risk groups include drug addicts, homosexuals, and children of immigrants where hepatitis B is endemic, especially South East Asia. Vaccination can be offered to people in high-risk groups including nurses working in renal units.

Tropical Diseases

Malaria

It is estimated that malaria affects perhaps 160 million people at any one time. It is caused by malarial parasites; *Plasmodium vivax*, *Pl. falciparum*, *Pl. ovale*, and *Pl. malariae*. The mode of spread is by the bite of an infected female anopheles mosquito which is necessary to complete the life cycle of the malarial parasite. The period of communicability in an infected human is as long as the infective gametocytes are present in the bloodstream and

this is dependent on the treatment given. Cases are still notified in Britain, half of which are contracted on the Indian subcontinent by immigrants revisiting their homes. There is increasing evidence of the emergence of more resistant strains of *Pl. falciparum*, especially in Africa, and infection may occur even whilst taking prophylactic drugs.

Prevention of the disease depends on the control of mosquitos. The World Health Organization has mounted large campaigns to curb the disease but administrative, political and financial difficulties have thwarted attempts and the worldwide situation remains essentially unchanged. Malaria eradication schemes have three main phases:

1 Treatment of environmental factors which encourage mosquito multiplication, such as draining swamps. Insecticides are also used including DDT which is prohibited in the USA because of associated health risks although it is still used in third world countries. Research continues into safer methods of insect control.
2 Visiting of all inhabitants in the area to monitor incidence of the disease and treat when necessary.
3 Preventive measures are continued to ensure that improvement is permanent. Widespread use of prophylactic drugs is not generally advocated as it has been found to lead to resistant strains.

Cholera

This is a bacterial infection spread from man to man by direct faecal contamination of water or food which is then ingested. Gastrointestinal infection causes severe abdominal cramps, dehydration and death if untreated. It is endemic in Lower Bengal, Burma and the Philippines and episodic epidemics occur in Africa, the Middle East, Turkey and parts of Europe. It is a disease of poverty caused by poor sanitation and is usually spread by carriers and people who have mild infection. International spread is usually through uncontrolled immigration, smuggling and pilgrimages.

Prevention of the disease depends on the provision of sanitary conditions in communities and at temporary gatherings of large numbers of people, such as religious pilgrimages in India and the East. Chlorination of the water supply is essential, 1–2 parts of chlorine in 5 million litres being recommended (potassium permanganate can also be used in contaminated wells). Vaccines are useful and recommended for visitors to certain countries but will not protect in insanitary conditions. Vaccination is contraindicated in areas where people have high levels of antibodies as it can cause adverse reactions. Quarantine of the infected person is important but in practice difficult to achieve.

Plague

This disease is endemic in Asia, India, South America and Central Africa. In the UK epidemics occurred mainly from the 13th to the 17th century and the last outbreak was in 1910. It is spread by rat fleas, *Xenopsylla cheopis*, which are carried by the black rat. The brown rat has been partially responsible for reducing the numbers of black rats. Prevention is chiefly through regular rat-proofing of ships which berth in the UK to reduce the possibility of rats reaching the shore.

Certain diseases are notifiable so that their incidence can be monitored and measures taken to prevent their spread. The Communicable Diseases Surveillance Centre was established in 1980 to coordinate national epidemiological investigations (including diseases which are not notifiable), to provide a reference for unusual problems, and to give advice and help in the investigation and control of communicable disease. It has links with European countries and the World Health Organization.

NON-COMMUNICABLE DISEASES

These diseases are more difficult to prevent because in many instances their cause is only partially understood. Often, prevention of the disease depends on behaviour and lifestyle (see Chapter 2 on general health measures). If prevention is not possible, early detection is important and this is dependent on the awareness and knowledge of the person concerned.

Coronary Heart Disease

The incidence of coronary heart disease has risen in the past 35 years in both men and women. Factors have been identified which appear to be associated with the development of this disease although the relationship is complex and often multifactorial. They include genetic factors, cigarette smoking, increase in body weight, stress, diet, high blood lipid levels, lack of exercise, diabetes and hypertension. There are marked differences in the incidence of coronary heart disease throughout the world. It is particularly high in Sweden, Scotland, Denmark, England and Wales and the USA, and relatively low in Egypt, Japan, Spain and France. The Black Report (Townsend and Davidson, 1982) showed that in the UK the incidence is highest amongst people in social class 5, dropping steadily to social class 1; this difference is most marked amongst women.

Cancer

The causation of neoplastic disease is unknown although certain predisposing factors are recognized. For instance, irritants and carcinogenic agents in cigarette smoke have been associated with cancer of the lung, viral genital warts with cancer of the cervix, smoked foods with cancer of the stomach, family history with cancer of the breast, antioxidants containing benzidine or naphthylamine with cancer of the bladder. The incidence is gradually rising and there is a marked increase in cancer of the lung (especially in women) and cancer of the cervix. However, the incidence of cancer of the stomach is falling steadily. The overall increase is partly attributable to increased life expectancy. There are marked differences between the social classes regarding mortality. In men the variation is greatest, with mortality highest in social class 5 and lowest in social class 1. Health measures to reduce mortality include health education, especially to discourage smoking. Screening services are essential where the disease can be detected at an early and treatable stage. In many health authorities women in the high-risk age groups are routinely sent appointments by a computerized recall system for cervical cytology (smear tests) (see Chapter 8).

Respiratory Diseases

Bronchitis is still responsible for many thousands of deaths each year in Britain although the incidence is falling. It is still more common amongst people in social class 5. The disease is characterized by coughing and expectoration, usually caused by prolonged irritation of the bronchial mucosa. This may be caused by cigarette smoking, industrial dust and air pollution (especially smoke and the emission of noxious gases such as sulphur dioxide and trioxide). In 1952 it was estimated that in the London area just under 4000 deaths were attributable to a 4-day smog. The Clean Air Act, 1956 has been responsible for reducing atmospheric pollution.

Diabetes

The incidence of diabetes is increasing, especially in social classes 4 and 5. The incidence is also increasing in children in western countries. The causation of the disease is unknown, but two important factors have been identified; hereditary factors and overnutrition. Prevention of the disease may not be possible where there are strong hereditary factors.

However, adult onset diabetes may be prevented through diet, exercise, and avoidance of obesity. When it cannot be prevented effective management can reduce the likelihood of associated disease. This may be achieved through a health visitor or district nurse or specialist diabetic nurse advising on diet to ensure that the condition is well controlled, as well as general health measures.

Mental Illness

Mental illness occurs in many forms, at all ages and in all types of people. The main types of mental illness are the psychoses — schizophrenia and affective disorders; neuroses — anxiety states and reactive depression; various personality disorders; drug addiction; and alcoholism. There are many factors which play an important part in the development of mental illness. These may be divided into intrinsic factors such as heredity and development, and extrinsic factors such as employment (or unemployment), domestic circumstances and environment. The highest incidence of mental illness is amongst men in social class 5 and there is a recognized association between unemployment and mental illness. A decrease in the number of people being admitted to psychiatric hospitals is mainly due to the trend towards community care.

Sickle Cell Disease and Thalassaemia

Both diseases are inherited disorders of haemoglobin synthesis and are believed to have developed because of the immunity which they afford the sufferer against malaria. Inheritance is through a recessive gene and many people have only the trait and not the symptoms associated with the disease. If both parents have a trait there is a one in four chance at each conception that the child will be affected by the disease.

Thalassaemia affects several million people around the shores of the Mediterranean, North Africa, the Middle East,

India, Pakistan and Thailand. There are two types: major and minor thalassaemia. Among the most severe and commonest forms is beta-thalassaemia. The disease disrupts the haemoglobin molecule which normally consists of two alpha chains and two beta chains. In beta-thalassaemia instead of two beta chains there are two delta chains. The disease presents in the first few months of life with anaemia and jaundice and the infant requires frequent transfusions of normal blood to survive. The disease can result in bone thickening due to bone marrow hyperplasia, impaired growth, delayed or absent puberty, and diabetes due to damage of the endocrine glands. Management includes regular blood transfusions and treatment to remove excess iron which tends to accumulate in the body and which can become toxic. Thalassaemia minor presents with mild anaemia which may be mistaken for iron deficiency.

Sickle cell disease affects mainly Africans where it occurs in a broad belt across the middle third of the continent. The carrier rate in this area is between 10 and 30% of the population. Sickle cell trait also occurs in approximately 10% of Afro-Caribbean people. It is characterized by the production of red blood cells which are mainly sickle-shaped and become rigid and unable to flow through small blood vessels. Clumping of blood cells can block the supply of blood to surrounding tissues and cause infarction. Children with sickle cell anaemia are particularly prone to pneumococcal infection. All black children should be screened for sickle cell trait before surgery because the change in oxygen tension may lead to complications.

There is no cure for the disease, only counselling and management. Crises can be brought on by stress, exercise, alcohol, dehydration or pregnancy. This usually involves painful swellings, especially of the hands and feet, anaemia, leg ulcers, gallstones, renal failure and jaundice, and it can precipitate infections such as pneumonia. During pregnancy a woman is especially prone to crises and it is therefore important that all women from the relevant ethnic groups are screened for the disease early in pregnancy so that they can be carefully monitored. Prenatal diagnosis of the disease is available using fetal blood sampling or amniocentesis and a woman has the option of termination. Women are more likely to go into premature labour and have light for dates babies, and there is a risk of both maternal and infant death. Postnatal complications include pulmonary embolism and deep venous thrombosis. Because of the risk of infection, children may require prophylactic antibiotics, and hospital admission to manage the crises. They also need counselling to come to terms emotionally with the disease. The increased risk of emboli contraindicates the use of the combined oral contraceptive pill and the intrauterine device for women with the disease. Those with only a trait may use these methods if their care is closely monitored.

ACCIDENTS IN THE HOME

Accidents in the home are almost always preventable. The Home Accident Surveillance System (Consumer Safety Unit) collects data on the number and nature of accidents and finds that the two groups of people most vulnerable are the very young and the very old (see Table 6). The highest incidence of accidents occurs in the under-five age group (especially boys), falls being the most common type of accident and the most common place being the living/dining room. The incidence of accidents gradually falls throughout the adult years until the age of around 69 when it rises steeply, especially amongst women. There is a higher incidence of fatal accidents at this age than at any other. Falls are the most common and tend to occur on steps or stairs. Deaths caused by a fall increased by about 10% for both sexes between 1982 and 1983 and accounted for about 60%

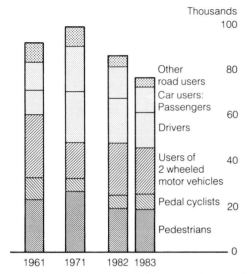

Figure 40. *Road users killed or seriously injured in Great Britain by type of road user. By permission of RoSPA.*

of deaths in the home and in residential accommodation.

ROAD TRAFFIC ACCIDENTS

The number of car drivers and passengers killed or seriously injured in Great Britain in 1983 was 20% lower than in 1982, and 17% lower than in 1961 despite there being about twice the number of motor vehicles on the road (see Figure 40). The recent fall can be attributed to the compulsory wearing of seat belts since 31 January 1983 for drivers and front seat passengers of cars and light vans. Young people aged 15–19 years are almost twice as likely as the next most vulnerable group (20- to 24-year-olds) to be killed or seriously injured riding a two-wheeled vehicle, especially motorcycles. Alcohol is a major factor in many road accidents, especially those involving young people (see Figure 41). Since October 1967 it has been an offence to drive with more than 80 mg of alcohol per 100 ml of blood. Another factor is fatigue and people who drive long distances, especially lorry and coach drivers, need regular rest stops. Accidents tend to be more common in November, possibly because of the short nights and poorer visibility. Children, teenagers and the elderly are the pedestrians most likely to be killed or serious injured.

SMOKING (see also Chapter 2)

Cigarette smoking is a major contributory factor in coronary heart disease, lung

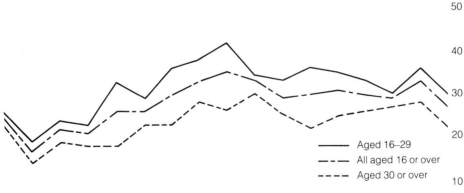

Figure 41. *Road traffic fatalities in England and Wales involving alcohol and young people.*

cancer and respiratory disease and is associated with other cancers including cancer of the mouth, oesophagus, bladder and cervix. The British Medical Association now estimates that 100 000 deaths a year in Britain are attributable to smoking (compared with an estimated 6500 deaths from alcohol abuse and 235 deaths from illegal drugs).

Passive smoking, that is the inhalation of smoke from other people's cigarettes, is also a recognized health hazard. It is known to trigger angina and asthma attacks in sensitive people, and non-smokers who work alongside smokers have been noted to have poorer lung function. Children of smoking mothers are more likely to be admitted to hospital with respiratory disease, and Butler and Goldstein (1973) found that at 11 years children whose mothers smoked during pregnancy were on average 1.5 cm shorter in height and 9 months delayed in reading and mathematical skills. Hirayama (1981) found that the non-smoking wives of smoking husbands were more likely to die from emphysema and lung cancer.

OBESITY (see also diet, Chapter 2)

There are a small number of people who are able to accept that they are greatly overweight and are perfectly happy with their body image and their style of life. However, for many people who become obese this is a major problem in their life. The problems associated with obesity can be all-encompassing. Some people talk of feelings of revulsion when they look in a mirror and see themselves, and feelings of depression and loss of confidence are typical, as are feelings of fatigue and weariness and breathlessness on exertion. Expectations of 'fat' people may conflict with how that person really feels. 'Fat' people are expected to be jolly — nothing ever gets them down; they are the listeners who everyone shares their problems with but nobody expects

them to have feelings to share; they are comfortable and easily pleased, not discerning or ambitious; and perhaps the most difficult expectation of all to cope with, they are figures of fun, not people to be taken seriously. These attitudes are difficult to cope with at any age but may be especially so during childhood and adolescence.

Obesity is associated with a number of health problems which include respiratory infections in infancy, diabetes, coronary heart disease, hypertension, reduced fertility, complications of pregnancy, complications following surgery, varicose veins, strokes, gall bladder disease, arthritis, hiatus hernia and diverticulitis. In general obesity is associated with a shorter life expectancy which is reflected by life insurance statistics.

Treatment for obesity depends on eating less food. Such a seemingly simple solution is however notoriously difficult to achieve. Crash diets have become very popular in recent years and most promise a dramatic immediate drop in weight. This is always likely to happen because the glycogen and water reserves are used up accounting for about 7 pounds of weight. The difficulties begin after the early weeks when weight loss drops as fat reserves begin to be used up. Ideally weight loss should be gradual and amount to only 1–2 pounds each week and so motivation needs to be very strong to continue. Group support can be very helpful and self-help groups such as Weight Watchers have been successful in offering guidelines for a safe, balanced slimming diet which can be adapted to suit one's lifestyle. Any diet which aims to lose weight should form the basis for a lifetime of healthy eating.

DRUG ABUSE

Virtually any substance taken into the body can be abused, indeed abuse might be taken to extend further than this, for instance to gambling, 'workaholism' and very fast driving. The World Health Organization identifies the following drugs: alcohol-barbiturate type, amphetamine, cannabis type, cocaine type, hallucinogenic type, khat type, morphine type, and inhalants and volatile substances. In 1969 the WHO defined drug dependence as 'a state, psychic and sometimes also physical, resulting from the interaction between the living organism and a drug characterized by behavioural and other responses that always include a compulsion to take the drug on a continuous or periodic basis in order to experience its psychic effects and sometimes to avoid the discomfort of its absence. Tolerance may or may not be present. A person may be dependent on more than one drug'. Although attention is often focused on physical dependence, it is usually psychological dependence which is the most difficult to deal with and constitutes the major problem in the long term.

Drug abuse is a major and rapidly growing health problem. The upward trend in drug abuse in the UK began around 1976 and affects people in every age group. According to Home Office statistics there are 5850 registered addicts in Britain, double the number in 1980. The number of street addicts is estimated to be at least ten times this number. The amount of heroin seized has increased considerably over recent years and there is evidence that it is relatively freely available on the streets in most large towns and cities and that teenagers and even children are being 'pushed' hard drugs. The current trend is to smoke heroin after heating it in silver paper ('chasing the dragon'). It is equally addictive administered by this route as by injection. About 30% of addicts are women and there is a growing number of babies being born to addicts. They are at an increased risk of perinatal mortality, sudden infant death syndrome, and they also experience withdrawal problems including hyper-irritability.

A drug currently causing considerable concern because of the rapid increase in its use is cocaine ('coke'). Cocaine is a powerful central nervous system stimulant and local anaesthetic. It can be administered in several ways including injection and smoking, but the most usual method is 'snorting'. It is said to give feelings of exhilaration which come on within 3 minutes and taper off inside an hour. Like amphetamines (speed) it gives a feeling of mental and physical potency and typical users snort repeatedly over any period of time which requires stamina, concentration, imagination or fun. Afterwards there are usually feelings of tiredness and melancholy. At high doses toxic psychosis can occur which can lead to feelings of paranoia and confusion. Dependence develops to the drug and withdrawal typically produces a long-term fatigue and depression.

A trend which has developed in the USA is the marketing of 'Designer Drugs'. Under US law all drugs are regarded as legal unless otherwise stated. Backstreet chemists are therefore able to take controlled substances and by making tiny adjustments in their molecular structure produce drugs which may have a greater potency than heroin, or similar effects to LSD, and which can be legally available. There is the potential for an infinite range of Designer Drugs.

Alcohol is a drug which, if abused, can be harmful to health. Glatt and Marks (1982) describe alcoholics as 'those individuals whose continual or frequent heavy drinking has led to a psychological and/or physical dependence and/or physical/psychological/social damage'. Excessive drinking in the longer term causes physical harm such as gastritis, liver disease and brain damage; social problems including financial worries, domestic arguments and difficulties related to employment; physical and psychological dependence making the problem particularly difficult to resolve. It has been noted that strokes in men sometimes occur following alcoholic binges. The aetiology is not fully understood but it could indicate a previously unrecognized health problem in relation to alcohol. In the last 20 years alcohol consumption in Britain has roughly doubled. This is in line with most western countries and many third world countries. Socioeconomic factors which lead to alcohol abuse are unemployment, competitive and stressful lifestyle, failure to adapt to a new environment, and depression. Certain occupational groups such as publicans, business executives, armed forces personnel and doctors are particularly vulnerable. In general, teenagers are starting to drink alcohol earlier and this is a growing concern. There is also an increasing problem amongst women, especially those in competitive careers and housewives whose children have left home.

IATROGENIC DISEASE

Virtually every medical procedure whether it is diagnostic or therapeutic has the potential for harm. Black et al (1984) states that iatrogenic disease is 'illness that would not have come about if sound and professionally recommended treatment had *not* been applied', and clinical iatrogenesis as 'all clinical conditions for which remedies, physicians or hospitals are the pathogens or sickening agents'. Iatrogenic disease can also be caused by nursing practice; administration of the wrong drug, ill-informed advice, infection as a result of faulty technique, e.g. catheterization, lack of care to prevent accidents happening in the ward and so on. Nurses are as accountable as doctors for the harm which they do to patients through their actions or lack of them.

Whenever medical or nursing intervention is necessary the potential benefits must be weighed against possible adverse effects. Crucial to this process is what the practitioner adjudges as reasonable, and what the patient chooses when provided with the necessary information. For instance, the DHSS estimates that adverse effects to whooping cough vaccine may affect one in 100 000 children.

This makes the risk less than that of not being immunized and risking the illness. Health workers therefore offer the vaccine but the final decision rests with the parent(s). Sometimes the side-effects associated with a drug are not realized, as with the tragedy of thalidomide which proved to be teratogenic and caused gross limb deformities.

NOISE POLLUTION (see also Chapter 13)

The factory floor still poses the greatest threat. Hearing damage is especially prevalent amongst workers in weaving, ship-building, boiler-making, forging, pressing and blasting. It is estimated that about 10–14% of workers in the UK suffer some loss of hearing as a result of their working environment. The Department of the Environment has set 90 dBA as the maximum steady noise for workers over a continuous 8-hour period. Ear protection is necessary for certain work and regular hearing tests are important. Hearing may also be damaged by gun shot if ear protection is not worn on shooting ranges. Concern has been expressed for the hearing of young people at discotheques where the sound is very loud. This is not believed to be a problem except for those who work in discos or who spend an exceptional amount of time there. Neither are personal stereos a problem; the noise levels do not reach those experienced in industry.

References and further reading

Adler, M. W. (1984) *ABC of Sexually Transmitted Diseases*, 3rd edn. Articles from the British Medical Journal. London: BMA.

Alcohol Problems. ABC of Alcohol (1982). Articles from the BMJ. Luton: Leagrave Press.

Black, N. et al (1984) *Health and Disease. A Reader*. Milton Keynes: Open University Press.

Butler, N. R. & Goldstein, H.(1973) Smoking

in pregnancy and subsequent child development. *British Medical Journal* **iv**, 573.

Consumer Safety Unit (1985) *Home Accident Surveillance System. Report of the 1984 Data*. London: Department of Trade and Industry.

Dally, P. & Gomez, J. (1980) *Obesity and Anorexia Nervosa. A Question of Shape*. London: Faber & Faber.

Glatt, M. M. & Marks, J., ed. (1982) *The Dependence Phenomenon*. Lancaster: MTP Press.

Hirayama, T. (1981) Non-smoking wives have a higher level of lung cancer: a study from Japan. *British Medical Journal* **282**, 183.

Home Office Statistical Bulletin (1984) 18/84. London: HMSO.

King, A. & Nicol, C. (1975) *Venereal Diseases*, 3rd edn. London: Baillière Tindall.

Manson, L. & Ritson, B. (1984) *Alcohol and Health. A Handbook for Nurses, Health Visitors and Midwives*. London: Medical Council on Alcoholism.

Manson-Bahr, P. E. C. & Apted, F. K., eds. (1982) *Manson's Tropical Diseases*, 18th edn. London: Baillière Tindall.

Meredith Davies, J.B. (1983) *Community Health, Preventive Medicine and Social Services*, 5th ed., London: Baillière Tindall.

Miller, D. et al, eds. (1985) *The Management of AIDS Patients*. London: Macmillan.

Myers, N., ed. (1985) *The Gaia Atlas of Planet Management*. London: Pan Books.

Phillips, K. (1985) Neonatal drug addicts. *Nursing Times* **82**, 12.

Shephard, R. J. (1982) *The Risks of Passive Smoking*. London: Croom Helm.

Smith, M. et al (1983) *The Effects of Lead Exposure on Urban Children*. Institute of Child Health, University of Southampton.

Social Trends (1983). London: HMSO.

Townsend, P. & Davidson, N. (1982) *Inequalities in Health. The Black Report*. Harmondsworth: Penguin.

Townsend, P. et al (1984) *Inequalities of Health in the City of Bristol*. Department of Social Administration, University of Bristol.

Tyler, A. (1986) *Street Drugs*. Sevenoaks: New English Library.

Volberding, P. (1986) In: Jones, P., ed. *Proceedings of the AIDS Conference 1986*. Newcastle upon Tyne: Intercept.

16

Health Statistics and Information Systems

Communities are made up of people each with their own unique personalities, expectations, desires, needs and wants. And yet, out of this individuality, patterns of commonality emerge. The term epidemiology comes from the Greek *epi* among, *demos* the people, *logos* science, and in medicine is concerned with the study of the distribution of diseases within populations and the factors which cause them. This information is used as the basis for formulating preventive strategies. In community nursing the techniques employed in epidemiology are extended to consider in more holistic terms the health and health needs of a given community and this forms the basis for health promotion and community care. It is the means by which health needs can be identified, priorities set, and by which trends in health can be measured. Without a comprehensive information base it is impossible to identify changing health trends or to judge whether the services being deployed are relevant, effective or even necessary.

INFORMATION BASE

The information necessary to build up a composite picture of the health needs in a community must be collected from a number of different sources which may be national or local. One of the difficulties is that it is generally easier to collect data on disease and ill-health than on positive health. Relevant information generally comes via two main routes; routinely collected data and specially conducted surveys. To assist comparison the same unit of population is used for statistical purposes. This unit is 1000 persons and is used for births and mortality rates. 'Statistics' is a science concerned with the collection, presentation, description and analysis of numerical data. It provides a great deal of the necessary information but does not tell the whole story.

POPULATION DATA

In the UK, as in many countries, all births, marriages and deaths must be registered.

Parents have a duty to register the birth of every child to the local registrar of Births, Marriages and Deaths within 42 days. (Stillbirths must also be registered.) Notification of births is made by the doctor or midwife in attendance to the District Medical Officer within 36 hours. This is to ensure that health services, especially the health visitor, are made available to support the family without delay.

Any death must be registered within 5 days of the death. The cause of death stated by the doctor on the death certificate provides the Registrar General with his records of mortality. Only when this has been done will a death certificate be issued and this must be shown to the undertaker before burial or cremation can take place.

The census, periodic counting of the population, has been a feature of many countries since antiquity. In Britain a census is carried out every 10 years by the Office of Population Censuses and Surveys (OPCS). Each head of household is obliged to provide information on the members of the household as well as details of basic household amenities. This information is essential for those concerned with planning services such as health, social services, housing and schools. It also forms the basis of population projections which make predictions about the size and structure of the population at different times in the future, such as the number of very elderly people. Information on specific geographical locations is produced, for instance regional and district health authorities, and local government authorities. 'Small area statistics' are available for electoral wards, parishes and enumeration districts and are particularly useful when planning health services for communities.

There are some limitations of census data; they can never reach 100% of the population (for instance homeless families are often overlooked); statements of occupation upon which social class analysis is based may be vague; ethnic minority groups, because of possible racist overtones, are defined only according to place of birth of the head of the household; and it is difficult to predict fertility levels and therefore the projected number of births and children under five.

In the years between a census being taken, the Registrar General is able to estimate the size of the population. Other large statistical surveys may also be carried out on behalf of the government. Much of this information is presented in two publications; *Population Trends* (published by the OPCS quarterly) which gives the latest population and vital statistics for Britain and the various regions as well as specialist articles on health topics, and *Social Trends* (published annually by the Central Statistical Office) which deals with many types of information and illustrates trends in subjects such as population, housing, leisure activities, personal income and wealth, and health. Census guides on particular groups of people are also published, such as *Britain's Elderly Population* (1981) which provides details of the current situation as well as projected figures for the future.

SOCIAL CLASS

To compare many vital statistics, and especially mortality, the Registrar General classifies the census population into five social classes based on the occupation of the chief wage earner of the household. These are:

- Class 1: higher professional and administrative, e.g. lawyers and doctors.
- Class 2: intermediate managerial and professional, e.g. sales managers, teachers and nurses.
- Class 3N: non-manual skilled occupations, e.g. clerks and shop assistants.
- Class 3M: skilled manual occupations, e.g. underground coal miners and bricklayers.
- Class 4: semi–skilled occupations, e.g. farmworkers and machine minders.
- Class 5: unskilled occupations, e.g. ticket collectors and general labourers.

Inequalities in health between people of different social classes are recognized. This information forms the basis of The Black Report (Townsend and Davidson, 1982).

BIRTH RATE

The birth rate is the number of children born per year per 1000 of the population. This may be expressed as:

$$\text{Birth rate} = \frac{\text{Number of births in the year} \times 1000}{\text{Mid-year population}}$$

In 1982 the birth rate was 12.6 compared with 28.2 in 1900. Over the same period infant mortality rates have dropped (see Figure 23). Birth rates vary considerably throughout the world and can be compared internationally (see Table 7).

MORTALITY DATA

In the UK the Office of Population Censuses and Surveys (OPCS) publishes annually statistics for births and deaths comparing local with national rates. It also presents data on deaths by cause within sex and age groups and so provides an overall picture of the major groups of conditions which cause death in the UK and trends in mortality rates. Causes of death are classified according to the International Classification of Diseases (ICD) and so can be compared internationally.

The crude death rate is the number of deaths per year per 1000 of the population. This may be expressed as:

$$\text{Death rate} = \frac{\text{Number of deaths in the year} \times 1000}{\text{Mid-year population}}$$

The crude death rate is of little value. For instance, a relatively high death rate may be usual in an area where there is a high proportion of elderly people. There is no perfect method by which death rates can be compared although the problem can to some extent be overcome by using the area comparability factor (published by OPCS) which produces an adjusted death rate. Mortality data is useful however when it is represented according to social class, age and cause of death. This information forms the basis of the Black Report (Townsend and Davidson, 1984) which highlighted the relatively high mortality rates in social class 5 compared with social class 1. It also noted that this difference was increasing (see Figure 42).

Specific mortality rates such as infant and perinatal mortality rates are more sensitive indicators of the relative health status of different districts. The infant mortality rate comprises deaths of all children under a year old per year per 1000 of the population. It is especially important because of its close correlation with social conditions. A deterioration in the social circumstances of any area, such as a sudden increase in the number of people unemployed, will rapidly be reflected in the infant mortality rate. Good paediatric services help in keeping the number of deaths down but social conditions are more important.

Separate periods within the first year are also defined:

Table 7. *International birth rates, 1979.*

Germany (Federal)	9.5	USA	15.8
Austria	11.4	Spain	16.1
Sweden	11.6	Malta	16.6
Switzerland	11.6	New Zealand	16.9
Italy	11.8	Yugoslavia	17.1
England and Wales	13.0	USSR	18.2
Germany (Democratic)	14.0	Poland	19.5
France	14.1	Israel	24.7
Japan	14.3	India	32.9
Canada	15.1	Venezuela	35.9
Australia	15.5	Egypt	41.0

From the *United Nations Demographic Yearbook*, 1979.

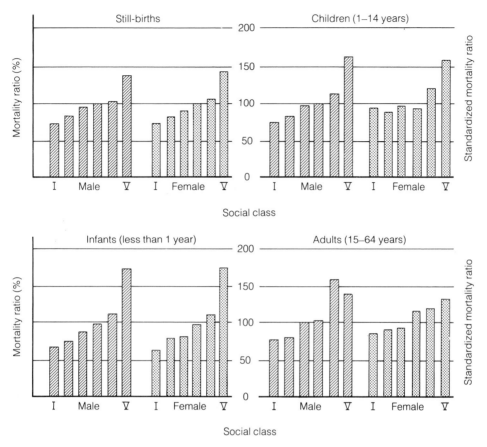

Figure 42. *Inequalities in health: mortality by occupational class and age. Relative mortality (%) is the ratio of rates for the occupational class to the rate for all males (or females).*

- Stillbirth — death of the fetus after the 28th week of pregnancy.
- Perinatal mortality — stillbirths and deaths within the first week of life.
- Neonatal mortality — deaths within the first four weeks of life. About two-thirds of deaths in the first year occur in this period and the rate is higher in boys than in girls.
- Post-neonatal mortality — deaths after 4 weeks and within 1 year.

The maternal mortality rate is the number of women who die from causes associated with childbirth per year per 1000 total births. It is a measure of the risk to the mother connected with childbirth and is influenced by many factors including antenatal care, social class and social conditions. Maternal mortality rates have fallen dramatically since 1935 (see Figure 23), although the rate among women in social class 5 is still nearly double that of social class 1.

MORBIDITY

Morbidity statistics provide a picture of the amount of illness, disability and injury within a population. Two terms are widely used:

- Prevalence — the proportion of existing cases of a health problem in a population.

• Incidence — the rate of new health problems developing in a population over a period of time (see Figure 39).

Morbidity figures are obtained from various sources. The main ones include:

1 *Notifications of infectious disease* (see list, Chapter 16).
2 *Notifications of congenital abnormalities.*
3 *General Household Survey.* The GHS collects information on issues such as education, leisure activities, employment, income and the family as well as health. The survey began in 1971 and involves interviews with a random sample of 15 000 private households (about 31 000 people) in Britain each year. The questions on health relate to medicine taking including self-medication, acute and chronic illness, disability, use of health and social services, and smoking habits. The survey provides invaluable information on health problems which do not reach the attention of the health services as well as people's changing habits. It may also indicate the effectiveness of national health promotion campaigns such as healthy eating or stop-smoking.
4 *General Practice data.* Most people in the UK are registered with a General Practitioner and about 60% of people on a GP list will attend for a consultation in the course of a year. Many general practices maintain an 'age-sex' register which is a file of the practice's population organized into males and females and age groups. It enables the practice to identify particular groups, for example underfives and people over 75 years of age. Many registers are held on computer and can be easily updated and cross-indexed. Some include additional information such as the immunization status of children, the presence of chronic illness such as diabetes, and social features such as housebound elderly. It may also provide a service such as cervical cytology recall and repeat prescriptions.

In 1970–1972 and 1980–1982 two National Morbidity Studies of General Practice were carried out. These collected morbidity data from 50 practices and provided a considerable amount of information on the level of sickness in the population, especially patterns of less serious illness. However, the practices were not a random sample and so the results may not be typical of the country as a whole. Information on the health status of people registered with a general practice is not routinely collected.
5 *Hospital data.* Four main sources of hospital data are currently available. These are the hospital activity analysis (HAA), hospital inpatient enquiry (HIPE), annual hospital returns, and the mental health enquiry. These have been reviewed by a Steering Group on Health Services Information (the Korner Committee) and, it is proposed, will be integrated into a new system by the late 1980s which will include information on all patient contacts in hospitals including outpatient departments. This should provide a much quicker and more comprehensive analysis of data than any previously obtainable.
6 *Community Services.* The Steering Group on Health Services Information has also recommended the routine collection of information on all client contacts by community services. This should provide much-needed information on services such as chiropodists and speech therapists as well as community nurses.
7 *Registers.* These include the National Cancer Registry at OPCS (containing data on age, sex, occupation, site of tumour, etc.), child abuse registers, and local authority registers of physically handicapped people including the blind. Many health authorities maintain an observation register of children with handicapping or potentially handicapping conditions so that they can be kept under special health surveillance.
8 *Social Security Statistics.* These relate to the amount and cause of sickness absence and show the causes of new spells

of certified incapacity and the commonest causes of working days lost. Certification of certain diseases for special benefits and allowances provides information on certain chronic diseases such as pneumoconiosis.

OCCUPATIONAL MORTALITY AND MORBIDITY

An association between occupation and disease has long been recognized. Information on the cause of death amongst people in particular occupations is made available by relating the numbers of deaths in a given occupation at a period at about the time of the census with the population counted in the census. Examples of such associations are as shown in Table 8.

HEALTH SERVICES ICEBERG

The term 'health services (or clinical) iceberg' has been used to describe the phenomenon whereby only a proportion of people with health problems make contact with health services. In particular only a small number make contact with hospital services which represent the 'tip of the iceberg' (see Figure 43). The process which leads people to seek health care and therefore to become represented in routinely collected information is complex and depends on many factors such as availability of health services, the person's perceptions of them, attitudes

to self-care, and increasingly the use of alternative therapies. Information on people who are ill but not seeking help is difficult to obtain. Even more difficult to obtain is information on the people who remain healthy and how they achieve this.

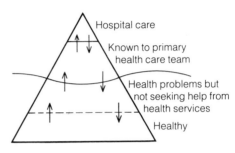

Figure 43. *The clinical iceberg.*

DATA PROTECTION

All information systems containing personal details, especially those relating to health, have always been subject to strict codes of confidentiality. The transfer of such sensitive information from manual filing systems to computerized systems is therefore an emotive issue. The concern that automated systems could be abused and lead to infringements in the codes of confidentiality led ultimately to the 1984 Data Protection Act. Under this act from 11 May 1986 all systems containing data from which an individual person can be identified must be registered with the

Table 8.

Occupation	Cause of death
Publicans	Cirrhosis of the liver and cancer of the lung
Pharmacists and doctors	Suicide
Coal miners (underground)	Pneumoconiosis
Steel erectors; riggers	Accidental falls

Data Protection Registrar. Personal data must:
1   be obtained fairly and lawfully,
2   be held for a specified and lawful purpose,
3   not be disclosed except for that purpose,
4   be adequate, relevant and not excessive for that purpose,
5   be accurate and up to date,
6   be held for no longer than it is needed.

In addition:

7   There are rights of access by an individual to any data held on that person (some health data may be exempt from this).
8   Security measures must be taken to prevent unauthorized use, alteration, disclosure or destruction of information.

PLANNING FOR HEALTH CARE IN A COMMUNITY

All health workers must identify priorities when planning health care for a community. These will be influenced by national, regional and district policies and will be based on information available both nationally and locally. For instance, the national perinatal and neonatal mortality rate highlighted by the Social Services Committee Report chaired by Renee Short (1980) prompted health authorities to give consideration to antenatal care, maternity services and special care baby units in order to reduce the number of baby deaths. However, an area with a particularly high perinatal death rate, such as an Asian community in an inner city area, may view this as a particularly high priority and choose to provide extra resources such as extra midwives, health visitors, community workers and interpreters with the specific aim of reducing the rate. Similarly, the projected increase in the numbers of very

elderly people makes this care group a priority for the future although towns such as Eastbourne and Bournemouth which have a relatively high proportion of elderly people living there must afford them an even higher priority.

Sources of information which are particularly useful in a local area are:

1   Small area statistics. These are available at the local library (see above).
2   Social and environmental indicators. The local planning office will have details of types of housing, leisure facilities, etc., as well as details of proposed plans for housing and industrial development.
3   Postal codes. Some education and health authorities are making use of the postal code system. For instance, by determining the number of children of a certain age in the catchment areas of schools education authorities can make reliable predictions of their forthcoming school entrance intakes. Health authorities can pinpoint the uptake of services such as immunizations and cervical cytology in particular areas and plan clinics and health promotion campaigns accordingly.
4   Local surveys. These are carried out on various health issues and by different groups including the Community Health Council.
5   General Practice based information. This varies from practice to practice (see above). It is generally available to all members of the primary health care team.
6   Observations of community health workers who are in close contact with the 'grass roots'.
7   Observations of local voluntary workers, neighbourhood groups, self-help groups, etc.
8   Expressed needs of the consumers. These may be presented by natural leaders from the community or from individuals who consistently make similar comments, such as a problem with dampness in their home.
9   Local levels of employment and

unemployment. Unemployment figures for electoral wards are available from Job Centres monthly.

10 Awareness of the impact of national political and economic policies on the local area. For specific issues, such as local pollution, this might involve communication with the elected member of parliament.

From this wealth of information health 'needs' emerge, priorities are decided and health care plans formulated. But first it is helpful to consider what is meant by a 'need'. Ewles and Simnett (1985) identify four kinds of need:

1 *Normative need.* These are needs defined by experts or professionals according to their own standards. For example a doctor or nurse may identify a need for people to stop smoking or eat a more healthy diet. Such needs may differ from those of the consumer.

2 *Felt need.* This is the need people feel or want. For example people may want postnatal support groups, or nightsitters to support carers at home. Felt needs may be limited or inflated by perceptions and knowledge about what could be available. For example young single mothers with low self-esteem may feel that there is nothing that can help them.

3 *Expressed need.* This is what people say they need. In other words it is a felt need which has been turned into a request or demand. This may be similar to, or in conflict with, the professional's normative needs. For example frail elderly people may express a need for a daily bath but the district nursing service may have set other priorities. Sometimes an expressed need prompts local people into Community Action. This is an organized approach to a local issue and may take place without the help of statutory health workers, for example a campaign by parents to improve safety standards at road crossings near local schools.

4 *Comparative need.* This is the differ-

ence between two comparable groups. For example an area with a nursery class may cause people in another area without such provision to feel relatively poorly off and 'in need' of a similar provision.

In order to identify the felt and expressed needs of a community some district health authorities are now employing health promotion officers with research skills to do fieldwork. They can identify specific health needs which will include positive health-related issues as well as health problems. Methods used may include questionnaires or interviews which are carefully designed to be unambiguous and which do not carry leading questions. Either the whole community or a random sample may be included in the study. The health promotion officer can then make recommendations for an acceptable plan of action and the means by which this can be evaluated. These methods mean that health initiatives are becoming increasingly consumer-led, are more sensitive to the needs of local people and arguably have the potential to be more successful. Health care planning in close collaboration with the consumers of the service has been described as the 'bottom-up' approach.

COMMUNITY DIAGNOSIS IN A THIRD WORLD COUNTRY

In third world countries information on the population and health needs is often scarce and one of the first tasks of the community health worker may be to gather such information. McCusker (1978) uses the term 'community diagnosis' to describe this process. Basic essential information which would include birth rate, percentage age structure, death rate, rate of natural increase and utilization of the health services might be obtained through a survey with follow-up surveys to note changes. In addition the community health worker may identify important health problems by:

1 Talking to and examining some or all of the people in the community. This may include specific questions such as whether anyone in the household has had a cough in the past few weeks to establish the prevalence of tuberculosis, and tests, for example skin snips for leprosy, and recording the weight and age of children for signs of malnutrition.
2 Talking to village leaders and local health workers for their observations and opinions.
3 Attending village gatherings and observing the people.
4 Looking at local medical records and treatments given.

A survey of the knowledge, attitudes and practice of local people may identify a need for health services as well as providing clues to the most sensitive approach.

THE PLANNING CYCLE (using the nursing process as a model)

This process (Figure 44) is interactive, continuous and constantly evolving. The effectiveness of community health work is largely dependent on the quality and quantity of available information. An understanding of community health needs begins with the collection of information from a variety of sources from statistical data to street-corner comments. It is the skill of the community nurse to select and interpret relevant information, establish priorities, take account of all the available resources, consider alternative policy options, decide on the most appropriate approach to enhance community participation, offer a service which will promote the health and wellbeing of the people in that community and then evaluate its effectiveness. In 1985 Dr Mahler, director-general of the World Health Organization made a statement that 'nurses lead the way' in primary health care. He suggested that nurses working together and sharing the same ideas and convictions could become a powerhouse for change. Nurses must work in harmony with the community so that they understand what the people want and adopt an epidemiological approach so that they can make a sound case for the provision of health services that are sensitive and relevant. Nurses hold the key to the goal of 'health for all by the year 2000'.

References and further reading

Catford, J.C. (1983) Positive health indicators — towards a new information base for health promotion. *Community Medicine* **5(2)**, 125–132.

Census Guide 1 (1981) *Britain's Elderly Population*. London: OPCS.

Donaldson, R. J. & Donaldson, L. J. (1983) *Essential Community Medicine*. Lancaster: MTP Press.

DHSS (1976) *Prevention and Health: Everybody's Business*. London: HMSO.

Ewles, L. & Simnett, I. (1985) *Promoting Health. A Practical Guide to Health Education*. Chichester: John Wiley.

Farmer, R. D. T. & Miller, D. L. (1983) *Lecture Notes on Epidemiology and Community Medicine*, 2nd edn. Oxford: Blackwell Scientific.

Florey, C. du V. et al (1983) *An Introduction to Community Medicine*. Edinburgh: Churchill Livingstone.

McCarthy, M. (1982) *Epidemiology and Policies for Health Planning*. London: King Edward's Hospital Fund.

McCusker, J. (1978) *How to Measure and*

Evaluate Community Health. London: Macmillan.

Meredith Davies, J. B. (1983) *Community Health, Preventive Medicine and Social Services*, 5th edn. London: Baillière Tindall.

Radical Statistics Health Group (1981) *The Unofficial Guide to Official Health Statistics*. London: Radical Statistics.

Social Services Committee (chairman Mrs Renee Short) (1980) *Perinatal and Neonatal Mortality*. London: HMSO.

Townsend, P. & Davidson, N. (1984) *Inequalities in Health. The Black Report.* Harmondsworth: Penguin.

Waters, W. E. & Cliff, K. S. (1983) *Community Medicine: A Textbook for Nurses and Health Visitors*. London: Croom Helm.

17

Health and Social Services in Britain

For most of the 20th century health care has been centred on hospitals and the dramatic advances which have come about through medical intervention at times of illness. In recent years however the emphasis has swung towards community-based care as the focus of the health care system. This has been facilitated by political, economic and social arguments which suggest that care at home is both preferable to institutional care and more cost-effective. But underlying this shift are fundamental changes in attitudes towards health care which are even more significant. There is unquestionably a growing realization that a holistic approach to the maintenance of health and its restoration is needed and that this includes an appreciation of that person's interaction with their family, the local community and their environment. There is also a growing recognition of the need for people to assume greater responsibility for their own health and in particular to lead their lives in such a way as to promote a sense of wellbeing. This increasing 'consumer' involvement heralds a new era of community care which is likely to become increasingly responsive to local needs and which will regard the users of the services as active participants rather than passive recipients. This will have a significant impact on the development of services. Changes brought about at the 'grass roots' have been described as 'bottom-up' as opposed to the 'top-down' planning of the past.

HISTORICAL ORIGINS OF THE HEALTH SERVICE

To understand the nature of community care it is helpful to view it in its historical context. It must also be remembered that the most significant improvements in health have come about through environmental changes and community-based initiatives. The following episodes are not intended as a comprehensive list but rather as a guide to some of the more relevant or more interesting passages in the development of community care.

The earliest references to community care date from feudal times when there is evidence of women healers throughout Europe. They were particularly skilful in the care of the sick and in midwifery and were called upon to teach and help other women. Their use of herbs and drugs such as belladonna, ergot and digitalis was based on empirical science. Women healers disappeared with the witch hunts which ravaged Europe during the 14th century and which ironically documented in the records of the trials the healing and beneficial nature of their work.

The Medical Officer of Health. In the period 1839–1843, Edwin Chadwick and Dr Southwood Smith, a London general practitioner, instigated reports into the living conditions of the poor which stressed the connection between chronic sickness and poverty. This led to a Royal Commission to inquire into the Health of Towns in 1843. One of its recommendations was the establishment of local control over sanitary conditions in towns which led, in 1847, to the appointment in Liverpool of a doctor responsible for the health of the community; the first Medical Officer of Health. Further outbreaks of cholera led to the first Public Health Act which established a central national body; the Board of Health. It had widespread powers to remove public health nuisances but had limited effect and was finally disbanded in 1858.

Epidemiology. In 1854 Dr John Snow demonstrated epidemiologically that cholera was spread by water. He did this by removing the handle of the Broad Water street pump thereby preventing people from drinking the contaminated water, and so prevented the spread of the disease. This was 30 years before the first discovery of the cholera vibrio. At about the same time, William Budd in Bristol also showed that typhoid fever was usually spread by water.

Health Visiting. During the 1840s there was a heightened public awareness of the plight of the poor and in particular the need to improve standards of cleanliness and hygiene. As a response sanitary missionaries or 'Bible women' appeared in London and Aberdeen. However, the origin of health visiting is usually taken to be the formation of the Manchester and Salford Sanitary Reform Association which was established in 1852 'to give information to the poor and aid the aged and feeble'. The female branch, the Ladies' Sanitary Reform Association founded in 1862, was particularly concerned with the dissemination of health knowledge among women and children. It appointed 'respectable working women' to go from door to door among the poorer classes to teach and help them as the opportunity offered. In 1893 Florence Nightingale considered the training of Lady Health Missioners to give instruction in 'the management of health of adults, women before childbirth, infants and children'.

Care of Children. One night in 1890

Barnardo found 73 homeless boys sheltering among empty boxes in Billingsgate Fish Market. This event led to the foundation of Barnardos Homes for children. The influence of voluntary bodies such as Barnardos, the NSPCC, the Shaftesbury Society and National Childrens Homes remains very strong although the direction of their work has moved away from residential care and towards day care and preventive work with families. They now complement the work of the social services department which has statutory responsibilities for children.

District Nursing. Before the NHS, home nursing was provided by nurses employed by voluntary nursing associations throughout the country. The service was financed by a scheme of weekly payments made by the residents of the neighbourhood supplemented by fund-raising activities together with payments made on behalf of patients by friendly societies, some employers, and for the very poor by public assistance. Collecting payments and subscriptions from those able to pay was part of the nurse's day. To prevent patients from consulting nurses instead of doctors, whose fees were higher, the nurse was forbidden to visit a patient who had not been seen by a doctor. Although this regulation no longer exists it continues to influence the autonomy of district nursing practice.

Midwifery. For centuries women in labour were looked after by other women who had no special training. The Midwives Act of 1902 made it illegal for unqualified persons to attend women in childbirth.

Family Planning. The first birth control clinic was opened in 1921 by Dr Marie Stopes. Her aim was to improve maternal and child health and to increase happiness in marriage. More clinics opened and by 1930 these were organized by a voluntary organization which became known as the Family Planning Association. These were subject to intense criticism from powerful influences in society and it was not until 1931 that local authorities began to provide clinics and not until 1967 that they were able to provide birth control on social as well as medical grounds and regardless of marital status.

Mass Immunization. The first mass immunization programme was carried out during the Boer War when thousands of soldiers were injected with a mixture of dead typhoid bacilli to prevent typhoid fever. Later during the 1940s and 1950s mass immunization was to play an important part in the reduction of tuberculosis and the eradication of diphtheria and poliomyelitis (see Figure 5). Selective immunization was largely responsible for the eradication of smallpox worldwide.

School Health. Since 1891 education has been compulsory and free for all children in the country. However, the Boer War provided the surprising catalyst for a school health service. For the first time in war it was decided to medically examine the young men who had volunteered to fight. The shocking consequence was that over 50% had to be rejected because of some serious medical defect. The School Health Service began in 1907 when education authorities were given power to provide a medical service which included systematic medical inspections of children. School meals were later provided.

Ministry of Health. This was established in 1919. Its policies included maternity services and a reduction in maternal mortality; child health services and a reduction in infant mortality; school health services; sanitation in the community; industrial health; prevention of infectious and non-infectious disease; promotion of health education; research projects; international health control.

The Peckham Experiment. In the years between the two world wars a small health club opened in a terraced house in Peckham, London. It was the brainchild of Dr George Scott Williamson who believed that persistent physical disorders were due to adverse environmental factors and that families therefore needed 'healthier' surroundings. The Pioneer

Health Centre followed and was a large leisure complex built around a swimming pool. It was intended as an extension to the home where leisure facilities could enrich people's lives. Membership was for whole families only; it involved an annual medical examination and a small weekly family subscription. A measurable improvement in health was observed but the health centre failed to attract sponsorship under the NHS and closed in 1951. This project is particularly interesting because it embodies ideas in relation to the family, leisure and positive health which are particularly relevant in the 1980s. In some areas the ideas of Williamson have been continued, such as the Templegarth Trust (see Mansfield, 1982).

National Health Service. The development of the National Health Service followed the Second World War when the inadequacy of existing services became apparent and when advances in medical science created a climate of optimism. Some believed that after an initial investment of resources health problems would disappear and costs for health care would inevitably reduce. The report proposing the organization of the NHS was prepared by William Beveridge in 1942 and agreed by all political parties. A final health service plan was drawn up by Aneurin Bevan and the National Health Service Act was passed in 1946. The service came into being in 1948.

Mental Handicap. During the 19th century asylums were built using voluntary subscriptions which provided an environment isolated from the outside world in which people could live and be taught a trade within a sheltered workshop. During Victorian times mentally handicapped people were viewed as a threat to society. It was believed that the propagation of the unfit would lead to national degeneracy. Between the two world wars 'colonies' developed in geographically remote areas where these people could be kept separate from mainstream society. These colonies were largely self-sufficient; 'high-grade' inmates were the skilled workers with relatively high status and 'low-grade' inmates did the menial tasks. During the 1950s recommendations were made that community care should replace the supervision and control being exercised by institutions. But it was not until the 1970s that determined efforts began to close long-stay hospitals and to provide true homes in the community for these people. In 1981 the DHSS document *Care in the Community* reaffirmed the basic principle that 'most people who need long-term care can and should be looked after in the community. This is what most of them want for themselves and what those responsible for their care believe to be best'.

Mental Illness. A significant change in attitudes to mentally ill people came about in the middle of the 20th century. Before this time institutional care had been the main approach to care and treatment. This was challenged by a number of interested parties who argued for a change to community care. Barton (1966) described a condition known as institutional neurosis which developed in people subjected to long-stay care in institutions and which resulted in them becoming totally dependent on others. Goffman (1961) in his book *Asylums* launched a scathing attack on institutional care which he argued was ruthless and authoritarian. Robb (1967) shocked people further with *Sans Everything*, which described the inhuman conditions in which some patients were forced to live. Another major factor was the development of new forms of treatment. Electroconvulsive therapy has been used since 1938, but arguably the most important breakthrough was the drug chlorpromazine, a major tranquillizer, which has been widely used since 1954. This has enabled many people with psychotic illnesses to live a relatively normal life in the community. Community care has also been possible because of specialist community psychiatric nurses who are able to offer skilled nursing care.

The Black Report. The Report of the Working Group on Inequalities in Health was submitted in 1980. Its main finding was that after 30 years of a national health service committed to offering equal health care for all there remained a class gradient in standards of health which in certain respects had become more marked. The poorer health experience of the lower occupational groups applied at all stages in life. Although the recommendations of report were never implemented the findings continue to stand as a major challenge to anyone involved in health care in Britain.

MANAGEMENT OF THE NHS

Since 1948 the NHS has undergone several administrative changes. It was completely reorganized in 1974 when the administration of all health services was unified. This was very significant for community care because it integrated into the NHS preventive and community health services which had previously been part of local authorities. This included district nursing, health visiting, domiciliary midwifery, health centres, ambulances, vaccination and immunization, and school health, as well as family planning services which had previously been a voluntary organization (the Family Planning Association). Day nurseries, childminders and home helps became part of the newly founded social services department.

The Government White Paper in 1980, *Patients First*, brought changes in the organization of the health service. In 1981 Area Health Authorities ceased to exist and their functions were taken over by District Health Authorities. Policy making was through a team of officers from different disciplines including nursing and medicine. Liaison and planning with other services such as education and social services continued. Nursing services were organized in specialist units under the administration of a Director of Nursing Services. In some District Health Authorities, but not all, community health services formed their own specialist community unit.

In 1984 the government requested a report on the community nursing services. This became known as The Cumberledge Report after its chairperson, Mrs Julia Cumberledge. The report suggested a system of neighbourhood nursing teams which would focus on communities of between 10 000 and 25 000 people. The team would consist of district nurses, health visitors and school nurses who would work closely together under the direction of a neighbourhood nursing manager. Together they would identify and meet the health needs of the people in that neighbourhood. Fundamental to the success of this is the proposal that the consumer voice should be represented through a Health Advisory Group and that the nurses would develop considerable sensitivity to the needs of the people in that area seeking to meet those needs through skillful and imaginative use of resources and without undue overlap of services. Primary health care teams would be retained.

THE PRIMARY HEALTH CARE TEAM

This is a multidisciplinary team of nursing and medical personnel, supported by receptionists, and sometimes with members of other professions who form the core of the comprehensive service of nursing, medical and social care in the community. Gilmore et al (1974) state that they 'share a common purpose and responsibility, each member clearly understanding his/her own function and those of the other members so that they all pool skills and knowledge to provide an effective primary health care service'. The membership is generally taken to be the health visitor, district nurse, community midwife and general practitioner. Other personnel who may be attached include the school nurse, community psychiatric nurse and social worker. The team may be based collectively at a health centre or separately with the GPs in surgeries and the nurses in a health clinic or at home. Many PHCTs meet regularly to discuss the care of patients and to establish or review health care strategies for the practice population. The people who they serve may live in a well contained geographical area or be scattered throughout several communities.

THE HEALTH VISITOR

The health visitor is a Registered General Nurse with obstetric experience who has undertaken an additional year of further education for the Health Visitor Certifi-

Table 9. *Community Health Services.*

District Health Authority

staffed by: managers, nurses, doctors, paramedical, ancillary, clerical
Includes: Nursing and medical care in the home, health centres, clinics and surgeries

Screening services	School health
Immunizations	Dental services
Health promotion	Physiotheraphy
Chiropody	Speech therapy
Maternal and child health	Mental health
Child and family guidance	Ambulances
Dietetic services	Medical loans
Family planning	Well women clinics
Continence advice	
Hostels for mentally handicapped people	

cate. If the work can be summed up in one word it is 'preventive'. In 1977 the following definition was agreed: The professional practice of health visiting consists of planned activities aimed at the promotion of health and the prevention of ill-health. It contributes substantially to individual and social wellbeing by focusing attention at various times on either an individual or social group in the community. It has three unique functions:

1 Identifying and fulfilling self-declared and recognized health needs of individuals and social groups.
2 Providing a generalist health agent service in an era of increasing specialization in the health care available to individuals and communities.
3 Monitoring simultaneously the health needs and demands of individuals and communities; contributing to the fulfilment of these needs by facilitating appropriate care and service by other professional health care groups.

The health visitor may be attached to a general practice and provide a service for that practice population or be based in a geographical patch. He/she assesses the needs of the community, establishes priorities and determines the structure of the work, who to visit and the visiting pattern. Referrals are made by other members of the primary health care team, other agencies, concerned family members and neighbours as well as self-referrals. Traditionally the health visitor has been concerned with maternal and child health although the role is one of a family visitor and involves work with groups such as pre-retirement, the elderly, the handicapped and people leaving hospital who require further health advice. Most of the work takes place in the family home although the health visitor is also responsible for certain clinics such as Child Health Clinics, Child Development Clinics and sometimes well woman clinics.

The method of working which the health visitor employs, whether he/she is considering the health of an individual, a family or a community, is an individualized, systematic approach which involves the four stages of the 'health visiting process': assessing, planning, implementing and evaluating:

1 *Assessment.* Because the health visitor often visits the family over a long period of time and in their own home, he/she is likely to have a more complete understanding of the various factors influencing health than is usual in nursing. Health needs are not only problem-centred, they are frequently preventive. The relationship between health visitor and client has to be one of mutual trust and respect with the reasons for visiting being clearly stated and understood by both parties. Part of the skill is to enable the client to become aware of their health needs and to express them. They can then be considered in the context of the family and local community.
2 *Planning.* This involves agreeing with the client priorities of need and deciding ways in which they might be resolved. The health visitor ensures that the client has all the relevant information on local resources so that the various options can be discussed. The specific actions decided upon might involve immediate, medium-term or long-term goals.
3 *Implementation.* This involves the client and health visitor putting their agreed strategies into action and may involve other family members, local support groups or other agencies.
4 *Evaluation.* Measuring the outcome against the agreed plan. This is shared by client and health visitor so that each can be aware of any progress and together reassess health needs and make further plans if necessary.

Several different nursing models have been used by health visitors, including Orem's self-care model and Roy's model which focuses on adaptation to stressors (see Chapter 1). (For a detailed account of a model for health visiting see Clark (1986).)

THE DISTRICT NURSE

The District Nurse is a Registered General Nurse who has undertaken post-basic training in a polytechnic (mandatory since 1981). He/she gives care to patients on the GP's practice list and is responsible for assessing the patient's nursing needs and carrying out skilled nursing care either in their homes or in the GP's surgery or in clinics. He/she is also involved in preventive and screening work such as diabetic and hypertensive clinics. Many district nurses are organized into district nursing teams which include a team leader, other RGNs, District Enrolled nurses and auxiliaries. Some District Health Authorities employ nurses to extend nursing care into the evening and in some areas there is a 24-hour nursing service. Most of the patients are referred by the GP and hospitals. Over recent years the work of the district nursing service has increased and the type of care offered has become more complex. Some of the reasons for this are:

1 Increasing numbers of very elderly people and a deliberate policy to avoid long-term hospitalization and residential care.
2 Shorter hospital admissions and an increase in day surgery leading to a greater need for aftercare in the community.
3 Greater awareness of previously hidden health problems such as incontinence.
4 Social and population changes including more women going out to work, and smaller families. Carers who are themselves aged increases the need for education and support.
5 Greater attention to the assessment

of the patient and family instead of the traditional task-orientated approach leading to increased expectations for health care.

The method of working employed by the district nurse is the nursing process through which the unique needs of the patient and family can be identified and met. At all stages the patient and family are involved and it is usual for the care plan to remain in the patient's home:

1 *Assessment.* This involves the nurse taking a history of the patient's health, making her own observations of the patient and carers and recording the family's use of other resources. A comprehensive base line assessment is the key to sound nursing care. It must include all relevant information so that when the nurse is not present the patient's health care needs will still be met.
2 *Planning.* It is usual in a nursing care plan to include the date when the problem was identified, the goal (which may be long- or short-term), the action to be carried out and by whom, and a review date. Communication with workers from other services which are involved is an essential part of planning care especially if several agencies are involved.
3 *Implementation.* It is usual for much of the care to be given by family members or other informal carers. The district nurse therefore has not only to implement her own care but to ensure that all the carers are effectively meeting the patient's needs.
4 *Evaluation.* The district nurse, patient and family continually evaluate the extent to which the care plan is meeting the health needs. Quality of care is a complex mix of the need expressed by the patient and the standards of care set by the nurse. This may be tempered by the limitations imposed on the district nursing service and the availability of other resources.

COMMUNITY MIDWIFE

The community midwife is a qualified midwife (SCM) who undertakes care of the antenatal mother, carries out deliveries in the home, and cares for the mother and baby postnatally, usually until the 10th day when the health visitor takes over. It is usual for the community midwife and health visitor jointly to organize Parentcraft Groups along with the obstetric physiotherapist. Health teaching in preparation for parenthood may also include teaching in schools as part of a health education programme and in some areas pre-conception clinics. The increasing demand for home deliveries promises to restore the community midwife to the role and status previously enjoyed in the community (see Hunter (1985)).

GENERAL PRACTITIONER

The General Practitioner offers a service to a population of usually between 2000 and 3000 and may intervene educationally, preventively or therapeutically to promote his patients' health. GPs tend to work in a group practice with others although there are still some single-handed practices, especially in inner city and rural areas. Most people in Britain are registered with a GP but the frequency with which they consult varies considerably and is usually patient-determined. Much of the patient contact is as a consultation in the surgery although he/she may also visit them at home, either as a self-initiated visit or because the patient requests it, and occasionally in hospital. The service is for patients of all age groups from before birth to death.

Traditionally the GP has recorded all patient contacts in chronological order on small buff cards which form the Family Practitioner Committee medical record. However, it may be difficult to establish a patient's current health problems, and some GPs are now using record cards which are A4 in size and contain a medical summary listing non-active and current health problems as well as treatment. In some health centres all members of the PHCT combine their records in one folder so that the involvement of those other health workers can be taken into account when planning care.

THE SOCIAL WORKER

Although employed by the Social Services Department, the social worker may be attached to a PHCT and if so is likely to be based in a health centre. The social worker accepts referrals from members of the PHCT as well as taking self-referrals. The methods employed in social work may be significantly different from the nursing process or the medical model although case work invariably involves seeing the problems from the client's point of view and enabling them to make the decisions. It may take them some time to resolve the problem of a frail and elderly person who wishes to remain at home, even though there is a risk of falling or hypothermia. Social workers have certain statutory responsibilities relating to clients at risk; for instance they must investigate reports of child abuse.

THE COMMUNITY PSYCHIATRIC NURSE

The CPN is a Registered Mental Nurse who may have undertaken a further course of community psychiatric nursing. They may be attached to one or several GP practices or may be based in a geographical patch. Traditionally CPNs were attached to consultant psychiatrists and visited their patients in the community. Much of this work was concerned with the care and treatment of psychotic patients requiring long-acting medication and careful monitoring of their mental and social health. However the work of the CPN has expanded considerably and, although with the closure of many long-stay psychiatric institutions this remains an important part of their work, they are becoming increasingly involved with people with other forms of mental illness as well as being involved in preventive work. Many CPNs are involved in support groups for people with phobias, alcohol and drug-related problems, people coming off minor tranquillizing drugs, and women with postnatal depression which is not severe enough to warrant hospital admission. CPNs are particularly interested in communities where there is a high incidence of mental ill health and part of their role is to consider with other community workers strategies for support, prevention of ill-health and the promotion of mental health.

THE SCHOOL NURSE

Although a school health service has been in existence for many years, the emergence of school nursing as a specialist branch of nursing is relatively recent. The Court Report (1976) recommended a full-time school nurse for all schools with a population in excess of 1000 children. In some areas this has been achieved. Many schools share a school nurse who divides her time between health promotion, health screening and the care of children with handicapping conditions. Sensory defects of vision and hearing are the most common complaints and screening for vision should be reviewed annually and hearing twice in the primary school. Screening for colour blindness is also carried out. The Warnock Committee (1978) recommended that children with special needs should be educated in a normal school wherever possible. These children may require careful monitoring to ensure that their needs are being met. The teaching of techniques such as self-catheterization may be required. As malnutrition and physical diseases have given way to psychological and social problems the

skills of the school nurse are increasingly moving towards counselling. Another very important sphere of work is health promotion and many school nurses work closely with teachers and parents to promote good health, to introduce children to the concepts of self-health and the principles of choice, and to tackle current health problems such as drug abuse and early unplanned pregnancy.

SPECIALIST NURSES

Over recent years a number of specialist nurses have appeared in response to specific needs such as stoma and mastectomy care, oncology, diabetes, infection control and continence advice. These nurses may either be based in the hospital and become involved in hospital care and aftercare, or they may be based in the community whilst maintaining close links with the hospital. Their role is typically multifaceted and includes direct involvement with patients requiring specialist nursing care, liaison between services, education of students and other health workers, research, management of their department and furthering the development of their speciality which may involve conferences at local, national or international level.

THE NURSE PRACTITIONER

The nurse practitioner has existed in the USA for some years but is a relatively recent development in the UK. The role is an extension of the traditional nursing role and seeks to meet health needs which are not currently being met by other health providers. In order to achieve this the nurse practitioner must be accessible to the community, and the role must be flexible enough to be able to respond to what the people want. The most important aim is to reach those people who are not making full use of the health services. These include homeless families, people in social classes 4 and 5 who are known to consult GPs less than other social groups in proportion to their health needs, and ethnic minority groups who may have difficulty in understanding the services or in communicating what they want. The nurse practitioner can enable people to take a more active role in their own health care and raise expectations of health.

Five areas of involvement were identified by Stilwell (1984):

1   An alternative consultant to the GP. The patient has the choice of who to consult. The nurse practitioner is able to offer more time and so is able to listen and share the whole problem. Health information or counselling may be all that is required.
2   Screening.
3   Managing minor and chronic ailments. This may involve the nurse in limited prescribing.
4   Health education.
5   Counselling.

A Marplan survey commissioned by the Community Nursing Review Group (1986) showed that confidence is high in the ability and skills of nurses to provide certain health services, as distinct from strictly medical services. Two-thirds of the sample said they were prepared to see or talk to a nurse instead of a doctor; 60% said they would actually prefer to see a nurse for certain purposes; and, of those, 40% gave as their reason that a nurse was more sympathetic and easier to talk to. The report made a recommendation that the principle should be adopted of introducing the nurse practitioner into primary health care.

SOCIAL SECURITY PAYMENTS

The present social security scheme was introduced after the Second World War although some benefits preceded this.

For instance the 'old age' pension was introduced by Lloyd George in 1908. The benefits payable are constantly being reviewed and modified. They are financed by the National Insurance scheme and through general taxation. The three main types of benefit are as follows:

1   *National Insurance (NI) benefits.* These can be claimed if you (or sometimes your husband or wife) have paid enough NI contributions.
2   *Means-tested benefits.* For these you have to give details of the money you have coming in and what your circumstances are. No NI contributions are needed.
3   *Non-contributory benefits.* These depend only on whether you meet certain conditions. No NI contributions are needed and there is no means test.

Types of benefits and the amounts payable are constantly changing. For accurate information on benefits the main sources are the local Department of Health and Social Security office (they can sometimes arrange home visits for people who are housebound) and the Citizens Advice Bureau. Some of the larger towns also have Welfare Rights Teams who can provide information and advice; in hospitals the medical social worker is the main source. Benefits are listed in a DHSS leaflet, *Which Benefit*, which is available in English, Urdu, Gujerati, Hindi, Punjabi, Bengali and Chinese. It is regularly updated and is available from the sources already listed.

SOCIAL SERVICES

The 'social services' cover three main groups:

1   Local authority social services departments which include a wide range of statutory, community and residential services for the elderly, children, physically disabled (including the deaf and the

blind), mentally disabled and the homeless. They are also responsible for medical social workers in hospitals, and social workers attached to health centres and child and family guidance clinics. Social Services Departments were established in 1971 as a result of the Seebohm Report which recommended the unification of the separate 'welfare' departments. They are usually organized into area social work teams which serve a population of between 50 000 and 100 000 people. The residential and day care services include:

a   Residential homes for the elderly, including homes for the elderly mentally infirm;
b   homes for the physically and mentally handicapped;
c   workshops for the disabled;
d   family group homes and fostering for children;
e   day nurseries;
f   registration of playgroups and childminders;

Fieldwork services include:

a   family and child care;
b   social work support for the disabled, homeless, elderly, mentally ill and mentally handicapped;
c   adoption;
d   home helps;
e   Meals on Wheels;
f   occupational therapy which is responsible for home adaptations and fitting of special equipment such as telephone aids, kitchen gadgets and bath rails or the installation of showers.

2   Probation and after care service which is attached to the courts and works mainly with adult offenders who are placed on probation as part of their sentence.

3   Voluntary bodies which may provide social services on a local or national basis. They include WRVS, NSPCC, PPA, Citizens' Advice Bureau and Age Concern. They work very closely with social services departments and are usually partly financed by them in the form of grants.

Recently some social services departments have begun to organize themselves on a 'patch' basis in order to be more accessible and responsive to local needs, to establish a partnership between professionals and users and to encourage public involvement. The essence of patch is locality and to be successful it needs to focus on a limited geographical area with about 10 000 people. The style of patch working is to develop flexibility in the various roles to meet local needs and to unify all the services including social work, home helps and residential and day care. Another essential feature is its capacity to recognize and support informal caring networks so that people learn to deal with their own problems more effectively and also to support, and in turn be supported by, their neighbours. (For a detailed description of a 'patch' system see Beresford and Croft (1986) *Whose Welfare.*)

CHILD ABUSE PROCEDURES

Child abuse, or non-accidental injury, created considerable public and professional concern in the 1970s. The case of Maria Caldwell in 1971–1972 led to the first of many enquiries into the handling of cases which ended in tragedy. These enquiries emphasized the importance of multidisciplinary cooperation; the need to have clearly defined procedures which are fully understood by all professionals concerned and those who later join the service; better training including periodic refresher courses; constant vigilance of the services involved — health, education, social services, police, probation; the value of a child protection register containing the names of families where child abuse had occurred or was suspected; and monitoring of the handling of child abuse cases by a review committee.

The features of high-risk families and the signs of child abuse are described in

Chapter 3. Child abuse is not solely a community problem. It concerns everyone involved with the families of children. Many such children are frequent attenders at hospital A/E departments or wards where they are investigated for conditions such as failure to thrive. Where there is any concern it is essential that discussion takes place between the agencies involved. This usually takes place at a case conference which gathers together everyone concerned with the family and may include the family themselves. Some health authorities employ a liaison health visitor who can develop communication systems between hospital and the community to prevent children 'slipping through the net'.

CONTINUITY OF CARE AND AFTERCARE

Hospital admission is usually only a small period in a person's life but for most it is a time of crisis; a life event. The time preceding admission when the person is aware of their illness is very variable but may span weeks or months of checking out their feelings with family or friends, consultations with their GP, outpatient appointments and perhaps also nursing care at home. Hospital admission time has been greatly reduced over recent years and the conditions treatable by day surgery have increased. It is therefore especially important that nurses in hospital and the community work together to ensure continuity of care. The team in the hospital needs to make careful plans before transferring a patient home if that person is to be dependent on informal carers or other agencies. A home assessment may be necessary when hospital and community workers can meet with the patient and his family at his home to finalize future plans. In some areas voluntary organizations such as Age Concern have developed schemes whereby a volunteer visits an elderly person return-

ing home from a hospital stay to settle them in and to ensure that they have basic amenities such as food and warmth. When patients require specialized care at home such as total parenteral feeding the district nurse may need to visit the patient in hospital to learn the nursing technique from hospital nurses.

Many conditions requiring hospital admission are the so-called 'life-style' diseases which are essentially preventable. Many are related to alcohol, smoking, obesity and stress. Further admissions may be prevented if the person adopts a healthier lifestyle. Some people are especially motivated to make some change following an acute illness and these people can be identified in hospital. It may be agreed with the patient that a health visitor will visit them at home to encourage them and perhaps put them in contact with local support groups. Whatever the type of aftercare required it is essential that the hospital nurse considers the needs of the patient when he returns home and accepts the transfer of care as part of her responsibility. The mandatory community experience in student nurse training has helped to ensure that this consideration is given.

TERMINAL ILLNESS

The care of people facing death is part of family life and therefore the normal setting is their own home. The problem is often in ensuring that all those involved receive the support they need, and that the patient receives the specialist care which will promote a good quality of life and freedom from pain and other untoward symptoms. The hospice movement has achieved these aims by providing specialist care which supplements the care given by the primary health care team and is particularly expert in symptom control and counselling skills. Hospice nurses spend most of their time in the community visiting patients in their own homes although hospices also have a small number of beds for short-term stays when required.

Nurses are also provided by the Marie Curie Foundation to care for cancer patients at home and are often especially appreciated at night when 24-hour skilled nursing care is required or when the relatives require a rest. There are also Macmillan nurses who specialize in the care of dying patients at home. They are named after Douglas Macmillan, one of the founders of the National Society for Cancer Relief. The society is involved in either the total or partial funding of the home nursing service. In addition both organizations have funds which can help towards the purchase of essential equipment (such as a liquidizer for a patient with difficulty in swallowing) for families experiencing financial hardship.

HEALTH PROMOTION

In most District Health Authorities health promotion is a district-based department which includes in-patient and community care and involves all care groups. Ewles and Simnet (1985) identify nine stages when planning for health education. The outline is very similar to the nursing process:

1 Identify consumers and their characteristics.
2 Identify consumer needs.
3 Decide on goals for health education.
4 Formulate specific objectives.
5 Identify resources.
6 Plan content and method in detail.
7 Plan evaluation methods.
8 Action!
9 Evaluate.

These stages form the basic framework for all programmes such as working with a school nurse to prepare a health education programme for a school or planning health education input into an outpatients department.

MENTAL HANDICAP

The idea that mentally handicapped people should live in their own homes in an ordinary community, living 'normal' lives marks a stark contrast with the attitudes of the past. The Nimrod project in South Glamorgan began in 1977 and aims to ensure that each handicapped person is helped to live and behave as normally as possible. To achieve this it is important that they have access to the full range of existing services as well as specialist services to offer advice and support. Some of the mentally handicapped people live with 'care families' in foster homes and others live together in groups of five or six in houses leased from the city council. Residential staff are trained to offer support and guidance whilst retaining a homely atmosphere and a sense of normality. 'Normalization' involves all aspects of fitting into community life including making use of local shops and leisure facilities, going to church, and being usefully employed. It also involves assuming a sense of responsibility for one's own health and learning to cope with feelings. Nurses may therefore need to give greater consideration to issues such as sexuality and contraception. Fraser and Ross (1986) describe a programme for teaching young mentally handicapped women about menstruation.

COMPLEMENTARY THERAPIES

This includes a wide range of therapies which complement conventional medicine. Homeopathy has always been available through the NHS but other therapies may only be available privately. They are relevant because people are increasingly turning to therapies which are gentle and which treat the whole person and not just the symptoms. Nurses working in the community may therefore find that their nursing care is only part of the total care for that patient. They may wish to find out more in order to discuss it with the patient or they may feel that knowledge of such therapies or acquiring those specific skills may help to further their nursing practice.

The Bristol Cancer Help Centre believes that stress plays a major role in the breakdown of the body's defences which can lead to cancer. It adopts a holistic approach and provides a tranquil and harmonious atmosphere where health is more easily restored. It uses a range of complementary therapies to promote healing including nutritional advice, counselling, meditation, guided visualization and healing.

It is important that only bona fide practitioners are consulted. A detailed account of the various complementary therapies available is beyond the scope of this book but the following is a brief guide to the more popular ones.

Acupuncture. Chinese acupuncturists believe that the life force of the body, Chi, circulates in 12 meridians or energy pathways and that all disease is a disturbance of these. Points along the meridian affect a specific organ in some way. Treatment of an illness is by stimulation of these acupuncture points, usually with fine needles, although it may also involve burning a herb called moxa on the points, or acupressure. Acupuncture has been used to reduce pain and to treat addictions. Shiatsu is a form of oriental massage and pressure which stimulates the acupuncture points and meridians.

Alexander Technique. This is a method of posture training which aims to harmonize mind and body and to rediscover basic, natural posture and movement patterns. This can reduce tension in the body and prevent physical ill-health.

Aromatherapy. Essential oils of plants are used in body or face massage inhalations, or occasionally by direct application.

Bach Flower Remedies. Distillations of plants are used to contribute to the healing of mental and emotional problems.

Biofeedback Training. This learned technique brings under conscious control bodily processes normally thought to be beyond voluntary command. It requires a measure of the particular physiological response and a method of conveying this accurately to the patient. It has been used in the treatment of hypertension, migraine, Raynaud's disease, retraining for continence, and to promote relaxation.

Chiropractic. This is a manipulative therapy which aims to correct distortions of posture, restore reasonable function to the spine and pelvic joints, and remove any irritation of nerves which might be causing pain or disturbed function throughout the body.

Healing. This is probably the oldest and still the most common form of complementary medicines. It usually takes the form of therapeutic touch healing. Krieger, a nurse–educator–healer at New York university describes it as a specific transfer of energy which forms part of the natural human potential and can be used by anyone with the intention of healing.

Herbal Medicine. An ancient worldwide system of medicine using plants to prevent and cure diseases. They may be administered as a tea, compress, infusion, gargle or external rub, and may be used to treat symptoms or to return the body's balance to normal.

Homeopathy. The basic principle is that like heals like. Research last century by Hahnemann found that agents which produce certain signs and symptoms in health also cured those signs and symptoms in disease. The substance is more powerful the more it is diluted and seems to act by triggering the body's natural healing processes. It is particularly effective in 'constitutional' disorders such as eczema. Dramatic results in children and animals dispel the notion that the effects are purely psychological.

Hypnotherapy. Hypnosis brings about an altered type of consciousness which induces compliance and heightened suggestibility. It is helpful for many different types of problems including weight control, phobias, addictions, anxiety, insomnia and smoking as well as disorders such as asthma.

Naturopathy. Treatment of illnesses depends upon the action of natural healing forces present in the body. Disease is simply a manifestation of the healing forces' efforts to restore the body to normal. Treatment is by discovering and removing the root cause of the disease which may be chemical (from faulty eating, drinking, breathing or elimination), mechanical (from poor posture, muscular tension, stiffness) or psychological.

Osteopathy. This therapy employs manipulation of the body and in particular the spine. A wide range of conditions can be treated although the most common is back pain.

Reflexology. This is an ancient diagnostic and therapeutic system in which the soles of the feet are deeply massaged. The reflexologist can detect points under the skin which relate to the organs of the body. Pain or lumpiness on the spots indicates that the organs may be affected by disease.

CONFIDENTIALITY

Early in childhood we learn the two essential elements of confidences; firstly, that to share a confidence with someone whom we trust makes us feel better in some way; secondly, that if that confidence is not respected, and we find that our secret has been shared with others, our trust in that person is damaged. Nurses, and all health workers, are constantly being entrusted with people's confidences. It is an essential part of the therapeutic role. The code of professional conduct for the nurse, midwife and health visitor states: 'respect confidential information obtained in the course of professional practice and refrain from disclosing information without the consent of the patient/client, or a person

entitled to act on his/her behalf, except where disclosure is required by law or by the order of a court or is necessary in the public interest'.

It is usual when a team of people is involved for essential information to be shared by team members. Primary health care team meetings often use this opportunity to discuss the care of families. It is essential that the consent of the family is obtained, and that they understand specifically the nature of the information which will be disclosed and who will be present at the meeting. At child abuse case conferences it is essential that in order to protect the child relevant information is shared and exchanged especially with the social services department, NSPCC and police. Information about the family which has no direct bearing on the current situation should not be disclosed. It is usual for the proceedings to be explained to the family beforehand, and increasingly for the family to be present at the conference. Anyone present at a conference should treat information as having been given in confidence and should not disclose it for any purpose without the express consent of the person who provided it.

The developing practice for nurses to write family notes in the home and for records to be kept there helps to safeguard the family from the collection and storage of information on them which they might take exception to. Social services departments are now beginning to make case notes available to their clients although there are safeguards for information gained from third parties and in rare situations where disclosure would not be in the client's best interests.

THE HEALTH OF COMMUNITY NURSES

Nursing in the community differs from nursing on hospital wards in many ways, not all of which are immediately apparent. A hospital is itself a community with its own subculture of different types of workers, uniforms, social life and so on. Nurses working in the community are isolated from this social system although some health centres may generate a similar atmosphere. Most of their work is carried out in the patient's own home with the nurse spending a significant part of her day isolated from colleagues. For some nurses this lack of peer support may be stressful, particularly if the appropriate care is time consuming and the nurse feels permanently hurried. Other problems specific to community nursing include a significant time spent driving with the accompanying stress and possibility of accident, inclement weather (especially snow and icy roads), back injuries caused by low beds and high baths, unlit passages, growling dogs, and time wasted trying to find people in unnamed flats. Increasingly district nurses, especially those working at night, are at risk of attack—sometimes by people desperate for drugs.

Health visitors relinquish their uniform and traditional nursing role. Their perception of themselves and the nature of 'nursing' therefore has to change. The preventive nature of their work means that results are less easily quantifiable. Moreover, the style of their work is to enable others to discover a greater awareness of health or to find answers to problems. The 'job satisfaction' is therefore subtly different from other branches of nursing. It is especially important that to maintain enthusiasm the health visitor has clear aims and objectives against which achievements can be measured. One of the most stressful factors in health visiting is the prospect of child abuse, in particular a concern that signs may be missed with tragic consequences. Peer support and effective and supportive management are essential to maintain staff morale.

BURNOUT

Burnout is being increasingly recognized as a potential problem in all branches of nursing. The process of burnout involves four stages—enthusiasm, stagnation, frustration and withdrawal—and culminates in a state of physical, emotional and mental exhaustion. The nurses most at risk appear to be those who are highly motivated, enthusiastic and perfectionist. This condition can be prevented if the symptoms are recognized at an early stage. Action which can be taken includes setting manageable objectives at work, developing leisure activities which cut out thoughts of work, reducing the amount of overtime worked, and having an effective peer group support system. Nurse management needs to be aware of this problem so that the expectations of a highly motivated nurse are not set too high. A careful note of levels of absenteeism is an important measure of staff morale and may pinpoint nurses who are continually shouldering extra responsibilities and who are therefore under stress. It is everyone's responsibility to be watchful of the signs of burnout in both themselves and colleagues and to act appropriately to prevent a condition which can rob nursing of a potential innovator and rob the nurse of health.

It is perhaps fitting that the final paragraph in a book on personal and community health should be reserved for the health of nurses. The greatest resource in community care is the carers, and in the health services this is nurses. What nurses have to give above all else is of themselves and the helping, healing relationships which they form with people of all backgrounds, creeds, ages, races and humours. Their involvement may enable people to find new dimensions in their personal sense of wellbeing, give comfort and strength through a period of illness, or help them to find peace at the time of their death. In order to fulfil these needs nurses must maintain and strengthen their own health and sense of wellbeing so that when their job is done and the people turn and say we did it all ourselves the nurses will simply smile.

References and further reading

Barton, R. (1966) *Institutional Neurosis*. Bristol; John Wright.

Beagle, P. (1981) *Nursing in the Community*. Key Facts Nursing Cards. London: Baillière Tindall.

Beresford, P. & Croft, S. (1986) *Whose Welfare*. Brighton: Lewis Cohen Urban Studies Centre.

Blattner, B. (1981) *Holistic Nursing*. Englewood Cliffs, NJ: Prentice-Hall.

Butterworth, C. A. & Skidmore, D. (1981) *Caring for the Mentally Ill in the Community*. London: Croom Helm.

Clark, J. (1986) In: Kershaw, B. & Salvage, J., eds. *Models for Nursing*. Chichester: John Wiley.

Clark, J. & Henderson, J., eds. (1983) *Community Health*. Edinburgh: Churchill Livingstone.

Court Report (1976) *Fit for the Future — Report of the Committee on Child Health Services*. London: HMSO.

DHSS (1986) *Neighbourhood Nursing — A Focus for Care*. Chairperson Mrs Julia Cumberledge. London: HMSO.

Edelwich, J. & Brobsky, A. (1980) *Burnout: Stages of Disillusionment in the Helping Professions*. London: Human Sciences Press.

Ehrenreich, B. & English, D. (1976) *Witches, Midwives and Nurses. A History of Women Healers*. Writers and Readers Publishing Cooperative.

Ewles, L. & Simnett, I. (1985) *Promoting Health. A Practical Guide to Health Education*. Chichester: John Wiley.

Fraser, J. & Ross, C. (1986) Time of the month. *Nursing Times* **82** (30), 56–57.

Gilmore M., Bruce, N. & Hunt, M. (1974) *The Work of Nursing Team & General Practice*. London, CETHV.

Goffman, E. (1961) *Asylums*. Harmondsworth: Penguin.

Hunter, B. (1985) Midwifery care study. *Nursing — The Add-on Journal of Clinical Nursing 2nd Series* **2**, 1056–1057.

Illing, M. & Donovan, B. (1981) *District Nursing*. London: Baillière Tindall.

Kershaw, B. & Salvage, J. eds. (1986) *Models for Nursing* (especially chapter 11, a model for health visiting). Chichester: John Wiley.

Krieger, D. (1979) *The Therapeutic Touch*. Englewood Cliffs, NJ: Prentice-Hall.

Mansfield, P. (1982) *Common Sense about Health*. Nottingham: Templegarth Trust (includes a chapter on the Peckham legacy).

Mathieson, S. & Blunden, R. (1980) Nimrod is piloting a course towards a community life. *Health and Social Services Journal* **90**, 122–124.

Meredith Davies, J. B. (1893) *Community Health, Preventive Medicine and Social Services*, 5th edn. London: Baillière Tindall.

Owen, G., ed. (1983) *Health Visiting*, 2nd edn. London: Baillière Tindall.

Report of the International Conference on Primary Health Care, Alma-Ata, USSR, 6–12 September 1978. Geneva: World Health Organization.

Robb, B. (1967) *'Sans Everything'*. London: Nelson.

Stanway, A. (1982) *Alternative Medicine. A Guide to Natural Therapies*. Harmondsworth: Penguin.

Stilwell, B. (1984) The nurse in practice. *Nursing Mirror* **158(21)**, 17–19.

Tierney, A., ed. (1983) *Nurses and the Mentally Handicapped*. Chichester: John Wiley.

Townsend, P. & Davidson, N. (1982) *Inequalities in Health. The Black Report*. Harmondsworth: Penguin.

Turton, P. & Orr, J. (1985) *Learning to Care in the Community*. London: Hodder & Stoughton.

United Kingdom Council for Nursing, Midwifery and Health Visiting (1984) *A Code of Professional Conduct for the Nurse Midwife and Health Visitor*.

Walker, A. ed. (1982) *Community Care. The Family, the State and Social Policy*. Oxford:

Basil Blackwell and Martin Robertson.

Warnock, M. (chairman) (1978) *Report of the Committee of Enquiry into the Education of Handicapped Children and Young Adults.*

London: HMSO.

Waters, W. E. & Cliff, K. S. (1983) *Community Medicine. A Textbook for Nurses and Health Visitors.* London: Croom Helm.

Index